Simon Stafford

Nikon D90

Magic Lantern Guides®

Nikon D90

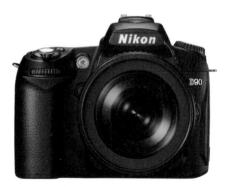

Simon Stafford

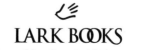

LARK BOOKS
A Division of Sterling Publishing Co., Inc.
New York / London

Editor: Rebecca Shipkosky
Book Design: Michael Robertson
Cover Design: Thom Gaines

Library of Congress Cataloging-in-Publication Data

Stafford, Simon.
  Nikon D90 / Simon Stafford. -- 1st ed.
      p. cm. -- (Magic lantern guides)
  Includes index.
  ISBN 978-1-60059-524-0 (pb-trade pbk. : alk. paper)
  1. Nikon digital cameras--Handbooks, manuals, etc. I. Title.
  TR263.N5S73254 2009
  771.3'3--dc22
                                          2008048903

10 9 8 7 6 5 4 3 2 1

First Edition

Published by Lark Books, A Division of
Sterling Publishing Co., Inc.
387 Park Avenue South, New York, N.Y. 10016

Text © 2009, Simon Stafford
Photography © 2009, Simon Stafford unless otherwise specified

Distributed in Canada by Sterling Publishing,
c/o Canadian Manda Group, 165 Dufferin Street
Toronto, Ontario, Canada M6K 3H6

Distributed in the United Kingdom by GMC Distribution Services,
Castle Place, 166 High Street, Lewes, East Sussex, England BN7 1XU

Distributed in Australia by Capricorn Link (Australia) Pty Ltd.,
P.O. Box 704, Windsor, NSW 2756 Australia

This book is not sponsored by Nikon.

If you have questions or comments about this book, please contact:
Lark Books
67 Broadway
Asheville, NC 28801
(828) 253-0467

Manufactured in the USA.

ISBN 13: 978-1-60059-524-0

For information about custom editions, special sales, premium and corporate purchases, please contact Sterling Special Sales Department at 800-805-5489 or specialsales@sterlingpub.com.

Contents

9

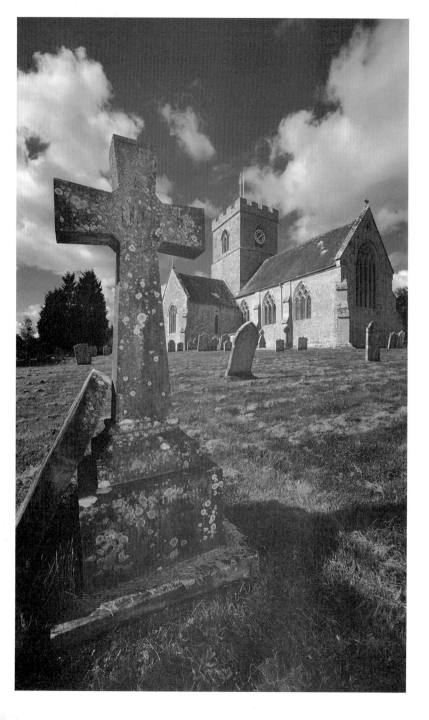

Introduction

The Nikon Corporation has accrued many years of experience building digital cameras, beginning with a variety of hybrid cameras produced in collaboration with Kodak and Fuji, but their breakthrough came in 1999 with the launch of the Nikon D1. This model represented their first fully independent digital SLR (D-SLR) camera design, which not only broke new ground technically, but also made high-quality digital photography financially viable for many photographers.

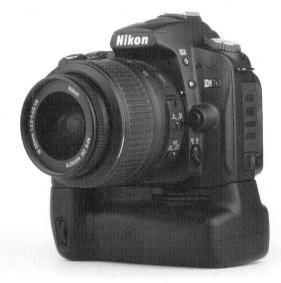

Shown here is the Nikon D90 with MB-D80 battery pack and Nikkor AF-S DX 18-55mm f/3.5-5.6G II lens, only two of a wealth of accessories that are compatible with the D90.

Since Nikon has never attempted to introduce new camera models at the frequency of some of its well-known competitors, the development of Nikon D-SLRs during recent years can be best described as a process of steady evolution. Nikon has unveiled a variety of models aimed at different sectors of the market, from the popular D100, launched in 2002, to the phenomenally successful D70 that arrived in 2004, and later to the mid-range D200 and D80, along with the professionally specified D2Xs. In light of this, the simultaneous release near the end of 2007 of the groundbreaking D3 and D300 models, followed by the introduction of the D60, D700, and the D90, all within the first nine months of 2008 represents a positive revolution!

The D90 has taken over the mantle from the highly successful D80 as Nikon's primary mid-range digital SLR camera for the dedicated enthusiast photographer. In the two years since the D80 was introduced, several new technologies have become commonplace among cameras in this class, including Live View and built-in sensor cleaning. So, it comes as no surprise that the D90 incorporates these features. The ground breaking step that Nikon has taken with the D90 in the inclusion of a video recording function is a first for any digital SLR camera.

Its video capability aside, the D90 is first and foremost a still camera, and in making it, Nikon has continued to maximize the economies of scale by using many tried and true components from existing camera models. For example, it has the same 12.3 million pixel CMOS sensor as the D300, as well as the same 420-pixel RGB sensor for its TTL metering and Multi-CAM 1000 module for its autofocus system as its predecessor, the D80. However, both the latter two systems are improved upon in the D90 by the inclusion of the innovative Scene Recognition System and improved data processing algorithms.

Thus, the D90 offers a comprehensive specification that makes it fully commensurate with its role as a camera for photographers with a wide range of experience and skill. Highlights include:

- DX-format (15.8 x 23.6 mm) CMOS sensor with 12.3 million pixels

- A shutter unit with the ability to cycle up to 4.5 frames per second

- An 11-point autofocus system with a 3D focus-tracking feature

- Self-cleaning mechanism for the optical low-pass filter

- Nikon's exclusive Expeed processing regime

- The Scene Recognition System, with its new, integrated Face Detection System, which enhances performance of the autofocus, metering, and automatic white balance functions

- The Picture Control System that provides a very high degree of control over the way the camera records an image

- A Live View function with three contrast detection AF options

- 720p HD (1,280 x 720 pixel) video recording (maximum clip duration is five minutes) at 24 frames per second

- An ISO range of 200 to 3200, with the ability to record down to an ISO equivalent of 100, or up to an ISO equivalent of 6400

- Accepts the optional MB-D80 battery pack to provide a second shutter release button and duplicated command dials to improve camera handling when shooting in a vertical format

- Compact and lightweight body

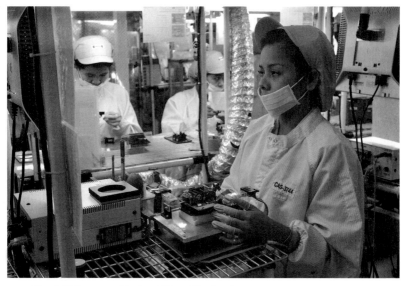
The D90 is assembled at Nikon, Thailand.

The D90 is a fully developed photographic tool with the flexibility to be used in either a completely automated way for point & shoot style photography, or with all of its features and functions under your direct control. Consequently, it is capable of meeting a broad range of requirements and photographic challenges.

Production of the Nikon D90

The D90 is assembled at Nikon's wholly owned production facility near Ayuthaya, Thailand. Ayuthaya is the old historical capital of Siam, about 50 miles (80 Km) north of Bangkok, Thailand's present day capital. However because a number of core parts of the camera such as the main printed circuit board, viewfinder optics, and lens mount are produced at the Nikon factory in Sendai, Japan.

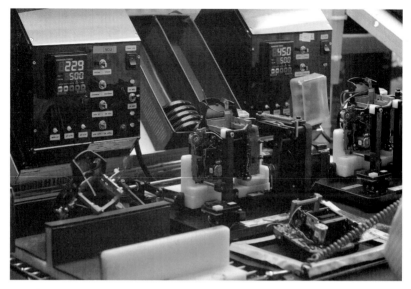

Before it is placed in the camera body, the shutter unit is tested repeatedly and fired so that it does not require a break-in period later when the camera is purchased.

The Nikon (Thailand) plant, which produced its first Nikkor lens back in 1992, currently has a workforce of over 15,000 people, most of whom are locals. At present, camera and lens production operates over three eight-hour shifts, 24 hours a day, seven days a week, assembling the D300, D90, D60, and D40 camera models and a number of consumer grade Nikkor lenses. A combined total of around 320,000 camera units are manufactured every month!

About This Book

To get the most from your D90, it is important that you understand its features so you can make informed choices about how to use them in conjunction with your style of photography. This book is designed to help you achieve this and should be seen as an adjunct to the camera's own instruction manual. Besides explaining how all the basic functions work, this book also provides useful tips on operating the D90 and maximizing its performance. The book does not have to be read from cover to cover. You can move from section to section as required, study a complete chapter, or just absorb the key features or functions you want to use.

The key to success, regardless of your level of experience, is to practice with your camera. You do not waste money on film and processing costs with a digital camera; once you have invested in a memory card, it can be used over and over again. Therefore, you can shoot as many pictures as you like, review your results along with a detailed record of camera settings almost immediately, and then delete your near misses but save your successes—this trial and error method is a very effective way to learn!

Conventions Used in This Book
Unless otherwise stated, when the terms "left" and "right" are used to describe the location of a camera control, it is assumed the camera is being held to the photographer's eye in the shooting position.

When referring to a specific Custom Setting, it will often be mentioned in the abbreviated form, CS xx, where xx is the identifying letter and number of the function. In describing the functionality of lenses and external flash units, it is assumed that the appropriate Nikkor lenses (generally, D- or G-type Nikkor lenses to ensure full compatibility) and Nikon Speedlight units are being used. Note that lenses and flash units made by independent manufacturers may have different functionality. If you use such products, refer to the manufacturer's instruction manual to check compatibility and operation with the D90.

When referring to software, either Nikon or third-party, it is assumed that the most recent iterations of each application are used. At the time of writing these are:

- Nikon Transfer (version 1.2.0)
- Nikon View NX (version 1.2.0)
- Nikon Capture NX2 (version 2.1.0)
- Nikon Camera Control Pro (version 2.3.0)

Acknowledgements

Finally, I would like to thank the following persons for their assistance and support during the writing of this book: At the Nikon Corporation (Tokyo), Mr. Tetsuro Goto, Chief Operating Officer and Vice President (Nikon Imaging Company) and his staff. At Nikon UK Limited, Mr. Michio Miwa, Managing Director and his staff; in particular, Mr. Jeremy Gilbert, Group Marketing Director (Imaging Division); Mr. Mark Fury, Professional Channel Manager; Ms. Jenny Grace, Press & PR; and Mr. James Banfield, Nikon Professional Support.

Simon Stafford
Wiltshire, England.

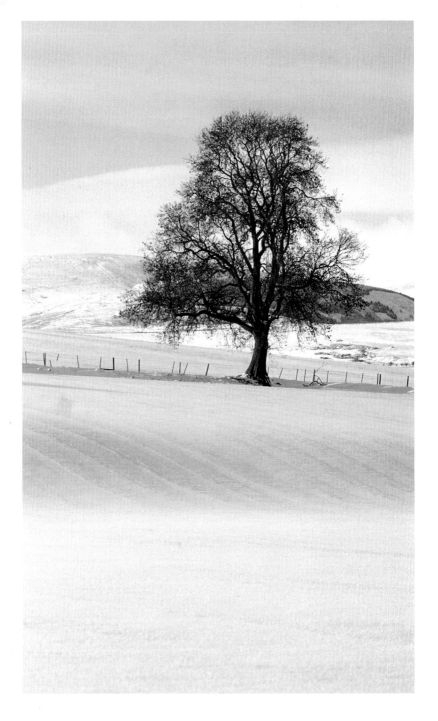

Introducing The Nikon D90

It is almost exactly two years since the introduction of the D80, predecessor to the D90, and it is a measure of how far development of the digital SLR has come, when you consider that features such as a 12MP sensor, built-in sensor cleaning, Live View, a 3″ (7.62 cm) LCD screen, and 3D autofocus tracking were to be expected in the new model rather than heralded as cutting edge!

The D90 draws heavily on the innovative engineering and progressive design of its more highly specified sibling, the multi-award-winning D300 model; however, it also takes features and functions, such as its user interface and range of options in the Retouch menu from the D60. Nikon's aim with the D90 is clear: To provide the broadest appeal to photographers ranging from the first time D-SLR user to the dedicated enthusiast who neither wants nor requires the sophistication, weight, and expense of the D300.

That said, Nikon has made no secret of the fact that the principal innovation of the D90, its ability to record video at 1280 x 720-pixel (720p) resolution, is there to test the demand for convergence of stills and moving picture technology in an SLR-type camera.

The first step to taking great pictures with the D90 is becoming familiar with its various features and functions and how to access them.

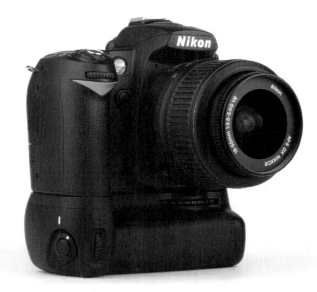

Shown here is the Nikon D90, with MB-D80 battery pack and Nikkor AF-S DX 18-55mm f/3.5-5.6G II lens.

Design

At first glance, the profile of the D90 is remarkably similar to that of the D80; and the similarity is not just skin-deep, as the D90 does share a few key components with the D80, such as the same 420-segment RGB senor for TTL metering and Multi-CAM 1000 autofocus module with 11-point AF system. Even these features, however, have benefitted from some significant enhancements, both to improve their performance and to combine their functions with the camera's Scene Recognition System, which is drawn from the D300. Other hand-me-downs from the D300 include the Nikon DX-format (APS-C size) 12.3MP CMOS sensor, built-in sensor-cleaning mechanism, 3-inch LCD screen, 3D-tracking autofocus, Expeed image processing, and Picture Control System. Furthermore, it shares the same design of built-in Speedlight flash. Improvements in the user interface intro-

Nikon D90 – Frontview

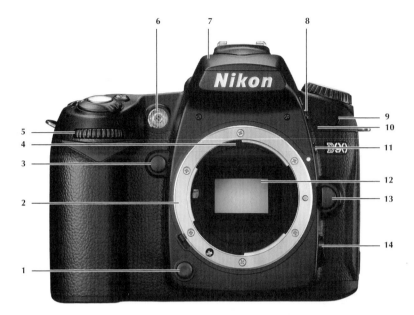

1. Depth-of-Field Preview button
2. Lens mount
3. Fn button
4. CPU contacts
5. Sub-command dial
6. AF assist illuminator / self-timer lamp / red-eye lamp

7. Built-in Speedlight
8. ⚡ flash mode / 🔆 flash compensation button
9. Infrared receiver
10. Microphone
11. **BKT** bracketing button
12. Mirror
13. Lens-release button
14. Focus-mode selector

Nikon D90 – Rearview

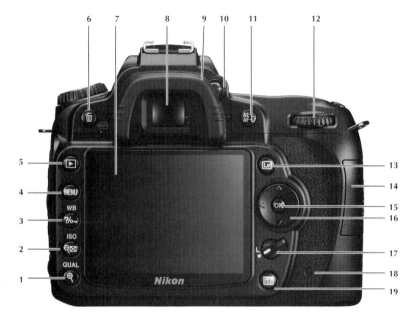

1. ⊕ playback zoom-in button
2. ⊠ playback zoom-out / thumbnail button
3. ?/₀₋ₙ help / protect button, WB white balance button
4. MENU button
5. ▶ playback button
6. 🗑 delete button / two-button format button
7. LCD monitor
8. Viewfinder eyepiece
9. DK-23 viewfinder eyepiece cup
10. Diopter adjustment control
11. AE-L/AF-L autofocus/ exposure lock button
12. Main command dial
13. Lv Live View button
14. Memory card slot cover
15. ⊛ button
16. Multi selector
17. Focus selector lock
18. Memory card access lamp
19. info information/quick settings display button

Nikon D90 – Topview

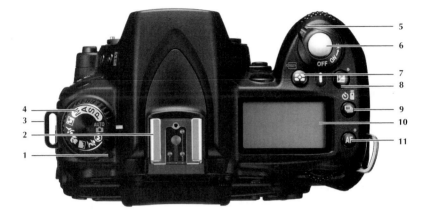

1. Focal plane mark
2. Accessory / flash shoe
3. Camera strap eyelet
4. Mode dial
5. Power switch
6. Shutter-release button
7. ⚅ metering button,
    FORMAT two-button format
    button

8. ⊞ exposure compensa-
    tion button, two-button
    reset button
9. ⊒ release mode button
10. Control panel
11. AF (autofocus) button,
    two-button reset button

duced in the D60 model earlier in 2008 have been enhanced further within the D90, as has the level of in-camera image editing.

It might be said that the D90 represents a meld of the best qualities of its esteemed stable mates; the result of an uncompromising design criteria harnessed to cutting-edge technology and the many years of experience accrued by Nikon in the manufacture of digital SLR cameras.

For a very compact camera, the D90 has a feels robust in the hand. It has dimensions of: (W x H x D) 5.2 x 4.1 x 3.0 inches (132 x 103 x 77 mm) and weighs approximately 22 oz (620 g) without battery or memory card. The 3-inch (7.6 cm) LCD monitor that dominates the rear of the D90 is probably its most notable external feature among the plethora of buttons, dials and switches, many of which will be familiar to users of previous Nikon D-SLR cameras.

The camera chassis is made from a sturdy magnesium alloy that imparts a solid, rugged feel to the polycarbonate body panels it supports. The sealing around all points to prevent the ingress of moisture and dust appears to be commensurate with a camera of this class, so the D90 is capable of withstanding some trying conditions!

Nikon has long been trumpeting that image quality in the digital world rests on three pillars: optical quality of the lens, sensor technology, and internal camera processing. The D90 epitomizes this in respect to the latter two aspects, while the sensor supports an in-built, 12-bit, analog-to-digital converter (ADC), all internal camera processing thereafter is handled at a 16-bit depth by a single ASIC. Nikon has dubbed this new image-processing system "Expeed," and it is at the heart of the camera's ability to record, process, and output high-quality images at a rapid rate. This fast data processing is combined with a mechanical shutter that enables the D90 to cycle at a maximum of 4.5 frames per second (fps). Furthermore, as part of the uncompromising design, the shutter unit is tested to perform at least 100,000 actuations.

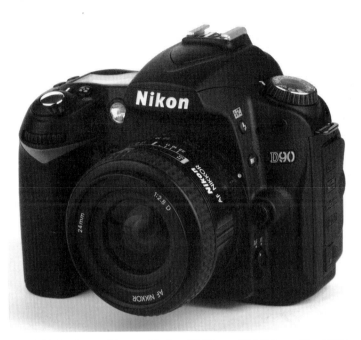

The D90 is pictured here with the AF 24mm f/2.8D lens. The D90 is the latest camera in a long series of SLRs which accept Nikon's F-mount lenses. While there is a huge variety of these lenses, some can only be used with the camera in manual (M) exposure mode.

The D90 has a Nikon F lens mount with an autofocus (AF) coupling and electrical contacts, the design of which can be traced back to the Nikon F introduced in 1959. The greatest level of compatibility is with either AF-D or AF-G type Nikkor lenses. Other lenses can be used, but provide a variable level of compatibility: AF and Ai-P type Nikkor lenses offer a slightly reduced functionality of the camera's TTL metering system because 3D Color Matrix is not available. Even manual focus Ai, Ai-s, Ai converted, and E-series Nikkor lenses can be used with the D90, although only in manual exposure mode; the TTL metering and autofocus systems, electronic exposure display, Depth-of-Field Preview function, and i-TTL flash control are not available.

The Sensor

The Complimentary Metal Oxide Semi-conductor (CMOS) sensor used in the D90 is not unique to the camera; as mentioned already, it is also used in the Nikon D300 model. There is a total of 12.9 million photo sites (pixels), of which 12.3 million are effective for the purpose of recording an image. Each photo site is just 5.49 microns (0.005 mm) square. This gives the camera a maximum resolution of 4288 x 2848 pixels, sufficient to produce a 17.8 x 11.8-inch (45 x 30 cm) print at 240ppi without interpolation (resizing).

The imaging area is approximately 0.66 x 1 inch (15.8 x 23.6 mm), producing a 2:3 aspect ratio. Nikon calls this their DX-format, which is often referred to as the APS-C format. The same "DX" designation is used to identify those lenses that have been optimized for use with their digital SLR cameras that have DX-format sensors. Due to the smaller size of the DX-format, the angle of view offered by any focal length is reduced compared with a lens of the same focal length used with the FX-format of the Nikon D700 and D3 camera models, or the 135-format on 35mm film. If it assists you to estimate the angle-of-view for a particular focal length in comparison with the coverage offered by the same focal length on the FX-format or a 35mm film camera, multiply the focal length by 1.5x.

The CMOS sensor of the D90 is actually a sandwich of several layers, each with a specific purpose:

Wiring Layer

Immediately adjacent to and in front of the layer of photo-diodes is the wiring layer that houses the electrical circuitry, which not only carries the electrical signal from each photo-diode to the analog-to-digital converter (ADC), but also amplifies it along the way.

Bayer Pattern Filter

Above the wiring layer is a colored filter layer. The photo-diodes on the CMOS sensor do not record color—they can only detect a level of brightness. To impart color to the image formed by the light that falls on the sensor, a series of minute red, green, and blue filters are arranged over the photodiodes in a Bayer pattern, which takes its name from the Kodak engineer who invented the system. These filters are arranged in an alternating pattern of red / green on the odd-numbered rows, and green / blue on the even-numbered rows. The Bayer pattern comprises 50% green, 25% red, and 25% blue filters; the intensity of light detected by each photodiode located beneath its single, dedicated color filter according to the Bayer pattern is converted into an electrical signal before being converted to a digital value by the ADC.

If the camera is set to record an NEF (Raw) file, the value for each photodiode is simply saved. When you open this file in an appropriate raw file converter, the software will interpret the value from each photodiode to produce a red-green-blue (RGB) value, which in turn is converted into an image that can be viewed. However, if the camera is set to record JPEG files, then the value from each photodiode is processed in the camera by comparing it with the values from a block of surrounding photodiodes, using a process called interpolation. The interpolation process produces a "best guess" for the RGB value for each sampling point (photodiode) on the sensor.

Micro-Lens Layer

Immediately above the Bayer pattern filter, there is a layer of micro lenses. Since the photodiodes on the sensor are most efficient when the light falling on them is perpendicular, each photodiode has a miniature lenses located above it to channel the light into its well to help maximize its light gathering ability; each micro-lens occupies an area larger than the photodiode-well below it, and there is virtually no gap between neighboring micro-lenses.

This effective ability to gather light, coupled with the relatively large, 5.49-micron pixel pitch of the camera's sensor allows it to scoop up photons very efficiently and contributes to the amazing image quality that can be attained at ISO 1600 or even 3200.

Optical Low-Pass Filter

Positioned in front of the CMOS sensor (which comprises the layers of photodiodes, the wiring layer, the Bayer pattern filter, and the micro-lenses), but not connected to it, is an optical low-pass filter (OLPF). An OLPF is also sometimes called an anti-aliasing filter.

When the frequency of detail in an image, particularly a small, regular, repeating pattern such as the weave pattern in a fabric alters at or close to the pitch of the photodiodes on the sensor, there is often a side effect that produces unwanted data (generally referred to as artifacts). This extra information in the image file occurs because of the way the in-camera processing converts the electrical signal from the sensor to a digital value via the ADC, and shows up in the final image as a wavy or striped color pattern known as moiré. Furthermore, the same in-camera processing can also result in a color fringing effect, known as color aliasing, which causes a halo of one or more color(s) alien to the image to appear along the edge of fine detail.

The OLPF is used to reduce the unwanted effects of color aliasing and moiré. However, the OPLF reduces the resolution of detail, so the camera designers must strike a balance between its beneficial effect and the loss of acuity in fine detail, which increases as the strength of the filter is increased. In the D90, Nikon appears to have adopted a relatively weak filter, which is manifest in the rather soft appearance of JPEG files taken at the camera's default settings. The OLPF also incorporates a number of important coating layers to help improve image quality:

• To help prevent dust and other foreign material from adhering to the surface of the OLPF, it has an anti-static coating made from Indium Tin Oxide.

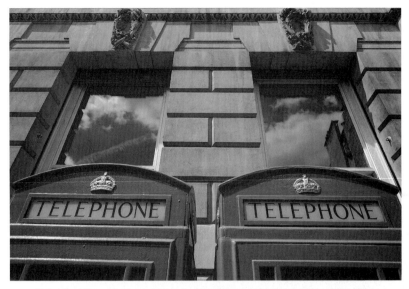

If the framing of your picture is crucial, consider using the Live View feature rather than composing by looking through the viewfinder. Since the viewfinder only displays 92% of the image as it will be captured, it does not give you a true preview of the final result.

- To reduce the risk of light reflecting from the front surface of the OLPF onto the rear element of the lens, which could then result in flare effects or ghost images, the filter has an anti-reflective coating.

- The CMOS sensor is sensitive to wavelengths of light outside the spectrum visible by the human eye. This light, which can be in either the infrared (IR) or the ultraviolet (UV) parts of the spectrum, will pollute image files and cause unwanted color shifts and a loss of image sharpness, so the OLPF has both an IR-blocking and a UV-blocking coat. These IR and UV blocking coatings are very efficient; consequently, the D90 cannot be recommended for any form of IR or UV light photography, which was possible with some earlier Nikon D-SLR cameras, such as the D1 and the D100.

The OLPF has a self-cleaning feature that vibrates it to help reduce the presence of dust and other unwanted particles on its front surface, which is the surface closest to the rear of the lens. Presence of dust on this surface is the bane of all digital photographers, because it causes dark shadow spots to appear in the final image; therefore, keeping the OLPF clean is fundamental to maintaining image quality and avoiding the necessity for time consuming post-processing (see page 363 for more details for OLPF cleaning options).

The Viewfinder

The D90 has a fixed, optical pentaprism, eye-level viewfinder that shows approximately 96% (vertical and horizontal) of the full frame. It is important to understand the consequence of this; reducing the viewfinder frame coverage to 96% in both linear directions actually results in a viewfinder that only displays about 92% of the image area recorded by the camera (0.96 x 0.96 = 0.92). As a result, it is not possible to frame an image in the viewfinder with complete accuracy, as there is a small but significant border area outside each edge of the viewfinder that will be included in the recorded picture. The prudent user will either make use of the Live View feature or the image review and playback options to ensure that their careful compositions have not been compromised!

Another very important thing to keep in mind about the viewfinder is that you must prevent light from entering the viewfinder eyepiece when the D90 is used remotely (i.e., your eye is not to the viewfinder eyepiece). Any excessive amount of light that finds its way into the viewfinder will influence the accuracy of the metering system adversely because its sensor is located in the roof of the viewfinder head above the eyepiece, so make sure the viewfinder eyepiece is covered with the supplied DK-5 cap when shooting this remotely.

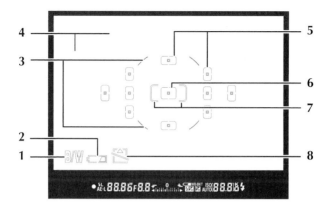

1. Black-and-white indicator
2. Battery indicator
3. Reference for center-weighted metering
4. Framing grid
5. Focus points

6. Center focus point for normal frame
7. Center focus point for wide frame
8. "No memory card" warning

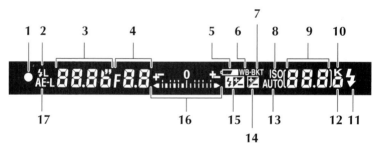

1. Focus indicator
2. FV (flash value) Lock indicator
3. Shutter speed
4. Aperture
5. Battery indicator
6. White balance bracketing indicator
7. Bracketing indicator
8. ISO indicator
9. Remaining exposures
10. Indicates more than 1000 exposures remain

11. Flash-ready light
12. ISO compensation indicator
13. Auto-ISO indicator
14. Exposure compensation indicator
15. Flash compensation indicator
16. Exposure scale display
17. AE (auto exposure) Lock indicator

The DK-5 eyepiece cover is shown here. To install the DK-5 onto the eyepiece, the DK-21 rubber eyecup must be removed. The diopter control dial for the viewfinder eyepiece is located to the right side.

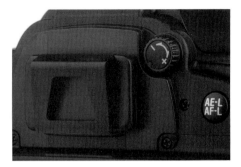

Adjusting Viewfinder Focus

The viewfinder has an eye-point of 0.77 inch (19.5 mm), which provides an excellent view of the focusing screen and viewfinder information for users who wear eyeglasses, plus there is a built-in diopter adjustment of –3.0 to +1.0 for adjusting the focus of the eyepiece to an individual user's eyesight. To do this, mount a lens on the camera and leave it set to its infinity focus mark. Switch the camera on and point it at a plain surface that fills the frame. Rotate the diopter adjustment dial to the right of the viewfinder eyepiece until the AF point and focus screen markings appear sharp. It is essential to do this to ensure that you see the sharpest possible view of the focusing screen. If the built-in correction is not sufficiently strong, optional eyepiece correction lenses, with the product code DK-20C, are available between –5 and +3; these are attached by slipping them onto the eyepiece frame (the standard DK-21 viewfinder eyecup must be removed first). The strength of these lenses may not match that of your prescription eyeglasses, so make sure you test one before making a purchase.

Focus Screen Displays

The viewfinder provides a magnification of approximately 0.94x, and the display includes all the essential information about exposure and focus (see illustration pages 38-39).

The camera is supplied with the Nikon type B Mark II Clear Matte Focusing screen, which is marked with two pairs of arcs to define a central 8 mm diameter circle, together with 11 pairs of brackets to indicate the location of the autofocus points. Nikon offers no alternative interchangeable focusing screen for the D90.

The D90 employs an LCD projection system to display and illuminate the AF point markings, viewfinder warnings, and grid lines over its focusing screen, which draws a very low level of power from the camera, even when the camera is switched off. If you remove the battery from the camera, the focus screen will dim and its markings will no longer be visible.

The Control Panel

The top control panel displays a wealth of shooting information including battery status, white balance setting, remaining picture count, and autofocus mode.

This large monochrome LCD display on the top plate of the D90, which Nikon calls the Control Panel, is used to display a range of information concerning the status of the camera. If the power is off, the only information shown is the number of remaining frames available with the installed memory card at the current settings for image size and quality, and [- E -] appears in the display if no card is inserted. As soon as the camera is powered on, the display shows a range of camera control settings, including metering pattern, focus mode, focus area mode, battery status, shutter speed, aperture, image size, image quality, white balance, and number of remaining exposures. Other controls will be indicated as and when they are activated, such as the exposure/flash compensation warning, multiple exposure indicator and GPS indicator. To illuminate the control panel display in low light, turn the power switch to the ☀ position, and then release it.

Control Panel A

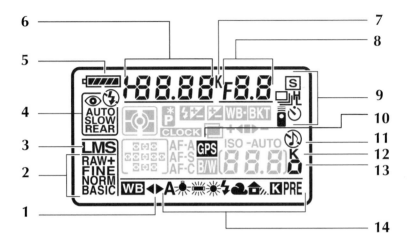

1. White balance fine-tuning indicator
2. Image quality
3. Image size
4. Flash mode
5. Battery indicator
6. Shutter speed, exposure / flash compensation value, number of shots in bracketing sequence, white balance color temperature / fine-tuning

7. Color temperature
8. Aperture
9. Release mode
10. GPS indicator
11. Beep indicator
12. Indicates more than 1000 exposures remain
13. ISO compensation indicator
14. White balance

Control Panel B

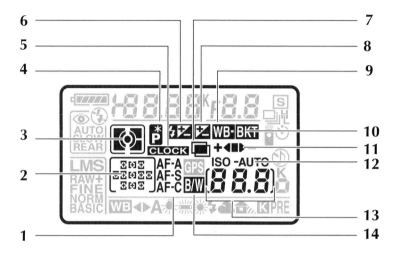

1. Autofocus mode
2. Focus points
3. Metering points
4. Flexible program indicator
5. Clock indicator
6. Flash compensation indicator
7. Multiple exposure indicator
8. Exposure compensation indicator
9. White balance bracketing indicator
10. Bracketing indicator
11. Bracketing progress indicator
12. ISO indicator
13. Number of remaining exposures
14. Black-and-white indicator

Shooting Information Display

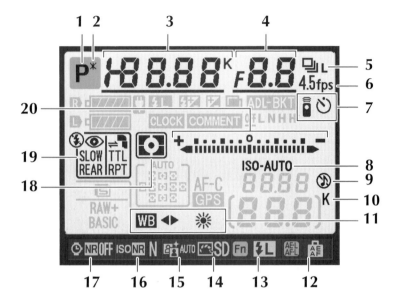

1. Exposure / shooting mode
2. Flexible program indicator
3. Shutter speed, exposure / flash compensation value, color temperature, number of shots in bracketing sequence
4. Aperture
5. Release mode
6. Continuous shooting speed
7. Remote / self-timer mode
8. ISO indicator
9. Beep indicator
10. Indicates more than 1000 exposures remain

11. White balance fine-tuning indicator
12. AE-L/AF-L button role
13. Fn button role
14. Picture Control indicator
15. Active D-Lighting indicator
16. High ISO noise reduction
17. Long exposure noise reduction
18. Metering
19. Flash mode
20. Exposure scale display

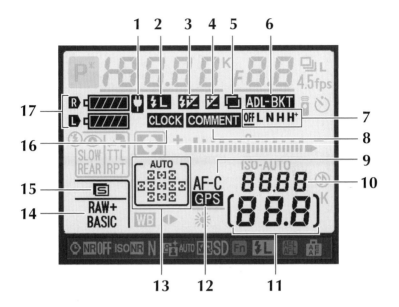

1. AC adapter indicator
2. FV (flash value) Lock indicator
3. Flash compensation indicator
4. Exposure compensation indicator
5. Multiple exposure indicator
6. Bracketing indicator
7. Active D-Lighting bracketing amount
8. Image comment
9. Autofocus mode
10. ISO
11. Remaining exposures
12. GPS indicator
13. Auto-area AF indicator
14. Image quality
15. Image size
16. Clock indicator
17. Battery indicator

*The **info** button is located on the rear of the camera, below the multi selector button lock switch.*

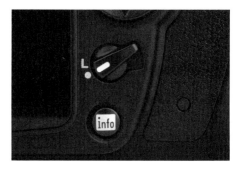

Shooting Information Display

The Shooting Information Display (SID) essentially replicates the display shown in the control panel, except it uses the 3-inch (7.62 cm) LCD monitor on the back of the camera, and therefore more information is displayed. You may also find it easier and more convenient to read than the control panel (see page 230 for details of CS-d8 [Shooting info display]). To display the SID, press the **info** button once.

Quick Settings Display

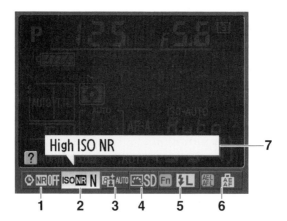

1. *Image quality*
2. *Image size*
3. *Vignette control*
4. *Release mode (single*

5. *Flash sync indicator*
6. *Exposure mode*
7. *Flexible program indicator*

The Quick Settings Display (QSD) allows you to access a number of key menu items directly from the SID, and apply changes to them without navigating the menu system. To display the SID, press the ▣ button; to highlight an item in the QSD, press the ▣ button again. Use the multi selector button to highlight the required item in the QSD and press the ⊛ button to open the associated menu item directly. To exit the QSD without opening a menu item, press the ▣ button a third time.

To display a reminder of role of the items displayed in the QSD, select [On] for CS-d5 [Screen tips]. This way, when an item is highlighted in the QSD, the screen will display a descriptive text caption and/or diagram to assist you.

Preparing the D90

In line with the stated aim of Nikon to make the D90 appeal to a very broad range of users with an equally wide span of skill levels, the specification the D90 includes the simple point and shoot 🅰 mode, six fully automated subject/scene orientated point-and-shoot exposure modes, plus four manual/semi-manual exposure modes for the more experienced photographer. This section is intended to assist those less experienced users who are eager to take some pictures with their new D90, but are either unable or reluctant to spend the time at this point to learn how to take control of the camera.

- **Charge and insert camera battery:** see pages 46-48 for full details on how to charge and insert the camera battery.
- **Choose a menu language:** see page 244 for full details on how to select and set a language for the camera menu system.
- **Set camera clock:** see page 243 for full details on how to set the internal clock of the camera.
- **Attach lens:** see pages 329-330 for full details on how to attach a lens.
- **Adjust viewfinder focus:** see page 34 for full details on how to adjust focus of the viewfinder eyepiece.

- **Select memory card:** see pages 271-275 for a list of compatible memory cards and memory card capacity.
- **Format memory card:** see pages 277-279 for instructions on how to format a memory card.
- **Select default settings:** see pages 141-142 for information about how to set the camera to its default settings.
- **Select a release mode:** see page 97 for full details on how to set the shooting mode; I recommend using single frame (S).
- **Select a metering mode:** see page 149 for full details on how to select a TTL metering mode; I recommend Matrix metering.
- **Select exposure mode:** see pages 160-164 for full details on how to select an exposure mode; the D90 offers the point-and-shoot simplicity of the fully automated $\overset{\text{AUTO}}{\blacksquare}$ mode, specific Scene modes for certain types of subjects, or four exposure modes (P, S, A, and M).
- **Select AF mode:** see page 178 for full details on how to select an AF mode; I recommend using single-servo (S) mode.
- **Select AF-area mode:** see page 183 for full details of how to select an AF-area mode; I recommend using single-point [ɿ] mode.

- **Compose and focus picture:** Make sure you are holding the camera firmly. The fingers of your right hand should wrap around the handgrip in such a way that your index finger is free to operate the shutter release button. Cradle the bottom of the camera and lens with your left hand, keeping your thumb and index finger free to operate the zoom and/or focus ring on the lens. Keep your elbows tucked in close to your body and stand with your feet about shoulder-width apart. Compose a picture and make sure that one of the AF point covers an area of the subject that you want to be in focus. Press lightly on the shutter release button, activating the focusing system. If the camera can acquire focus, the focus indicator ● will appear in the viewfinder. If ● (blinks) is shown, the camera has not been able to acquire focus; re-compose the picture, place the selected AF point over an alternative part of the subject, and press lightly on the shutter release button again.

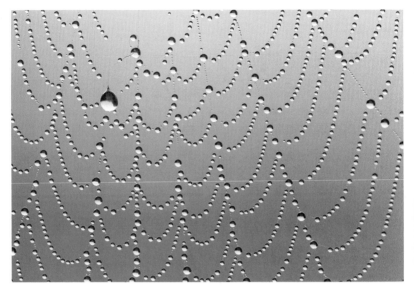

Proper hand-holding technique is one of several very important elements to getting good, sharp images.

- **Release shutter:** The shutter button has a two-stage release mechanism; pressing it down halfway activates the AF and TTL metering systems, while pressing it down all the way operates the shutter. Avoid stabbing you index finger down on the shutter release button, as this will increase the risk of camera shake. Practice the good hand holding technique described above and simply roll the tip of your index finger smoothly over the edge of the shutter release button to take the picture. The green access lamp on the back of the camera will illuminate as soon as an exposure has been made, indicating the camera is saving the image. To make another exposure, lift your index finger clear of the shutter release button and repeat the process described above.

- **Review picture:** see page 126 for full details on how to play back pictures.

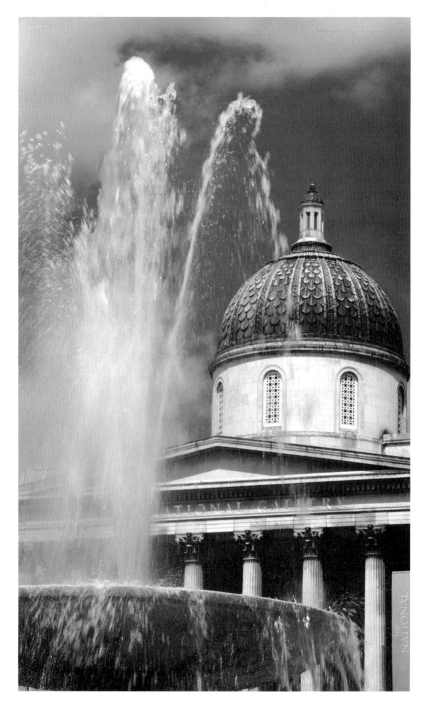

Powering the D90

Battery and Chargers

The D90 can be powered by a variety of sources. The battery supplied with the camera is the rechargeable lithium-ion EN-EL3e (7.4V, 1500mAh), which weighs approximately 2.8 oz (80g). The profile of the battery ensures that it can only be inserted the correct way into the camera. It is charged with the dedicated MH-18a Quick Charger, also supplied with the camera; its slightly larger predecessor, the MH-18, is also compatible. The MH-19 Multi-Charger, which supports both AC and DC power supplies can also be used. A fully discharged EN-EL3e can be completely recharged in approximately 135 minutes using the MH-18a or MH-18.

The EN-EL3e does not require conditioning prior to its first use (it is supplied partially charged). However, it is advisable to ensure that the initial charge cycle for a new battery is continued until the battery cools down before removing it from the charger. Do not be tempted to remove it as soon as the charging/charged indicator lamp on the MH-18a / MH-18 / MH-19 stops flashing to indicate charging is complete, as the battery is unlikely to have reached a full 100% charge.

Making the right choices regarding power sources for your D90, based on the situation, can mean the difference between capturing the images you want and not getting any photos at all.

An EN-EL3e battery is shown here, next to the empty battery chamber of the D90; note the diagram on the inside of the chamber cover.

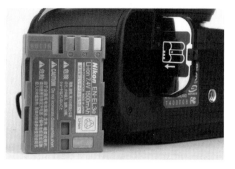

Using the EN-EL3e Battery

Whenever you insert or remove an EN-EL3e, it is essential that you set the camera's power switch to the off position.

To insert an EN-EL3e into the D90:

1. Invert the camera and push the small button on the battery chamber lid toward the tripod socket. Turn the camera back over and the battery chamber lid should swing open.
2. Open the lid fully and slide the battery into the camera, observing the diagram on the inside of the chamber lid.
3. Press the lid down (you will feel a slight resistance) until it locks (you will hear a click as the latch closes).

To remove an EN-EL3e from the D90:

1. Repeat Step 1 (above).
2. Hold the lid open, turn the camera upright, and allow the battery to slide out, taking care that it does not drop.
3. Close the battery chamber lid.

Note: If you are in the process of making any changes to the camera settings and the battery is removed or the power supply from the EH-5a / EH-5 is interrupted while the power switch is still set to the on position, the camera may not retain the new settings. Likewise, if the camera is in the process of transferring data from the buffer memory to the storage media when the power is interrupted, image files are likely to be corrupted or data lost.

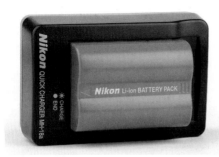

To charge an EN-EL3e:

1. Connect the MH-18a or other compatible charger to an AC power supply.

Note: The MH-18a / MH-18 / MH-19 can be used world-wide, connected to any AC power supply, at any voltage from 100V to 250V, via an appropriate power socket adapter.

2. Align the slots on the side of the battery with the four lugs (two on each side) on the top of the MH-18a / MH-18 / MH-19 and lower the battery before sliding it toward the indicator lamp until it locks into place. The charge lamp should begin to flash immediately, indicating that charging has commenced.

Lithium-ion batteries do not exhibit the same charge-memory effects associated with certain other types of rechargeable batteries, therefore a partially discharged EN-EL3e can take a top-up charge without any adverse consequences to battery life or performance. However, I do recommend that you avoid giving a battery a top-up charge when its charge level is at 90% or more; likewise, do not repeatedly run a battery down to a charge level of 10% or less before recharging it. In the former case, there is a risk of reducing overall battery capacity, and in the latter, successive charging of a battery from near exhaustion to full charge will likely reduce its life expectancy. The EN-EL3e battery has an electronic chip in its circuitry that allows the D90 to report detailed information regarding its status. To access this information, select [Battery Info] from the Setup menu (see page 248 for more details).

Hint: If you carry a spare EN-EL3e, always ensure that you keep the semi-opaque plastic terminal cover in place; without it, there is a risk that the battery terminals may short and cause damage to the battery.

It is a good idea to carry a spare EN-EL3e battery and rotate them regularly so that they are both in use.

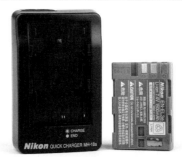

Note: The EN-EL3 and EN-EL3a battery types for some earlier Nikon D-SLR cameras such as the D100, D70 series, and D50 models are not compatible with the D90; if you attempt to insert either of these into the battery chamber of the D90, it will not fit. However, the EN-EL3e battery supplied with the D90 is backwards compatible and can be used in those earlier camera models.

Battery Performance

Operation of the D90 is totally dependent on an adequate electrical power supply. Obviously, the more functions the camera has to perform the greater the demand on its battery, so reducing the number of functions and the duration for which they are active is fundamental to reducing power consumption. This can be an important consideration, especially if you are travelling with your camera or expect to spend any extended period away from a AC electrical supply.

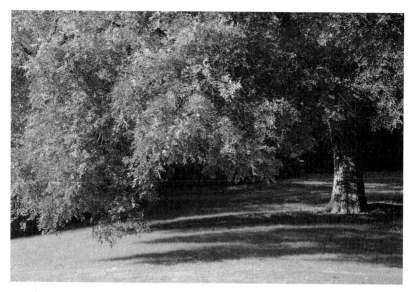

If you anticipate not having access to a means of charging your battery for a length of time, practice some of the suggestions set out here to conserve battery power.

Listed below are some of the principal causes of battery power drain together with a few suggestions as to how you can conserve battery power.

• The Movie mode (video recording) feature of the D90 is without a doubt the most demanding camera operation in terms of power consumption. In addition to requiring the camera to run in Live View mode, when recording is active, the camera is also writing data to the memory card continuously. To compound matters, it is almost always necessary to use the Vibration Reduction (VR) feature when shooting video with a hand-held camera; VR is second only to video recording as far as power consumption is concerned. A fully charged EN-EL3e can be reduced to near exhaustion after about 20 minutes of video recording when VR has been running continuously as well.

- In a similar vein, when shooting still pictures, the Live View feature draws a considerable amount of power from the battery, so consider rationalizing its use in situations when battery power preservation is important.

- Using the camera's color LCD monitor when shooting stills also increases power consumption significantly. Unless you need it, turn the monitor off. Consider setting the [Image review] item in the Playback menu to [Off]; the default setting is [On]. If [On] is selected, press the shutter release button lightly as soon as you have finished assessing the picture, since this returns the camera to its shooting mode, switching the LCD monitor off immediately. To help reduce time spent scrolling through the camera's menu system, I recommend consolidating those menu items you use frequently within ▓ My menu so that you only need to consult a single menu list.

- Recording NEF draws far more power compared with recording JPEG or TIFF (RGB) files. Although the power management of the D90 appears to have been enhanced in this respect compared with previous camera models, saving NEF files still places a significant burden on the camera's battery. There is nothing that can be done to mitigate this issue other than ensuring that if you habitually shoot using the NEF format you carry at least one spare battery.

- While driving the autofocus mechanism of lenses draws relatively little power because the demand on the battery is delivered in peaks of very short duration, the Vibration Reduction (VR) feature available with some Nikkor lenses is another matter. The VR function draws power from the camera battery and it tends to be active for far longer periods compared with AF operation. Consequently, VR can reduce battery life by approximately 10-15% when active.

- Using the built-in Speedlight flash unit will also place a significant demand on the battery and shorten the duration of any shooting session considerably.

- Low temperatures cause a change to the internal resistance of a battery, which impairs performance. Lithium-ion batteries are fairly resistant to cold conditions. However, to ensure that you can keep shooting, particularly in freezing conditions (i.e., below 0°C/32°F), keep at least one spare battery in a warm place such as an inside pocket; and as the performance of the battery in the camera dwindles, exchange it with the warm one. Allow the used battery time to warm up again and keep rotating between the batteries to maximize the shooting capacity.

Despite my warnings above, in my experience, shooting in an average ambient temperature range of 60° to 75° F (16° to 24° C), using autofocus with Vibration Reduction (VR) switched on, moderate use of the LCD screen for picture assessment, occasional use of Live View, and support of a GPS unit, a single EN-EL3e battery will still deliver sufficient power for approximately 500 exposures. Obviously, shooting capacity is increased significantly if a pair of EN-EL3e batteries is used in the MB-D80, but this does increase both the weight and bulk of the camera considerably.

Battery Storage
A fully charged Nikon Lithium-ion EN-EL3e battery in good condition will retain its full capacity over a short period of a few days. However, if the battery is left dormant for four weeks or more, regardless of whether it is installed in a camera or not, expect it to suffer a noticeable loss of charge; so ensure that it is recharged fully before use (see comments concerning top-up charging above). If you expect to store a camera battery for an extended period, avoid leaving it fully charged or heavily discharged. Storing a fully charged battery can have a long-term effect on its overall capacity, while storing a heavily discharged battery can risk it shifting to a deeply discharged state, which can damage it. The optimum charge level for a battery that will be stored for four weeks or more is between 20 and 80%. Always store your camera and batteries in a well-ventilated, cool, dry place and be sure that the protective terminal cover is in place.

Alternative Power Supplies For The D90

The MB-D80 Battery Pack

The MB-D80 battery pack is shown here with the battery chamber door open and two EN-EL3e batteries installed.

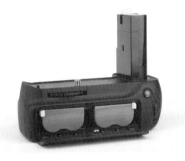

The MB-D80 is a battery pack/grip that is compatible with the D80 and the D90. Attaching to the base of the D90 body via the tripod socket, it requires the battery chamber door and the battery installed in the camera to be removed first, so that the shaft of the battery pack, which has electrical contact pins located on its top face, can be inserted in to the battery chamber to make connection with the camera. To prevent loss of the battery chamber door while the MB-D80 is attached to the D90, stow it in the slot set into the side of the shaft of the battery pack.

The MB-D80 battery pack features a second set of controls for vertical shooting.

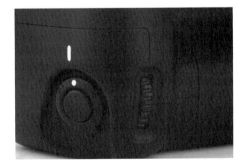

The MB-D80 battery pack can accommodate either one or two EN-EL3e batteries. Installing an extra EN-EL3e in the MB-D80 has no effect on the maximum frame rate, which remains at 4.5 fps (frames per second) but two fully charged EN-EL3e batteries provide the highest possible power level (a combined maximum of 3000mAh) to extend the potential shooting duration of the camera.

In addition to providing extra battery capacity, the MB-D80 has a shutter release button, main and sub-command dials, and an AE-L/AF-L button to improve handling when the camera is held in the vertical (portrait) orientation. Another potential benefit of the MB-D80 is that it can help to improve camera handling when using longer, heavier lenses because of the extra bulk and weight it adds to the D90.

Alternatively, it can accept six AA batteries that must be fitted in the MS-D80 battery holder (supplied with the MB-D80). There are four compatible AA battery types: LR6 (Alkaline), HR6 (Nickel Metal Hydride), FR6 (Lithium), and ZR6 (Nickel Manganese). Regardless of which type of AA battery is installed, it is important that the [MB-D80 Battery Type] item at CS-d12 is set appropriately to ensure proper camera operation. There is, however, no requirement to use this custom setting when the EN-EL3e battery is used instead. It is

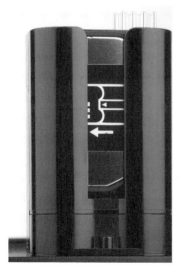

The battery chamber door of the D90, which must be removed to attach the MB-D80, can be stowed in a slot set into the shaft of the battery pack.

often possible to attain a very slightly higher frame rate with the D90 when using absolutely fresh or fully charged HR6 (Nickel Metal Hydride) or FR6 (Lithium) AA batteries; however, any advantage will be short lived, as the level of battery charge drops with use.

Hint: I strongly recommend that if you use AA batteries, you avoid the LR6 (Alkaline) and ZR6 (Nickel Manganese) types unless there is no alternative. It is important to be aware that in cooler ambient temperatures (i.e., below 20°C / 68°F) the performance of these batteries is impaired significantly and they may even cease to function in cold conditions. Regardless of the ambient temperature, they will offer the lowest shooting capacity compared with other AA battery types.

Note: The status of the batteries installed in the MB-D80 can be checked using the [Battery Info] option of the Setup menu (see page 248 for more details).

External Power Supply – EH-5A / EH-5 AC Adapter

The Nikon EH-5A and EH-5 AC adapters, which are optional accessories, can also power the D90; either version of this AC adapter, which are both rated for an input of 100 – 240V, AC 50-60Hz, is particularly useful for extended periods of shooting, such as time-lapse photography, image playback, or data transfer direct from the camera to a computer. The adapter connects to the DC-In socket, which is located beneath the large rubber terminal cover on the left side of the camera. The EH-5a /EH-5 is also useful to prevent the camera from powering off while the reflex mirror is raised for inspection or cleaning of the optical low-pass filter (see page 369 for more details).

To prevent data loss or file corruption during shooting or data transfer as a result of the power from the EH-5 / EH-5A being disconnected inadvertently, leave a fully charged EN-EL3e battery in the camera to maintain a power supply. Always ensure that the power switch is set to the off position before connecting/disconnecting the EH-5A / EH-5 to the DC-In socket. There is a risk that the camera's circuitry could

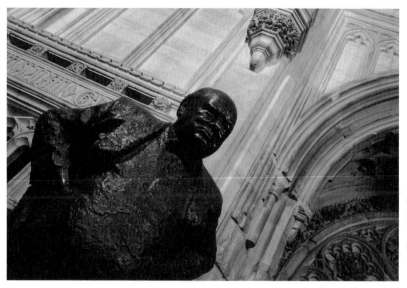

To extend the overall life of your batteries, when transferring images directly from the camera to a computer, use the EH-5 or EH-5 AC Adapter.

be damaged if you plug/unplug the AC adapter while the power switch is set to the on position.

Effect of Static Charge

All electronically controlled cameras very occasionally exhibit strange behavior, with unexpected icons or characters appearing in the LCD display or the camera ceasing to function properly. This is usually due an electro-static charge. To remedy the situation, try switching the camera off, removing and replacing the battery, or disconnecting and reconnecting the AC supply, before switching the camera on again. If normal operation does not resume, it will be necessary to have the camera checked by a qualified technician.

Internal Clock/Calendar Battery

The D90 has an internal clock/calendar that is powered by a fixed, internal, rechargeable battery; fully charged, it will power the clock/calendar for about three months. This battery requires charging for approximately 48 hours via the camera's main power supply: this can be either a single EN-EL3e inserted in the camera body or MB-D80 battery pack, two EN-EL3e batteries in the MB-D80 battery pack, or the EH-5a / EH-5 AC adapter. Should the clock battery become exhausted, **CLOCK** will flash in the control panel and the clock is reset to a date and time of 2008.01.01 00:00:00. If this occurs, insert at least one fully charged battery and leave it in place for a few days, or plug the camera to an AC outlet using one of the AC adapters and turn it on. The clock/calendar will need to be reset to the correct time via the [World time] item in the Setup menu (see page 243 for more details).

Note: Should the internal clock/calendar battery fail and not retain a charge, the camera must be returned to a Nikon approved service center for a replacement battery to be fitted, since this battery cannot be changed at home.

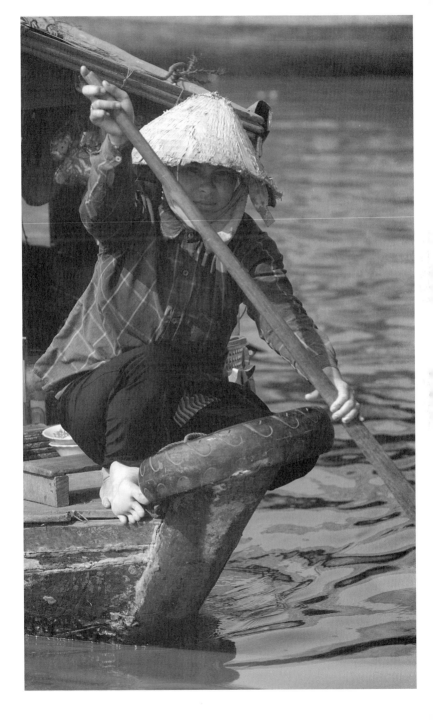

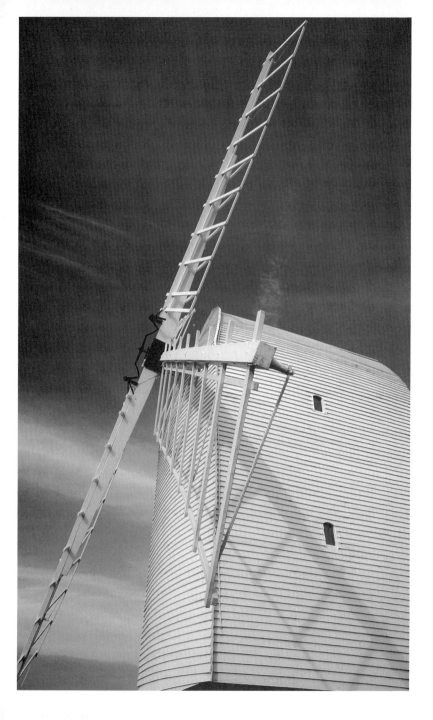

White Balance

We are all familiar with the way the color of sunlight changes during the course of a day from the warm orange/yellow colors immediately after sunrise, through the cooler (blue) color of light around midday, returning to the orange/yellow colors that appear as the sun sets. These changes are significant and our eyes can see them quite clearly. However, the color of light (not to be confused with the color of the objects from which it is reflected) changes in subtle ways at other times of the day and in different climatic conditions. Furthermore, artificial light sources such as a household lightbulb or a an electronic flash unit emit light with a wide range of different colors. The color of light is referred to as its color temperature (see "What is Color Temperature?" on page 60). In many instances, our eyes and brain are remarkably good at adapting to these changes in the color temperature of the light, so they are not visibly apparent to us. Think about what you see when you stand outside a building in which the interior lamps are switched on in daylight—the light the lamps emit often appears very yellow. But, if you look into the same building after dark, the light from the lamps now appears to be white. This is an example of the adaptive process that our eyes and brain apply to light, one which cameras, regardless of whether they use film or a digital sensor, cannot perform!

☞ *Understanding the D90's white balance settings will allow you to control how colors will be rendered in your photos.*

The white balance (WB) button is located on the rear of the D90, immediately below the MENU *button.*

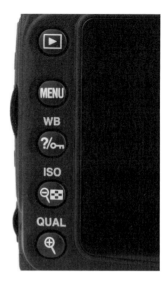

Cameras have a fixed response to the color temperature of the light they record. Film has a response limited to a specific color temperature (for daylight-balanced film, this is equivalent to direct sunlight at midday under a clear sky). Digital cameras, such as the D90, are far more flexible; they can process the picture data to equate to a variety of specific color temperatures, either automatically or by settings made manually by the user. This function is known as white balance control.

What is Color Temperature?

The color of light is often referred to as its "color temperature," which is expressed in units called degrees Kelvin (K). It sounds counter-intuitive, but warm light (red/orange colors) has a low color temperature and cool light (blue tones) has a high color temperature.

Why is this? Well, the color temperature of a light source equates to the color of something called a "black body radiator"—a concept used by scientists that involves a theoretical object that can re-emit 100% of the energy it absorbs. As heat is applied to this black body radiator, it becomes hotter and its color changes from black, to red, orange, yellow, through to blue. The color temperature of a particular light source is said to approximate the color of a black body radiator at the same temperature. Thus, at a low temperature, the color of the light emitted would contain a high proportion of red wavelengths; at a high temperature, the light would contain a high proportion of blue wavelengths.

Generally, film is balanced to either direct sunlight under a clear sky at mid-day (a color temperature around 5500K) or the light emitted by a tungsten photoflood lamp (a color temperature around 3400K). If you were shooting film and the temperature of the ambient light under which you were shooting differed from these values, your photographs would take on a color cast (unnatural tint) and you would need to use color correction filters to counter the effects.

Note: The color temperature of daylight will vary according to a number of factors, including time of day, time of year, latitude, altitude, and the prevailing atmospheric and climatic conditions. The color temperature of 5500K, to which daylight film is balanced, is a somewhat arbitrary value and should only be used as a rough guide.

Digital cameras are far more versatile and can either automatically adjust their response to light within a range of different color temperatures, or allow you to set a specific color temperature. This feature is known as the white balance control. Assuming that the color temperature value of the chosen white balance corresponds to the color temperature of the prevailing light in the scene, it will be rendered without any noticeable color cast. You can also use the white balance feature creatively by setting an alternative value, which does not correspond to the prevailing light, thereby inducing a deliberate color shift.

Selecting a White Balance Option

The white balance options of the D90 camera can be selected in one of two ways: Via the Shooting menu or using the WB button. To access the white balance setting via the Shooting menu, open the Shooting menu and navigate to the [White Balance] option. Press ⊕ on the multi selector and highlight the option you want from the displayed list by pressing either ▲ or ▼ (you must take this route if you want to alter the color temperature value for the Fluorescent option). Then, press ⊕ to open the fine-tuning control and set any desired adjustment (see the next section). Finally, press ⊕ to confirm the selection.

Alternatively, and in my opinion the quicker method, use the WB button on the back of the camera to select a white balance option. Press and hold the WB button and rotate the main command dial until the relevant white balance icon is displayed in the control panel.

White Balance Options

The white balance control of the D90 offers nine principal white balance options: Auto, Incandescent, Fluorescent (with seven sub-options), Direct Sunlight, Flash, Cloudy, Shade, Choose Color Temp, and Preset manual. In addition to these options, the white balance control has a fine-tuning function. The approximate color temperature for each option (except Choose Color Temp and Preset manual) is given in parentheses in the following list of descriptions for the various white balance options.

A Automatic (3500 – 8000K)
Unlike previous Nikon D-SLR cameras, the D90 benefits from the newly developed Scene Recognition System (SRS), which enhances the abilities of its long-established, 1005-pixel, RGB metering sensor. For example, the system helps enable the D90 to distinguish between the greens of foliage and the green wavelengths produced by a florescent lightbulb.

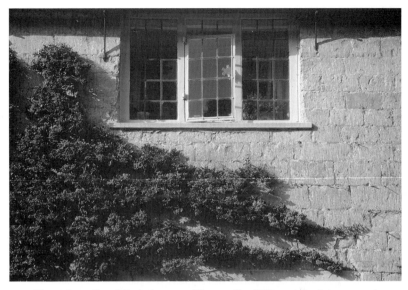

The automatic white balance setting on the D90 usually does a great job in normal daylight conditions.

Nikon states that the effective color temperature range of the automatic white balance option on the D90 is 3500 to 8000K. In practice, while I have found this option to be very effective and more reliable than on any previous Nikon D-SLR, when shooting in the middle of that range (i.e., typical daylight conditions) I would suggest that in practice the color temperature range is closer to 4000 to 6500K. For example, in lighting conditions with low color temperature values, typically incandescent lighting, I find the D90 consistently sets a color temperature that is too high, resulting in an overly warm (too much yellow) cast. As with all automatic features, you will need to override the automatic white balance settings of the D90 when the lighting situations necessitate it: For example, indoors under normal domestic-type electric lighting, the color temperature of light sources is likely to be lower than 4000K; or alternatively, outdoors in bright overcast conditions and at high altitudes, the color temperature of daylight can often exceed 6500K.

☀ Incandescent (3000K)

Use this option when shooting under typical household incandescent lighting, as its color temperature is a better match; however, you may find that results still look too warm (i.e., the red content is too high).

☲ Fluorescent (2700K – 7200K)

The light emitted from fluorescent tubes is notorious for causing unwanted color casts. This is due to the way these tubes work and the variability in the color temperature of the light they produce. In an effort to increase the accuracy of color rendition under the wide variety of fluorescent bulbs, the D90 has seven sub-options available under the [Fluorescent] white balance option in the Shooting menu. To access these options, open the Shooting menu and navigate to the [White Balance] option, press ⊚ on the multi selector button and highlight [Fluorescent], and then press ⊚ again to display the seven bulb types. Highlight the required bulb type and press ⊚ to open the fine-tuning control. Make any desired adjustment before pressing ⓞⓚ to set the bulb type and fine-tuning factor (if selected). The bulb type will be displayed in the Shooting menu, as ☲ next to a number from 1 to 7 (see table below). Selecting [Fluorescent] by pressing the WB button and rotating the main command dial will select the bulb type set via the [White Balance] option in the Shooting menu, but only ☲ is displayed in the control panel.

The details of the seven bulb types found in the [Fluorescent] white balance option is as follows:

Bulb Type	Color Temperature	Shooting menu display
Sodium-vapor lamps	2700	☲ 1
Warm-white fluorescent	3000	☲ 2
White fluorescent	3700	☲ 3
Cool-white fluorescent	4200	☲ 4
Day white fluorescent	5000	☲ 5
Daylight fluorescent	6500	☲ 6
High temp. mercury vapor	7200	☲ 7

☀ Direct sunlight (5200K)

This option is intended for subjects or scenes photographed in direct sunlight during the middle part of the day (i.e., from around two hours after sunrise to two hours before sunset). At other times, when the sun is low in the sky, the light tends to be "warmer" – using this setting at those times will produce pictures with a higher red content.

Hint: White balance is a very subjective issue, but to my eye, Nikon's color temperature for the Direct Sunlight option is too low. When shooting in these conditions, I often prefer to use either the [Flash] or the [Cloudy] option. I recommend you experiment to find a setting that meets your requirements.

⚡ Flash (5400K)

As its name implies, this option is intended for use whenever a flash (Nikon refers to their own flash units as Speedlights) is the main lighting source.

Hint: Like the [Direct Sunlight] option, I consider the color temperature of the Flash option to be slightly too low. The color temperature of light emitted by Nikon Speedlights is generally in the range of 5500 – 6000K; therefore, I often select the [Cloudy] option when working with Nikon flash units as the main lighting source.

☁ Cloudy (6000K)

This white balance option is intended for shooting under overcast skies, when daylight has a high color temperature. It ensures that the camera renders colors properly without the typical cool tone, which can impart a blue appearance to a photograph, particularly in pale skin tones.

🏠 Shade (8000K)

This option applies a greater degree of correction than the [Cloudy] option, and is intended for those situations when your subject or scene is in open shade beneath a clear or nearly clear blue sky. Under these conditions the light will have a very high blue content, as it is principally comprised of light reflected from the blue sky above.

ⓚ Choose Color Temp. (2500 – 10,000K)

The [Choose Color Temp] option under the [White Balance] option in the Shooting menu enables you to select from thirty-one different predetermined color temperature values, ranging from 2,500K to 10,000K in increments of approximately 10 MIRED (see "What is MIRED?" panel, later in this chapter). If you know the specific color temperature of the light source(s) illuminating the subject / scene, the camera can be set to match it.

Open the Shooting menu and navigate to the [White Balance] option, then press ⊙ to display the choices. Highlight the [Choose Color Temp] option and press ⊙ to display the color temperature values. Press either ▲ or ▼ to highlight the required value and press ⊙ to open the fine-tuning option, make any needed adjustments, then press ⓞⓚ to save the setting.

Alternatively, press and hold the WB button and rotate the main command dial to select the [Choose Color Temp] option in the control panel display. To select the required color temperature, press and hold the WB button and rotate the sub-command dial; the color temperature value is displayed in the control panel while the WB button is pressed.

PRE Preset

This option allows you to obtain a measurement of the exact color temperature of the light illuminating the subject or scene using a test exposure or an existing image. This probably provides the most accurate way of setting a white balance value in conditions with mixed lighting sources or any type of lighting that has a strong color bias.

Using the Preset Option

The camera can store up to five different values for a preset white balance. The white balance value measured most recently will be stored as d-0. This can be copied to any one of the other four white balance files, d-1, d-2, d-3, and d-4.

Likewise, a white balance copied from an existing photograph can also be copied to these same white balance value files.

Hint: The Nikon instruction manual suggests that you can use either a white or gray card as a reference target for the Preset manual white balance option. I strongly recommend that you use only a gray card for two reasons. First, white cards often contain pigments used to whiten them, which can cause the camera to render colors inaccurately. Second, it is more difficult to expose correctly for a pure white subject. To try to compensate for this, the D90 will automatically increase exposure by 1Ev when measuring for the Preset manual white balance (in manual exposure mode, be sure to adjust exposure, so the analog scale display is set to ±0), but errors in exposure can affect the white balance reading you obtain from the test target.

Hint: In place of a test target such as a gray card, there are a number of products that can be attached directly to the lens and allow the camera to not only obtain a white balance measurement but also to take an incident reading for the ambient light, using its TTL metering system. Probably the best device I have used for this purpose is the ExpoDisc (www.expodisc.com).

Create a new preset value: To measure a Preset manual white balance value, select the [Preset manual] option (as described above), then place your test target in the same light that is illuminating the subject to be photographed. The exposure mode you use is not critical, but I suggest you use Aperture-priority auto (A). Press the WB button on the rear of the camera and rotate the main command dial until **PRE** is displayed in the control panel. Release the WB button briefly, then press and hold it until **PrE** begins to flash in the viewfinder and control panel displays. Point the camera at the reference target (make sure you do not cast a shadow over the test target card) and make sure that it completely fills the viewfinder frame. There is no need to focus on the test target, simply press the shutter release button all the way down. If the camera is able to obtain an adequate measurement and set a white balance value, **Good** will be displayed in the control panel, while "Gd" will appear in the viewfinder; both icons will blink. If the camera is unable to set a white balance value, it probably means that the light level is either too low or too high and **no Ŀd** will blink in both the viewfinder and the control panel. In this case, repeat the process, adjusting either the illumination of the test target or the exposure level until a measurement is achieved.

The white balance is now set for the prevailing light falling on your subject and this value will automatically be stored and retained in d-0, replacing any previous value stored there until you make another preset option measurement. To use the new white balance value immediately, ensure that d-0 is selected for the preset white balance file by pressing the WB button and rotating the sub-command dial until d-0 is displayed in the control panel.

To retain the value at d-0 and store it as one of the other four preset values, d-1 to d-4, open the [White Balance] option in the Shooting menu before taking a new white balance measurement and select the [Preset manual] option, then press ⊚ . Highlight the destination preset (d-1 to d-4) using the multi selector button, and then press the ⊕ . Finally, highlight [Copy d-0] and press ⊛ . If a comment has been attached to the Preset manual white balance value stored at d-0, it will be transferred to the selected preset value.

Note: If no white balance value is measured for d-0, the color temperature will be set to 5200K (the same as the Direct sunlight option).

Use an existing image: If you want to use the white balance value of a photograph previously recorded by the D90, open the [White Balance] option in the Shooting menu, highlight the [Preset manual] option, and then press ⊚ . Highlight the destination preset (d-1 to d-4) to which you want to save the value and press the ⊕ button. Highlight [Select image] and press ⊚ to display a thumbnail view of all images stored on the installed memory card (press the ⊕ button if you wish to display the image full frame on the screen). Highlight the photograph desired as the source of the white balance value by using

68

the multi selector button (a narrow yellow border will surround it) and press ⊛ to copy the white balance value and any stored comment to the selected preset.

Selecting a White Balance Preset Value

You can select a stored preset white balance value in one of two ways: Via the menu system or by using the WB button in combination with the main command dial.

To use the menu system, open the [White Balance] option in the Shooting menu and highlight the [Preset manual] option, then press ⊛ . Highlight the desired preset (d-0 to d-4) value and press the ⊖ button. Highlight [Set] and press ⊛ to display the fine-tuning options, adjust if required and finally press ⊛ to save the settings.

Alternatively, press the WB button and rotate the main command dial until **PRE** is displayed in the control panel. Press the WB button again and rotate the sub-command dial to display the preset value (d-0 to d-4) in the control panel.

Attaching a Comment to a Preset Value

To help identify a preset value, a comment of up to 36 characters can be attached to it. Open the [White Balance] option in the Shooting menu and highlight the [Preset manual] option, then press ⊛ . Highlight the required preset value and press the ⊖ button. Highlight [Edit comment] and press ⊛ . Use the displayed characters and controls displayed at the bottom of the screen to create a comment. Press ⊛ to save the comment.

Hint: The ability of the D90 to store preset white balance values is very useful. If the camera is to be used in a variety of different lighting conditions during the course of an event, a white balance value can be measured, stored, and named for each location in advance. Then, you only have to recall the appropriate preset value for each location as the event progresses. This is also applicable if you frequently return to a particular location; the white balance value for the lighting can be stored and recalled at will on each visit.

Fine-Tuning White Balance

This feature allows you to fine-tune the white balance to compensate for variations in the color temperature of a particular light source or to create a deliberate color cast in a picture. The system effects change in equally spaced MIRED values, which offers considerably more precise and consistent results when compared with the somewhat arbitrary and counter-intuitive method employed in previous Nikon D-SLR cameras. If you have become familiar with the previous system, where positive and negative values created cooler and warmer results respectively, you will need to invest some time to learn the new one—the results may not be what you expect.

The fine-tuning of white balance can be achieved via two different routes: The [White Balance] option in the Shooting menu or the WB button and sub-command dial. The [White Balance] option in the Shooting menu will provide the greatest control over the level of fine-tuning for both color temperature and color. Open the Shooting menu and navigate to the [White Balance] option; press (⊙) to display the list of options. Highlight the desired white balance option, then press (⊙) to display a color graph; its horizontal axis is used to fine-tune for the level of amber (A) and blue (B), while the vertical axis is used to adjust the level of magenta (M) and green (G).

The [Fluorescent], [Choose color temp], and [Preset] options each require one additional step to be performed before the color graph is displayed:

- If you opt for the [Fluorescent] option, select a bulb type and press (⊙) .
- If you opt for the [Choose color temp] option, highlight a color temperature value and press (⊙) .
- If you opt for the [Preset] option, select a preset value (see below) and press (⊙) .

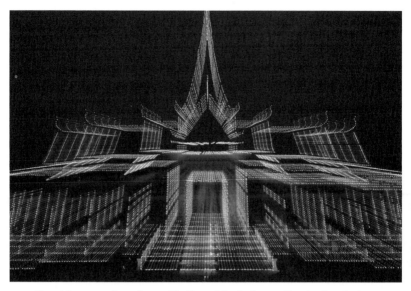

Consider experimenting with the white balance fine-tuning feature for creative effects.

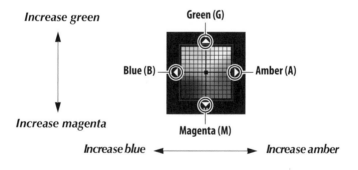

Once the graph is displayed, using the multi selector, select a value between 1 and 6 along each axis of the color graph, working from the central point (see graphic above). Color temperature is fine-tuned by shifting along the amber (A) – blue (B) axis, while color is shifted along the green (G) – magenta (M) axis. Adjusting the color through this fine-tuning option is similar to using color-compensating (CC) filters. A combined color temperature and color shift is possible by moving the cursor of the graph display into one of the four quadrants of the graph. Once you have set the fine-tuning adjustment, press ⊙ button to save the setting and return to the Shooting menu.

The alternative fine-tuning method uses the WB button in combination with the sub-command dial, but only provides the ability to fine-tune the color temperature (not the color), so the image looks either warmer or cooler. However, this method is not available for either the [Choose Color Temp], or [Preset] white balance options. If you use this method, the values A1 - A6 (amber) and b1 – b6 (blue) are displayed in the control panel. Each increment is equivalent to about 5 MIRED; the higher the number, the greater the color shift. Two opposing arrowheads are displayed beneath the WB icon in the control panel when the fine-tuning is active. Select 0 if you do not wish to apply a fine-tuning factor.

What is MIRED?
MIRED (Micro Reciprocity Degree) is a method of defining a shift in color in such a way that each shift in MIRED value is equivalent to the difference in color we perceive. The disadvantage of degrees Kelvin (K) is that a relatively small shift in Kelvin value at low color temperatures (e.g., less than 4000K) creates a much larger perceived shift in visible color than the same small shift in Kelvin value at high color temperatures (e.g., more than 6000K). The MIRED value is calculated by multiplying the reciprocal of the color temperature by ten to the power six (10 6). For example, the difference of 1000K between a color temperature of 3000K and 4000K is equal to 83 MIRED, whereas the difference between 6000K and 7000K is only 24 MIRED.

Creative White Balance

Feel like getting creative? It is easy with the white balance control on the D90. You don't necessarily have to set the white balance to match the color temperature of the prevailing light. Try mismatching it instead! For example, rather than shooting a subject or scene lit by daylight using one of the daylight white balance values, set the white balance to incandescent – now your picture will have a strong blue color cast. The great appeal of digital photography is the ability to experiment!

Remember, if the color temperature of the prevailing light is lower than the color temperature of the white balance value set on the camera, the subject or scene will be rendered with a warmer appearance. Conversely, if the color temperature of the prevailing light is higher than the color temperature of the white balance value set on the camera, the subject or scene will be rendered with a cooler appearance.

White Balance Bracketing

The white balance-bracketing feature on the D90 creates multiple copies of a single image recorded by the camera, but each copy has a different white balance value (as determined by the selected settings). The bracketing feature is not available with the following image quality settings: NEF (RAW), or NEF (RAW) + JPEG; selection of any of these options will cancel white balance bracketing. White balance bracketing only affects color temperature on the amber / blue axis; there is no effect on the green / magenta axis.

Select the [WB bracketing] option at CS-e4 (Auto Bracketing Set). Press the **BKT** button and rotate the main command dial to select the number of different white balance values to be created by the bracketing process. A scale will be displayed in the control panel to indicate the number of images that will be created. (Remember, only one exposure is made – the camera applies the different white balance

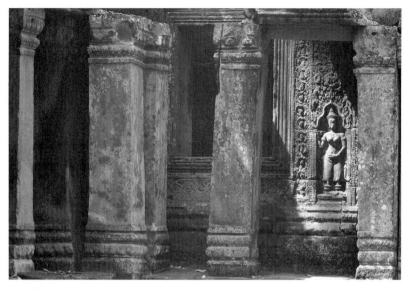

If you are unsure about the light temperature of the ambient light, try bracketing to see which white balance value produces the best image.

values as it processes the image data from a single exposure.) At a setting other than zero, "WB-BKT" is displayed in the top and rear control panels.

To select the adjustment level to be applied to the white balance value, press the **BKT** button and rotate the sub-command dial. Each increment is approximately equal to 5 MIRED. Choose from increments of 1 (5 MIRED), 2 (10 MIRED), or 3 (15 MIRED); higher 'A' values correspond to an increased shift in color temperature toward a warmer rendition of the image (i.e., more amber), while higher 'B' values shift color temperature toward a cooler rendition (i.e., more blue).

After making the single exposure, the camera will process the data to create the number of shots that you specified in the sequence. Each file will have a different white balance value according to the increment selected.

Control panel display	No. of shots	White balance increment	Bracketing order (Evs)
OF 1	0	1	0
b2F 1 +◀■	2	1B	0/1B
A2F 1 ■▶-	2	1A	0/1A
3F 1 +◀■▶-	3	1A, 1B	0/1A/1B

Note: The effect of applying a white balance fine-tuning factor and white balance bracketing are cumulative (i.e., the bracketed values will be added to the fine-tuning factor for each file the camera creates).

Note: If the number of shots in the bracketing sequence is greater than the remaining capacity of images on the installed memory card, shooting will stop when the card is full; simply insert a new memory card, format it, and you can resume shooting the white balance bracketing sequence.

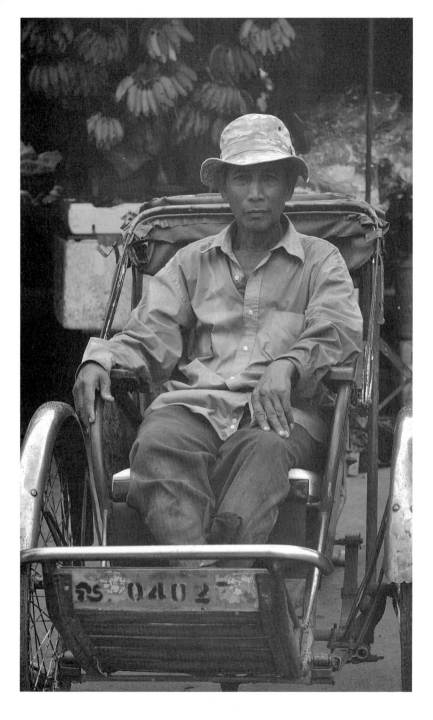

The Picture Control System

The Picture Control System (PCS) replaces the color mode options and optimize image features in previous Nikon D-SLR cameras, which were used to influence the appearance of pictures in terms of sharpening, contrast, brightness, color saturation, and hue.

The purpose of the PCS is to provide a single, all-encompassing solution for obtaining consistent results with different Nikon cameras, while also integrating Nikon software, particularly View NX and Capture NX2. Once you have adjusted settings to achieve your desired result on one camera, they can be replicated and used to produce pictures with identical attributes. Furthermore, within Nikon Capture NX2 software, it is possible to apply the same settings to an NEF (RAW) file recorded by any Nikon D-SLR camera that has the PCS.

It is important to mention that full integration of the PCS with Nikon View NX and Nikon Capture NX or NX2 means that the settings made within the PCS on the D90 are only relevant if you shoot in the JPEG format. The values for the various parameters are embedded in those file types and cannot be altered at a later stage, at least not without a lot of trial and error, and even then there is no guarantee that the process will be successful. Since the full range of the PCS settings is replicated in View NX and Capture NX2, it is possible to adjust all PCS settings at will if pictures are recorded by the D90 in the NEF format.

The D90's Picture Control System offers a level of in-camera manip-ulation that was previously only available as part of post-processing computer software.

Note: If you use an alternative RAW file converter (e.g., Adobe Camera RAW 4.6 or 5.1, or Lightroom 2.1), the embedded JPEG within the NEF file (which is used for preview purposes) will not match the converted NEF file unless the PCS settings on the camera were at their default values. This issue is compounded by the fact that many third-party RAW converters do not reproduce Nikon's white balance settings with precision, so color may look a little off compared with an NEF file converted by View NX or Capture NX2.

Features of the PCS

The Picture Control System offers six basic picture control options: Standard, Neutral, Vivid, Monochrome, Portrait, and Landscape. Depending on which option is selected, a range of attributes can be adjusted including sharpening, contrast, brightness, saturation, and hue. The monochrome option offers controls to simulate traditional contrast filters and toning effects used for black-and-white photography. The Standard, Vivid, Portrait, and Landscape Picture Controls also offer quick adjustment features that allow their effects to be either intensified or toned down. Plus, there is an automated option to adjust sharpening, contrast, and saturation. Finally, a graphical display available on the camera's LCD monitor maps contrast against saturation to help you understand how one group of settings relates to another.

The full flexibility of the PCS comes with the ability to modify the six default picture control options and create your own Custom Picture Controls within the D90. A maximum of nine custom picture controls can be saved in the camera; they can also be copied to a memory card and transferred to other compatible cameras, or to a computer for use with Nikon View NX or Nikon Capture NX2. Likewise, Custom Picture Controls can be created using the Picture Control Utility within View NX or Capture NX2 software and uploaded to the camera.

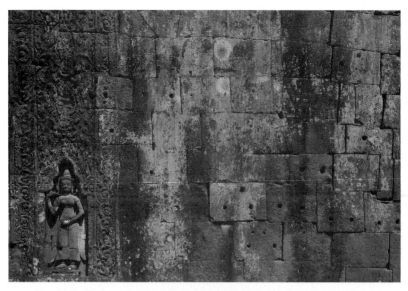

The D90 offers a number of picture control options, including Vivid, Portrait, and Monochrome (black and white).

Nikon has also issued a Picture Control that emulates the results produced by the D2X camera model. This can be downloaded for free from any Nikon technical support website along with comprehensive instructions on how to install it into the D90. Essentially, once the relevant Picture Control file has been downloaded, it entails copying that file to the top (root) level of a memory card, pre-formatted in the D90, by connecting the card to the computer using a card reader. After inserting the memory card in the camera, you use the [Copy to camera] option of the [Load/save] option in the [Manage Picture Control] item of the Shooting menu. The new Picture Control must then be assigned to one of the unused locations in the Picture Control menu list (see below for full details).

Selecting a Nikon Picture Control

Open the Shooting menu and navigate to the [Set Picture Control] option, then press ⊕ to display the six basic picture control options: Standard, Neutral, Vivid, Monochrome, Portrait, and Landscape. Highlight the required option and press ⊛ . To access the graphical display of contrast and saturation, in order to compare the selected option with the others, press and hold the ⊞ button (if the Monochrome option is selected, only the value for contrast is shown).

Option	Sharpening	Effect
▣SD Standard	3	Probably the most useful option for most shooting situations. Modest levels are applied to image attributes such as color, saturation, and contrast.
▣NL Neutral	2	Provides a good starting point for any image that will be subjected to extensive post-processing, as processing is applied in-camera is very minimal.
▣VI Vivid	4	Useful for images that will be printed directly from the camera. Saturation and contrast are relatively high.
▣MC Monochrome	3	Use for producing black-and-white images directly from the camera.
▣PT Portrait	2	Color rendition is optimized for skin tones, while sharpening is reduced.
▣LS Landscape	4	Saturation of blues and greens tends to be boosted, plus sharpening level is raised.

Hint: There is no indication in the control panel or viewfinder as to which picture control is selected, but if you press the [Info] button, the information will be shown in the shooting information display.

Modifying a Picture Control

The PCS enables you to modify any one of the six basic Nikon Picture Controls to create a Custom Picture Control; furthermore, once a Custom Picture Control has been saved, it can be modified at any time subsequently. However, it is not possible to create an entirely new Picture Control, but only modify an existing set of parameters provided by the Nikon Picture Control settings.

Start by navigating to the [Set Picture Control] option in the Shooting menu, and then press ⊕ to display the stored Picture Control options. Highlight the required option and press ⊕ to display the settings: Use ▲ and ▼ to select the desired attribute and use ◄ and ► to adjust its value. Alternatively, where available, you can use the quick-adjust to select a preset combination of settings; these will be displayed against each attribute as you adjust the level in the quick-adjust option. If at any time you want to restore a Picture Control to its original settings, press the 🗑 button, highlight [Yes] and press ⊛ . Press the ⊛ button to save the settings you have selected. When you adjust the level of a Picture Control setting, a yellow line is displayed beneath the previous level for your reference. If a Picture Control is modified from its default, or original settings in the case of a Custom Picture Control, it will be marked with an asterisk.

Note: If you modify a Picture Control and do not see the results you expect, it is probably due to the default setting for the monitor brightness being too high. Try reducing the brightness of the screen display to a value of [-1]. Also remember that while the screen has greater resolution than previous Nikon D-SLR cameras, it is still not capable of displaying the full gamut of colors defined by the Adobe RGB color space, with greens being restricted in particular; its capabilities are closer to approaching the narrower gamut of sRGB.

The settings available for each of the picture control options is outlined in the following table:

Option	Settings
Quick adjust	Choose values between ±2 to reduce (negative value) or enhance (positive value) the effect of the selected Picture Control. This option resets any manually adjusted settings and is only available with the Standard, Vivid, Portrait, and Landscape options.
All Picture Controls	
Sharpening	A (auto), or a manually set value between 0 and 9; the higher the value the greater the degree of sharpening.
Contrast	A (auto), or a manually set value between ±3; negative values reduce contrast, while positive values increase contrast.
Brightness	Choose values in the range of ±1 to reduce (negative value) or enhance (positive value) brightness of an image.
Picture Controls (except Monochrome)	
Saturation	A (auto), or a manually set value of ±3; negative values reduce saturation, while positive values increase saturation.
Hue	Manually set value between ±3; see description of the effect below.
Monochrome Picture Controls only	
Filter effects	Use to emulate the effects of contrast control filters used with traditional black-and-white photography.
Toning	Use to emulate the effect of chemical toners used in traditional black-and-white photography

Adjustments Available in all Picture Controls

[Sharpening]: Sharpening is a process applied to digital data that can increases the apparent sharpness (acuity) of a picture. It is applied to correct the side effects of converting light into digital data, which often causes distinct edges between colors, tones, and objects in a digital picture to look ill-defined (fuzzy). The process identifies an edge by analyzing the differences between neighboring pixel values. It then lightens the pixels immediately adjacent to the brighter side of the edge and darkens the pixels adjacent to the dark side of the edge. This adjustment causes a local increase of contrast around the edge, making it appear sharper; the higher the level of sharpening applied, the greater the contrast at the edge. Sharpening is not a method for rescuing an out-of-focus picture—remember, once out-of-focus always out-of-focus!

If you select the automatic setting for this option, you surrender all control to the camera and have no way of ensuring consistency in the degree of sharpening it applies; the camera will vary the amount of sharpening according to the nature of the scene being photographed. Scenes with a high degree of fine detail will receive a greater degree of sharpening, compared with scene that contains large area(s) of continuous tone.

Hint: There is no single level of sharpening that is appropriate for all shooting conditions. With JPEG files, it is fixed by in-camera processing and any sharpening applied in post-processing will be cumulative. With an NEF file, the original in-camera sharpening can be removed, but only by selecting a different Picture Control option within Nikon Capture NX 2 and then adjusting the settings. The level of sharpening should be based on your ultimate intentions for the image (i.e., display on a website, publication in a book or magazine, or producing a print for framing). Therefore, it is often preferable to only apply sharpening during the final stages of post-processing, particularly if you want to work on images for a range of different output purposes.

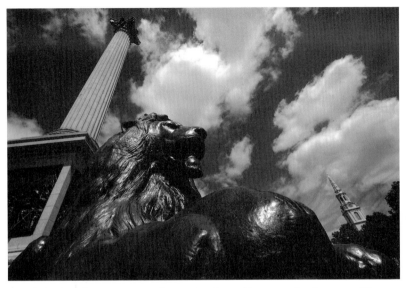

It is often better to save sharpening for post-processing because it is much easier to judge whether or not it is necessary once all other editing is done and you're looking at the image on a full-size monitor, rather than the camera's 3-inch LCD screen.

I would make the following suggestions with regard to in-camera sharpening when shooting with the D90:

- For general photography, using JPEG format files: If you intend to work on these images in post-processing, set sharpening to zero or a low value. If you intend to print pictures direct from the camera without any further post-processing, set sharpening to a mid-range value.
- On occasions when you need to expedite the output of pictures for publishing on a website or in newsprint, use the JPEG format and set the sharpening level in the mid- to high range. In this specific case, a slightly stronger degree of sharpening is probably more appropriate, as images will be viewed on computer screens or at low reproduction resolutions. It is probably also more prudent because it will save valuable time in post-processing.

- If you shoot in the NEF file format, I recommend setting sharpening to zero. Otherwise, there is a risk that any in-camera sharpening, applied by a RAW file converter, will create a cumulative effect with any further sharpening that is applied.

Note: Nikon appears to have changed direction somewhat in terms of in-camera sharpening with the D90, as it is noticeably less aggressive with JPEG files compared with other Nikon D-SLR cameras. The result is that at the default settings for the Nikon Picture Controls, JPEG images can look rather soft. So, if you expect to use these images direct from the camera, you may wish to increase the level of in-camera sharpening; try a level of 5 or 6 as a starting point but I do recommend you experiment for yourself to determine the most appropriate level for your purposes.

[Contrast]: The contrast control allows you to adjust the distribution of tones in an image, and works by applying a curve control similar to those used in software for post-processing. The D90 tends to err toward too much contrast when left to set it automatically and with the exception of the [Neutral] option, the default level of contrast in the other Nikon Picture Controls is also slightly high; therefore, I recommend that this control be used judiciously. It is important to remember that it is far easier to increase contrast than reduce it. This is especially important if you intend to subject the image to further contrast adjustments in post-processing.

Note: If Active D-Lighting is in operation, the contrast option in all Picture Controls is disabled; the contrast adjustment scale display is replaced by "ACT. D-LIGHT," indicating that Active D-Lighting has been selected. To adjust contrast manually for the Picture Control, switch Active D-Lighting to [Off].

[Brightness]: The brightness (luminance) control is used to make an overall image lighter or darker, while the contrast control is used to increase or reduce the difference between lighter and darker tones in an image. Adjusting the brightness affects all three color-channels (red, green, and blue); a positive value increases brightness and a negative value decreases brightness. Adjusting the brightness level of an image does not affect the exposure.

Adjustments Available in All Controls Except Monochrome

[Saturation]: Adjusting the saturation of an image changes the overall vividness (chroma) of color without affecting the brightness of an image. A positive value increases saturation and a negative value decreases saturation. As with contrast, I have found the D90 sets saturation a little too high for my liking in both the automatic option and at the default settings in the Standard, Vivid, and Landscape Nikon Picture Controls. I suggest you exercise restraint with the saturation control—overdoing it will make returning an image to a more natural looking color a difficult task.

There will always be a degree of subjective opinion when assessing color, but I find the D90 tends to produce a slightly oversaturated color. In otherwise accurate colors produced by the [Neutral] option and the Adobe RGB color space, saturation seems appropriate, and this probably represents a good reference point when adjusting other Picture Controls.

[Hue]: The RGB color model (sRGB or Adobe RGB) used by the D90 to produce images is based on combinations of red, green, and blue light. By mixing two of these colors, a variety of different colors can be produced. If the third color is introduced, the hue of the final color is altered. For example, by applying a positive adjustment, reds will look more orange, greens more blue, and blues more purple. If you apply a negative adjustment, the hue shifts so that red is more purple, blue is more green, and green is more yellow.

Hint: Personally, unless you need to produce images directly from the camera, I believe it is better to leave adjustment of contrast, saturation, brightness, and hue until post-processing. Appropriate software offers a far greater degree of control over these adjustments.

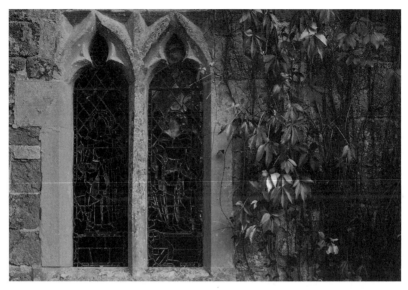

Use filter effects to enhance contrast in black-and-white photos. Here, a red filter effect was applied to increase contrast in the green foliage.

Adjustments for Monochrome Only

[Monochrome – Filter Effects]: In the Monochrome Picture Control, there are options to select filter effects that emulate the results of using contrast control filters with traditional black-and-white film. These filters modified the tonal response of the film to certain wavelengths of light.

The options available on the D90 are [Off] (default), [Yellow], [Orange], [Red], and [Green]. Just like their optical filter counterparts, these filter effects reduce the amount of their complimentary color in the image. For example, the yellow, orange, and red options reduce the level of blue, making a blue sky appear darker; the yellow filter has the least effect and the red the greatest. The result of this effect is an increase in the level of contrast between the blue sky and any white clouds, making the clouds more prominent. The green option reduces the amount of red, making red and orange colors appear darker. This option can be useful for enhancing the range of skin tones in a portrait picture and making them appear more natural and separating the tones of the various shades of green in landscape photography. My advice is to experiment with these options to determine how and when they will best suit your needs.

[Monochrome – Toning]: In addition to the filter effects described above, the [Monochrome] Picture Control also offers a range of options that emulate the effects of traditional chemical toning of black-and-white prints. The options include [Black-and-white] (default), [Sepia] (yellow/brown), [Cyanotype] (blue tint), [Red], [Yellow], [Green], [Blue-green], [Blue], [Purple-blue], and [Red-purple] (similar to selenium toning). Once you have selected the [Toning] option and selected the desired tone, press ▼ to display a saturation control and use ◄ and ► to adjust the saturation of the toning effect (this is not available with the [Black-and-white] option).

Note: Regardless of the black-and-white option selected under the [Monochrome] Picture Control option, the D90 always saves a black-and-white picture recorded in the NEF format as an RGB file. Therefore, it can always be converted back to a full-color image using the Picture Control utility in View NX or Capture NX2.

Creating Custom Picture Controls

The six basic Nikon Picture Controls can be modified and the new settings saved to create a Custom Picture Control. Starting from the Shooting menu, navigate to the [Manage Picture Control] option then press ⊚ to display the available options, and highlight [Save/Edit] and press ⊚ . Highlight the required Picture Control and press ⊚ to open the options, adjust these as required and then press ⊛ to display the [Save As] list (if you do not wish to modify the highlighted Picture Control press 🗑 in place of ⊙). Up to nine different custom Picture Controls (C-1 to C-9) can be stored by the D90.

Highlight the destination of the Custom Picture Control and press ⊙ to display the text-entry dialog box. Use the controls beneath the text field to create a name for the Custom Picture Control, with a maximum length of nineteen characters. Press ⊙ to save the name and return to the Picture Control list.

Sharing Custom Picture Controls

Custom Picture Controls can be created in Nikon View NX or Nikon Capture NX2 software using the Picture Control Utility, or created in another compatible camera and then saved to a memory card, before being loaded into the D90. To copy a Custom Picture Control to the D90, highlight the [Manage Picture Control] option in the Shooting menu and press ⊙ to display the options. Highlight [Load/Save] and press ⊙ , then highlight [Copy to camera] and press ⊙ . Highlight the desired custom Picture Control and either press ⊙ to display the current Picture Control settings, or press ⊙ . Select the destination for the Custom Picture Control and press ⊙ to display the text-entry dialog box. Name the custom Picture Control as described previously under Creating Custom Picture Controls. Finally, press ⊙ to save the name and return to the Picture Control list.

To copy a Custom Picture Control to a memory card, display the [Load/Save] menu as described above, highlight [Copy to card], and press ⊙ . Highlight the required custom Picture Control and press ⊙ to display the [Choose destination] list. Select the destination for the Custom Picture Control from one of the 99 locations listed and press ⊙ to save the Custom Picture Control to the memory card. If you select a destination that already has a Custom Picture Control saved to it, it will be overwritten by the new save command. A maximum of 99 custom Picture Controls can be stored on a memory card.

Managing Custom Picture Controls

To rename a Custom Picture Control, highlight the [Rename] option in the [Manage Picture Control] option of the Shooting menu and press ⊚ . Highlight the required Picture Control and press ⊚ to display the text-entry dialog box. Create the new name for the Custom Picture Control. Finally, press ⓄⓀ to save the name and return to the Picture Control list.

To delete a custom Picture Control from the camera, highlight the [Delete] option in the [Manage Picture Control] option of the Shooting menu and press ⊚ . Highlight the desired Picture Control and press ⊚ to display the Yes/No options. Highlight [Yes] and press ⓄⓀ to confirm the action.

Note: The six default Nikon Picture Controls (Standard, Neutral, Vivid, Monochrome, Portrait, and Landscape) cannot be renamed or deleted.

To delete a Custom Picture Control from a memory card, highlight the [Load/Save] option in the [Manage Picture Control] option of the Shooting menu and press ⊚ . Highlight the [Delete from card] option and press ⊚ to display the list of Custom Picture Controls stored on the card. Highlight the desired Custom Picture Control and either press ⊚ to display its settings, or press ⓄⓀ to display the Yes/No options in the Delete from card dialog box. Highlight [Yes] and press ⓄⓀ to confirm the action.

Color Space

A color space (sometimes called color gamut) defines the range of colors that are available for reproduction and what particular RGB values should represent those colors in the digital image file. For most photography, I recommend using the Adobe RGB color space option on the D90 – it provides the widest range of colors, permitting more subtle rendition and well-graduated tonal transitions. This increases the flexibility of an image file that will be subjected to post-processing and the quality of any print made from that image file produced by an appropriate printing process. The sRGB color space is ideal for an image that will be used directly from the camera with no post-processing or for display on a website.

To choose a color space, highlight the [Color space] option in the Shooting menu and press ⊚ to display the two choices: sRGB (default) and Adobe RGB. Highlight the desired option and press ⊚ to confirm the selection, returning to the Shooting menu.

Note: While it comes very close, the Adobe RGB color space option on the D90 does not appear to be capable of reproducing the complete gamut of the full Adobe RGB color space, as the camera does not replicate some of the green values; however, the camera's Adobe RGB color space option is still significantly broader than its sRGB color space.

Hint: The LCD screen on the D90 gets close to the sRGB color space but it certainly cannot display the full gamut of the Adobe RGB space, so do not attempt to make a critical assessment of color from the camera's display.

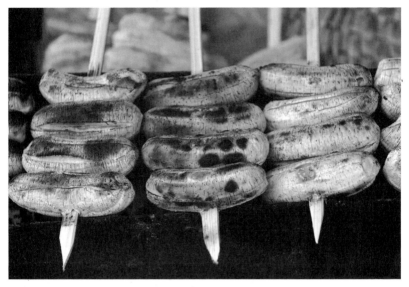

Use the Adobe RGB color space for images that are likely to be subjected to post-processing.

Hint: It is essential that any software used for post-processing be set to the same color space as the image file recorded by the camera. Otherwise, it is more than likely that the application will assign its own default color space and you will lose control over the rendition of colors in your images.

Active D-Lighting

Active D-Lighting (not to be confused with the D-Lighting option available in the Retouch menu) applies a localized adjustment to contrast to improve the rendition of areas of deep shadow and bright highlights. It can be thought of as an automated dodge and burn effect, as opposed to a global adjustment to brightness and contrast. It is only available with Matrix metering, which is used to assess scene contrast, and is intended for use in situations where the scene has a high level of contrast. If necessary, it will modify exposure by reducing it accordingly. The adjustment is quite modest, typically 0.3 Ev or 0.7 Ev to preserve highlight detail; and then after the exposure has been made and the image data is being processed, the shadow and middle tones are adjusted to optimize the dynamic range by adjusting the tone curve applied to the image data.

I recommend choosing either the Low or Normal setting if you're recording JPEG files, since this function modifies the exposure settings before recording an original file, unlike the normal D-Lighting feature in the Retouch menu where a copy file is created from the original, to which the adjustments are then applied. Any Active D-Lighting setting applied to an NEF file can always be modified later, using Nikon Capture NX2 software. If the effect of the Active D-Lighting setting is too strong, it may compromise the tonal range of the entire image, especially if the contrast in the scene is very high.

To select Active D-Lighting, highlight the item in the Shooting menu and press ⊙ to display the options: [Off], [Low], [Normal], [High], [Extra high], and [Auto]. Highlight the desired option and press ⊛ to confirm the selection and return to the Shooting menu.

Note: In M exposure mode, a setting of [Auto] is equivalent to [Normal].

It is possible to bracket exposures with and without Active D-Lighting; select [ADL Bracketing] under the CS-e4 [Auto bracketing set] item. The camera will record two images; the first will be recorded with the current setting for Active D-Lighting while the second is taken with Active D-Lighting switched off.

Note: Using Active D-Lighting increases recording time and reduces buffer memory capacity.

Hint: To maintain image quality, avoid using Active D-Lighting at ISO settings above 800.

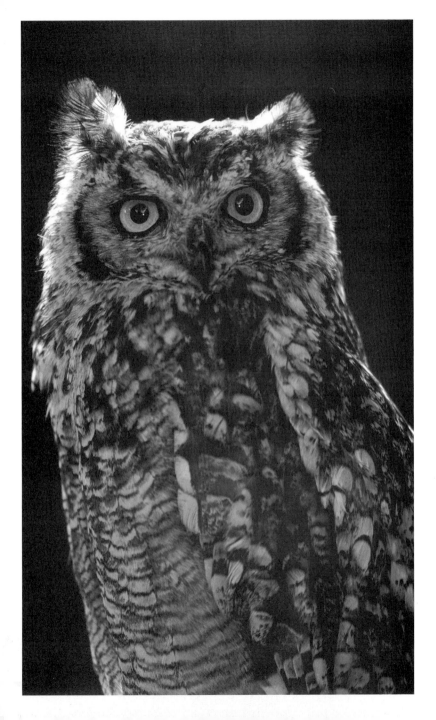

Shoot and Review

The Shutter

The specification of the electronically timed, mechanical shutter used in the D90 is impressive for a camera of its class; its lag-time is just 65 milliseconds (ms), with a viewfinder (mirror) blackout time of approximately 120 ms, and a maximum flash-sync speed of 1/200 second (assuming Automatic Hi-speed FP Sync mode is not active). The shutter blades are constructed from a durable composite of Kevlar™ and carbon-fiber material, which provides great strength and low mass to ensure both durability and accuracy; the unit is tested and proven to at least 100,000 cycles.

The shutter speed range of the D90 runs from 30 seconds to 1/4000 second and can be set in increments of 1/3 or 1/2 Ev. There is also an option for exposures beyond 30 seconds using the **bu L b** setting; the D90 has a long exposure noise reduction feature, which should be used in such circumstances (see page 208 for more details). However, there is a practical limit to the duration of a single exposure due to the fact that the noise reduction feature, which is essential to maintain image quality, uses a 16-bit counter to map the exposure time in increments of 1/10 second. Hence, after a little over 109 minutes, the noise reduction process ceases.

One of the greatest novelties of digital photography is the ability to view the results right away. But be careful not to spend so much time reviewing your pictures that you miss the next great shot!

Shutter Release

The main shutter-release button of the D90 is located conventionally on the top-right end of the camera, where the power-switch collar surrounds it. If the MB-D80 battery pack is attached, it provides a second shutter-release button located on the front-right corner of the camera, which is intended for use when the camera is held vertically, to improve camera handling (it has a lock on a collar to prevent inadvertent operation of the shutter). When the camera is switched to [ON], a light pressure on the shutter-release button that depresses it halfway will activate the metering system and initiate autofocus (assuming an autofocus mode is selected). Once you release the button, the camera remains active for a fixed period of time, the duration of which depends on the selection made within CS-c2 [Auto Meter-off Delay]; 6 seconds is the default setting.

If you continue to press either shutter-release button down fully, the shutter mechanism will operate and an exposure will be made. There is a very short delay (Nikon states it is approximately 120 milliseconds) between pressing the button all the way down and the shutter opening; this delay is usually referred to as "shutter lag." The following are some of the factors that may cause an extended shutter lag.

- The capacity of the buffer memory is probably the most common cause of shutter delay. It does not matter whether you shoot in single- or one of the continuous- release modes (see below for description); once the buffer memory is full, the camera must write data to the memory card before any more exposures can be made. As soon as sufficient space for another image is available in the buffer memory, the shutter can once again be released. For this reason, using memory cards with a fast data write speed is recommended. The D90 supports a maximum data write speed of approximately 14 Mbps (megabytes per second), so using any card that can sustain a write speed of 20 Mbps (x133) will ensure the maximum performance as far as clearing the buffer memory is concerned (a card with a faster write speed will deliver no benefit, since the camera imposes the limiting factor).

- If the camera is set to single-servo autofocus mode, the shutter is disabled until the D90 has acquired focus. In low-light or low-contrast scenes, the autofocus system will often take longer to achieve focus, particularly if one of the outer single-line sensor type AF points is used, adding to the delay (see pages 173-175 for a full explanation).
- In low-light conditions, the D90 can activate its AF-assist lamp, or that of an external Speedlight or the SC-29 TTL flash control cable, which can introduce a short delay while the lamp illuminates and focus is acquired.
- The Red-eye reduction function (one of the flash modes available on the camera) introduces an additional one-second delay between pressing the shutter-release button and the exposure being made (see page 313 for a full explanation).

Release Modes

Obviously, unlike a 35mm film camera, the D90 does not have to transport film between exposures using a motor-drive, but the shutter mechanism still has to be cycled. The camera offers a range of release modes: to set them, hold down the ⊒ release mode button and rotate the main command dial until the icon for the required release mode is displayed in the control panel: S single frame, ⊒L continuous low-speed, ⊒H continuous high-speed, ☉ self-timer, ☋ delayed remote, and ☋ quick response.

S Single Frame
A single image is recorded each time the shutter-release button is pressed. To make another exposure, the button must be released and pressed again. You can continue to do so until the buffer memory is full, in which case, you must wait for data to be written to the memory card. The shutter-release button will also lock if the memory card becomes full.

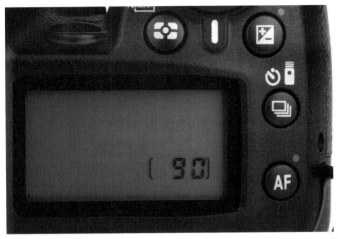

The release mode button is located on the top of the D90 to the right of the control panel LCD.

Hint: You do not have to remove your finger from the shutter-release button completely between frames; by raising it slightly after each exposure but maintaining a slight downward pressure, you can keep the camera active and be ready for the next shot. If you want to take a rapid sequence of pictures in single-frame mode, avoid stabbing your finger down on the button in quick succession. Keep a light pressure on the button and roll your finger over the top of it in a smooth, repeating action. This will reduce the risk of camera shake spoiling your pictures.

⊒L Continuous Low-Speed

In this mode, if you press and hold the shutter-release button down, the D90 will continue to record images, up to a maximum rate of 4 frames per second (fps). The actual frame rate is set via CS-d6 [CL Mode Shooting Speed].

⊒H Continuous High-Speed

In this mode, if you press and hold the shutter-release button down, the D90 will continue to record images up to a maximum rate of 4.5 fps.

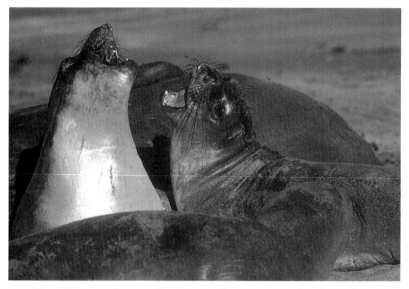

The D90's continuous shooting modes are great for those times when any picture is better than no picture, because the shutter will release even if focus has not been acquired. This doesn't necessarily mean your shots will be out of focus, though. Even if the camera hasn't achieved what it considers to be perfect focus, you'll find that pictures taken using this method will often be in acceptable focus.

Note: The quoted frame rates for the D90 are based on the camera being set to manual focus, manual or Shutter-priority exposure mode, and a minimum shutter speed of 1/250 second. It is important to remember that the selected shutter speed, use of the Vibration Reduction (VR) feature available on some Nikkor lenses, the buffer capacity, other auto-exposure modes, and autofocus (particularly in low-light) can, and often will, reduce the maximum frame rate significantly.

☉ Self-Timer

The self-timer option is used to release the shutter after a predetermined delay. The default delay is 10 seconds, but it can be adjusted to 2, 5, or 20 seconds via CS-c3. Traditionally, the self-timer has been used to enable the photographer to be included in the picture, but there is another very useful function for this feature. The self-timer enables you to release the shutter without touching the camera, thus reducing the chance of camera shake. This is particularly useful for long exposures when the subject is static and precise timing of the shutter release is less critical. To use the self-timer, the camera should be placed on an independent means of support such as a tripod. Compose the picture and ensure focus is confirmed before depressing the shutter-release button (in single-servo AF mode, the shutter release will be disabled unless focus is acquired).

Hint: Make sure you do not pass in front of the lens when setting the self-timer, as autofocus operation may shift the point of focus and prevent the camera from operating. I recommend that the camera be set to manual focus mode when using the self-timer feature.

Note: If the P, A, or S automatic exposure mode is used in conjunction with the self-timer feature, it is essential to cover the viewfinder eyepiece to block extraneous light from entering the viewfinder and influencing the camera's TTL metering sensor. Nikon makes a cover for the eyepiece: The DK-5. However, fitting the DK-5 requires removal of the DK-20 rubber eyecup; this is a nuisance and increases the risk that the eyecup might be lost. I find it far quicker and more convenient to keep a small square of thick felt material in the camera bag to drape over the viewfinder eyepiece when using the self-timer mode.

After the shutter-release button is pressed, the self-timer lamp will begin to blink (if the audible warning is active, as set via CS-d1 [Beep], it will also sound) until approximately two seconds before the exposure is due to be taken. At this point, the light stops blinking and remains on continuously (the frequency of the audible warning beep will increase) until the shutter is released. To cancel the self-timer operation during the countdown, turn the release-mode dial to another release mode.

Using a Remote Release

The benefit of mounting a camera onto a tripod or other type of rigid camera support to increase image sharpness will be compromised if you touch the camera to press the shutter-release button; to eliminate or reduce camera vibration to an absolute minimum, it is advisable to use a remote release to operate the shutter. The D90 has two options: the Nikon ML-L3 wireless infrared (IR) remote release, which is also compatible with several other Nikon D-SLR cameras, or the MC-DC2 remote-release cable.

Using the ML-L3 Infrared Remote Release: Pressing the transmit button on the ML-L3 sends an IR signal to the receiver on the camera, which is located behind a small widow on the front-left side of the camera, just above the camera's badge. The system has a maximum effective range of approximately 16 feet (5 m).

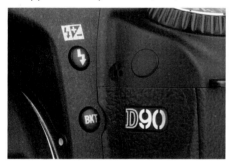

The sensor for the IR remote release is located behind the small window on the front of the D90, just above the camera's badge.

The ML-L3 can be used to release the shutter in two different ways:

- 🔲☉ **Delayed remote:** The shutter is released with a delay of approximately two seconds after you press the transmit button on the ML-L3 remote control. The self-timer lamp will illuminate for approximately two seconds before the shutter is released.

101

- 🔲 **Quick-response remote:** The shutter is released as soon as you press the transmit button on the ML-L3 remote control. The self-timer lamp will flash immediately after the shutter is released.

Regardless of which remote release mode you choose (Delayed or Quick-response), the D90 will cancel it automatically after a fixed period of camera inactivity. At the default setting, this period is one minute but you can also set it to five, ten, or 15 minutes via CS-c5 [Remote on duration].

Hint: Though it is most effective when there is an unobstructed line of sight between the ML-L3 and the receiver on the camera, it is not essential; it is possible to bounce the IR signal from the ML-L3 off of a reflective surface such as a wall or window.

Note: If you require a flash unit to be used with either of the remote release options, ensure that it is switched on and that the flash ready light in the viewfinder or on an external Speedlight is illuminated before you press the release button on the ML-L3.

Hint: If you want to make extremely long exposures, select Manual exposure mode and set the shutter speed to **bu L b**. Then, select either [Delayed remote] or [Quick-response]; a pair of dashes replaces **bu L b** in the control panel and shooting information display. To start the exposure, press the transmit button on the ML-L3 once; then, press it a second time to end the exposure (the maximum duration of a single exposure is 30 minutes). A single flash of the AF-assist lamp confirms completion of the exposure. Before attempting any long exposure, make sure the battery is fully charged and activate the noise reduction feature available in the Shooting menu.

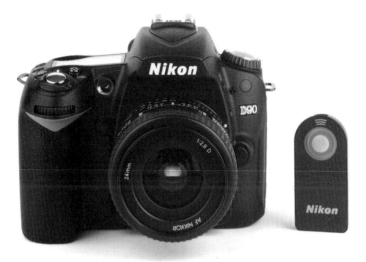

The ML-L3 Infrared Remote Release is one of two remote release accessories that are compatible with the D90.

Using the MC-DC2 Remote Release Cable: The one disadvantage of the ML-L3 is that it must be pointed toward the camera's IR receiver, which is located on the front-left side of the camera. The receiver's location can make using it somewhat awkward, as you need to reach in front of the camera to use it. However, the D90 also has a dedicated terminal for connecting the MC-DC2 Remote Release Cable located underneath the rubber cover on the left side of the camera.

This useful accessory enables the shutter to be released remotely, which is essential when shooting from a tripod and using a shutter speed of 1/30 second or slower,, where the effects of camera vibration are most likely to occur. Furthermore, the MC-DC2 has a lockable release button so it can be used with the **bu L b** setting to lock the shutter open for exposure times of over 30 seconds in duration (the longest timed exposure available on the D90).

The D90 has a terminal on the left side of the camera located under the small rubber cover for connecting the MC-DC2 remote release.

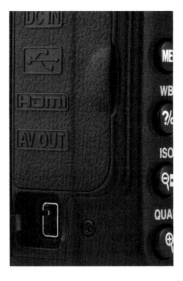

Hint: To help reduce the effect of internal camera vibrations caused by the movement of the reflex mirror, consider using CS-d10 [Exposure delay mode], which causes the shutter opening to be delayed by approximately one second after the shutter release is pressed (including the release button on the MC-DC2) and the reflex mirror being raised.

Note: The D90 is not compatible with the MC-DC1 remote release available for the D80 camera.

Multiple Exposure
The Multiple Exposure feature of the D90 enables either two or three exposures, shot in sequence, to be combined into a single image. The images are not saved individually, but rather as a single combined image.

To use Multiple Exposure:

1. Highlight [Multiple Exposure] in the Shooting menu, and press ⊙⃝ .
2. Highlight [Number of Shots] and press ⊙⃝ , then use ▲ and ▼ to select either [2] or [3].

3. Press ⊛ to confirm the selection and return to the [Multiple Exposure] menu.
4. Highlight [Auto Gain] and press ⊜ , then highlight either [On] or [Off] and press ⊛ to confirm the selection and return to the Multiple Exposure menu.

Hint: When Auto Gain is turned [On], the camera will automatically make adjustments to the exposure level of each image recorded in the sequence, so the final cumulative exposure is correct. This useful feature eliminates the need to make exposure calculations to compensate for the cumulative effect of combining the individual exposures.

5. Highlight [Done] and press ⊛ .
6. Frame and shoot the images you wish to combine. In either of the continuous-release modes, the camera can record all exposures in a single sequence and will stop once the designated number has been recorded. In single-release mode, an exposure is made each time the shutter release is pressed; you must continue to take pictures until the designated number has been recorded.

To cancel the multiple exposure feature without taking a multiple exposure, press the Menu button to highlight the [Multiple Exposure] option in the Shooting menu and press ⊜ to display the [Reset] option. Press ⊛ to confirm the action.

A small double exposure icon ▬ will appear in the control panel when the multiple exposure function has been set. When the selected number of exposures has been completed, it will disappear from the control panel, and the multiple exposure feature is automatically turned off. To create another multiple exposure sequence at different settings, you will need to repeat steps 1-6 above. However, to shoot another multiple exposure sequence using the same settings for [Number of Shots] and [Auto Gain], simply select [Done] from the options under the [Multiple Exposure] item and press ⊛ .

The LCD Monitor

On the rear of the D90 is a 3-inch (7.62 cm), 920,000-dot, color TFT, LCD monitor that offers a viewing angle of 170°. Unlike the viewfinder display, this screen shows virtually 100% of the image when it is reviewed. Pictures can be displayed either as a single image or in multiples. When used to display a single image, the review function has a zoom facility that allows you to enlarge the image by up to 27x ([Large] size images only); lower magnifications are available for [Medium] (20x) and [Small] (13x) size images.

The maximum magnification of a [Large] size image is equivalent to a 400% view, so to examine the image at 100% (i.e., actual pixel level), press the ⊕ button until the maximum magnification is reached and then press the ⊝ button twice to reduce the image to a 100% view.

Use the multi selector to scroll through a range of pages containing shooting information, which are superimposed on any image reviewed in single-image playback mode (see page 200 for more details). Pictures can be edited while they are still held in the camera by reviewing them on the LCD monitor, with the option to delete them or protect them from being deleted unintentionally (see pages 136-137 for more details); they can also be modified using the items in the Retouch menu (see pages 252-267 for more details).

In addition to the display of images and image information, the LCD monitor is used to display the various camera menus (see pages 193-194 for more details).

Live View

The D90 also uses the monitor for its Live View (LV) feature, which provides a real-time video signal from the camera's sensor to the camera's monitor. The picture displayed on the monitor refreshes at 24 fps, showing a view of the scene the lens is pointed towards (i.e., the same view seen

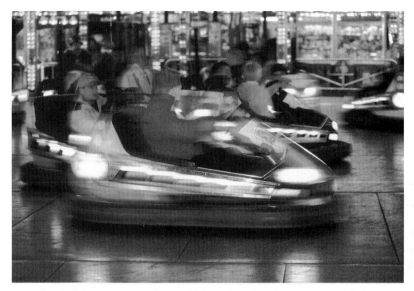

The D90 is the first D-SLR to feature the ability to show a real-time image of the scene before it is photographed.

through the camera's optical viewfinder). This enables pictures to be composed in situations when using the optical viewfinder is difficult, such as when the camera is in a very low position. It is also helpful at times when the enlarged view offered by the monitor and the ability to magnify the image displayed in it in Live View mode will assist in precise focusing, particularly when using the camera for close-up photography.

In Live View, the D90 uses contrast-detection autofocus exclusively instead of the phase-detection autofocus method that the normal AF system uses, and has three mode options: [Face Priority], [Wide area], and [Normal area]. Alternatively, it is possible to use manual focus.

Contrast-detection autofocus uses information from the camera's CMOS sensor to assess contrast in the vicinity of the selected AF point, the point of focus is then adjusted based on the level of detected contrast, and focus is confirmed when the highest level of contrast is achieved beneath the AF point. Although the contrast-detection autofocus is noticeably slower than the phase-detection method the D90 uses for its normal autofocus, it does have the advantage that the point of focus can be selected from anywhere within the total frame area and is not restricted to one of the 11 fixed AF points. It is also important to understand that in Live View autofocus, the D90 always uses single-servo AF mode (see page 179 for full details), which for most intents and purposes limits it to photographing stationary subjects, since as soon as the camera has acquired focus, the focus distance will be locked; so if the subject to camera distance should change after that, focus will be inaccurate. The only circumstances under which Live View autofocus might be successful with a moving subject is when the subject is moving laterally across the frame area and the camera-to-subject distance remains constant.

The other factor that inhibits use of Live View autofocus when photographing a moving subject is the delay that occurs between pressing the shutter-release button down fully and the shutter opening. This delay occurs because camera must first lower the reflex mirror, switch off the Live View signal from the sensor, then activate the sensor to record a still picture, and finally raise the mirror and open the shutter to make the exposure. All these actions take a short time, but it is of a sufficient duration to make timing the exposure with precision a rather hit or miss affair!

In my opinion, Live View is most useful when the D90 is mounted on a tripod and shooting can be conducted under controlled conditions with a static subject. While it can certainly be used with a hand-held camera, it can be a bit awkward to position the focus point, magnify the monitor view, and adjust controls like exposure compensation, all while holding the camera in front of your face.

Notes on Live View

The degree and nature of user control the D90 offers once it is in its Live View mode is altered compared with normal shooting; the following apply:

- After pressing the [Lv] button to activate Live View, it is possible to change the following: The Live View auto-focus mode ([Face priority], [Wide area], or [Normal area] – these AF modes are only possible in Live View); exposure mode (P, S, A, and M); the Scene modes; the shutter speed and aperture value according to the selected exposure mode (P, S, A, and M modes only); and white balance.
- After pressing the [Lv] button to activate Live View, it is not possible to alter the metering mode or ISO value, so ensure these are set as required before activating Live View.
- Depth-of-Field Preview is not available in Live View, regardless of the focus mode used.
- Exposure can be locked in Live View by pressing the AE-L/AF-L button; any of the options for locking exposure under CS-f4 [Assign AE-L/AF-L button] can be used. Probably the most useful of these in respect to using Live View is [AE lock (hold)], because once it's activated there is no necessity to keep the AE-L/AF-L button pressed to lock exposure, which improves camera handling.
- Exposure compensation can be applied in P, S, A, and M exposure modes using the [±] and rear command dial to set the required level of exposure adjustment; the effect of exposure compensation is reflected in the LCD monitor view, which will brighten or dim depending on whether a positive or negative exposure compensation is applied. The exposure compensation value is displayed along the bottom of the screen display when it is being set or when the [±] button is pressed.
- To help offset the effects of internal camera vibration, particularly when shooting at high subject magnification—when using a very long focal length or shooting close-up pictures, for example—I recommend using CS-d10 [Exposure delay mode] because the one-second

delay it introduces between raising the reflex mirror and opening the shutter will allow the effects of such vibration to dissipate, especially if you're using a tripod.

- The brightness of the monitor display in Live View can be adjusted by pressing and holding down the ▶ button to display a scale on the rightside of the screen. Press ▲ to increase brightness and ▼ to reduce brightness; this has no effect on the exposure level of pictures taken in Live View.

- The Live View feature of the D90 is also supported by Nikon Control Pro 2 software, enabling the screen view of the camera to be replicated on a computer screen. This way, all camera controls can be performed from the computer via a hard-wire connection. The D90 requires version 2.3 of Camera Control Pro (also check compatibility with the operating system on the computer).

- When the shutter is released in Live View mode, the reflex mirror is lowered first before the normal cycle of raising the mirror, opening the shutter, and then lowering the mirror. The sound this creates can be misinterpreted as a double exposure but it is normal and only a single exposure is made.

- If the D90 is connected to an HDMI device, the camera's monitor will turn off automatically and the Live View display will be shown only on the screen of the HDMI device.

Using Live View

The first step in using Live View is to set the desired metering mode and ISO values, as these cannot be altered once in Live View.

To activate Live View mode, press the 🔲 button. The reflex mirror will be raised, blacking out the optical viewfinder; the view through the camera's lens will be displayed on the LCD screen, together with a range of information about camera settings. This is the default shooting information page in Live View.

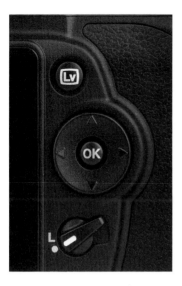

Press the *button to activate Live View, but remember to set the desired metering mode and ISO first, because these things cannot be changed once the D90 is in Movie mode.*

Beginning in the top-left corner of the screen and working around in a clockwise direction, the following will be displayed, overlaid on the Live View image:

• **Shooting/exposure mode:** The exposure mode currently selected via the mode dial is displayed.

• **Time remaining:** Only displayed if Live View shooting will end automatically in 30 seconds or less, to prevent damage to the camera's electronic circuits as a result of overheating.

• ▨ : The "No movie" icon is displayed if the camera determines that it cannot record a video sequence.

• **Live View autofocus mode:** ▨ , ▨ , or ▨ will be displayed to indicate the current autofocus mode.

• **Image size:** Only applies if the camera is set to record JPEG or NEF + JPEG; L, M, or S is displayed. No size is displayed if NEF is selected for image quality.

• **Image quality:** The current setting for image quality is displayed.

• **White balance:** The current setting for white balance is displayed.

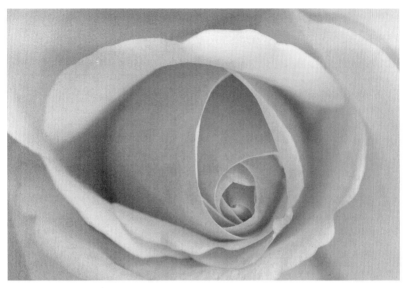

The D90's Live View mode features three autofocus modes: Face priority, Wide area, and Normal area. For close-up shots, I recommend Normal area autofocus.

- **Audio recording indicator:** Indicates whether or not sound will be recorded with video.
- **Time remaining:** Only applies to the Movie mode and indicates the amount of recording time remaining at the current quality setting.
- **Monitor brightness:** Only displayed if the ▶ button is pressed and held; use ▲ and ▼ to adjust accordingly.
- **Along the bottom edge of the projected image three reminders are displayed:** press ⊛ to record in Movie mode, press 🔲 to exit Live View, and press ▶ with ▲ and ▼ to alter screen brightness.
- If the camera battery level drops to ▭ this icon will be displayed in red in the lower-left corner of the display.

Immediately below the Live View image, the screen displays a number of other camera settings. From left to right these are as follows:

- Metering pattern
- Shutter speed
- Lens aperture
- **⊠** if set
- ISO value
- Number of remaining exposures (or buffer memory capacity if the shutter release is pressed down halfway)

The next stage in using Live View is to select the required autofocus mode. Press the AF button and rotate the rear command dial until the appropriate icon is displayed, as follows:

Live View AF mode	Description
⊚ Face priority	The D90 automatically detects and focuses on any human face(s) orientated toward the lens.
	The focus point is displayed as a yellow square with four quadrant marks inside it (it is only displayed if the D90 detects a face within the image area).
WIDE Wide area (default)	The focus point covers a larger area compared with the **NORM** setting; this option is useful for general shooting with a hand-held camera in situations where the subject is not too close to the camera.
	The focus point is displayed as a large square: upon activating Live View, it is shown as solid and in red; once autofocus is performed, the square will change to green when focus is acquired or blink red if the camera is unable to focus.
NORM Normal area	The focus point covers a smaller area compared with the **WIDE** setting; this option is most useful for shooting when the camera is mounted on a tripod and precision in positioning of the plane of focus is essential—in close-up photography, for example.
	The focus point is displayed as a small square; its color and nature of display are the same as for [Wide area] autofocus, as described in the box above.

To position the focus point in [Wide area] and [Normal area], rotate the focus selector lock, located immediately below the multi selector button, to the ● position. Press ✥ to position the autofocus point anywhere within the frame area displayed in the screen. Once the position of the focus point has been set, rotate the focus selector lock to its 'L' position to prevent any inadvertent shift of the focus point.

If [Face-priority] autofocus is selected, the camera will only display the focus point, which appears as a yellow square with four quadrant marks inside it, if it detects a face within the image area. If there are multiple faces in the scene (the camera can detect up five), the point of focus will be positioned on the face deemed by the D90 to be the closest.

After selecting the Live View autofocus mode and positioning the focus point as required in [Wide area] and [Normal area] focus modes, press the shutter-release button down halfway to initiate autofocus. The focus point square will change from red to green when focus is acquired or blink red if the camera cannot achieve focus.

In [Face-priority] autofocus, the camera will set both focus and exposure for the face it detects within the focus point. If it does not detect a face or no longer detects a face in the scene because, for example, the subject has turned their face away from the lens, the yellow [Face-priority] autofocus point will no longer be displayed. In this situation, if the shutter-release button is pressed down halfway, the camera will focus using the [Wide area] focus point, which is positioned at the center of the frame area (it cannot be shifted elsewhere). If focus can be acquired on the part of the scene covered by the [Wide area] focus point, focus will lock and the focus point will be displayed in green. If the camera cannot focus, the focus point is displayed blinking in red (as long as the shutter-release button is depressed).

To check the accuracy of focus, it is possible to magnify the image displayed in the screen up 6.7x by pressing the

⊕ button. To return to the normal full-frame view, press the ⊖ button. While the magnified view is displayed, a navigation window is shown in the lower-right of the screen. To scroll around the image in a magnified view, press ⊕ .

To record a picture in Live View, press the shutter release down all the way. The monitor display is turned off and the camera will shoot in the release mode set currently on the camera; if this is 🖳L or 🖳H continuous release mode, the camera will record pictures successively until the shutter-release button is released or the buffer memory becomes full. Once shooting is finished, the last recorded picture will be displayed on the screen for 4 seconds or until the shutter-release button is pressed down halfway. The D90 will then return to its Live View mode. To exit the Live View mode, press the 🔳Lv button.

Shooting Information Display in Live View

Three pages of shooting information can be shown in Live View by pressing the 🔳Info button repeatedly to scroll from page to page, while the live View image is displayed in real time on the screen.

The page order is as follows:

- **Shooting Information Display on:** The information described in the section entitled "Using Live View Mode" is displayed.
- **Shooting Information Display off:** Only displays the metering pattern, shutter speed, lens aperture, 🔳 if set, ISO value, and number of remaining exposures (or buffer capacity if the shutter release is pressed down halfway) along the bottom of the screen.
- **Framing Guides:** A grid pattern of vertical and horizontal lines is shown superimposed over the image to assist composition, while the AF point is also shown. This grid pattern can be more useful than the grid lines displayed under CS-d2 [Viewfinder grid display] because the lines cover the central area of the frame. The exposure mode and Live View autofocus modes are also displayed, as

well as the low-battery warning in red when appropriate. It is not possible to magnify the Live View image when the framing guides are displayed.

General Notes on Using Live View

Caution: Never point the camera at the sun or other strong light source when using the Live View mode. Doing so risks damage to the sensor and/or associated circuitry.

- The contrast-detection autofocus in Live View may not be able to function properly if any of the following apply: the subject contains lines parallel to the long edge of the frame, the subject lacks contrast, the subject covered by the focus point has areas with significantly different levels of contrast, the subject is smaller than the focus point, the subject has a geometric pattern, a special effects filter is used on the lens, or the subject is moving.
- Live View will cause the internal circuitry of the D90 to become warm, especially over an extended period of operation. This may lead to an increase in the level of noise and/or a distortion of colors recorded by the camera. Live View mode can be used for a maximum period of 60 minutes. If you exceed this time period, protective circuitry in the camera will automatically shut down Live View mode (providing a 30-second countdown) to prevent the camera from overheating. In extremely high ambient temperatures, this feature may activate as soon as the Live View mode is switched on.
- If you remove the lens from the camera when it is set to Live View mode, shooting will cease immediately.
- Under certain types of light sources that emit light in a series of charge and decay cycles (i.e., fluorescent, mercury vapor, and sodium lights), you may observe distortion and/or banding effects on the screen. These effects occur because the frequency of light emission does not coincide with the 24 fps refresh rate of the image displayed on the monitor.
- If you pan the camera in Live View mode or a subject moves across the frame at a high speed, you may observe

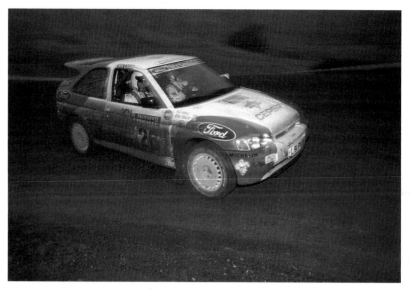

A moving subject can make it difficult for the D90 to focus when it is in Live View mode because it uses a different type of autofocus than does the camera's normal shooting mode.

distortion and/or banding effects on the screen. Similarly, very bright light sources may create ghost images if the camera is panned. These effects are due to the fact that the image displayed on the monitor is refreshed at 24 fps (i.e., it is not a continuous image).

- In [Face priority] Live View autofocus mode, the camera may be unable to detect a face (or faces) if they are partly hidden by sunglasses or other obstructions such as the low brim of a hat. Likewise, the camera may be unable to attain focus if the face or faces occupy too much or too little of the frame area. In these circumstances, autofocus will revert to [Wide area].

Movie Mode

Much of the marketing hype that surrounded the launch of the Nikon D90 centered on the camera's ability to capture video, which was a first for any D-SLR. The following benefits of the D90 Movie mode make it better in some respects than even high-end movie cameras, capable of broadcast quality recording:

- Its ability to record in a High Definition (HD) resolution of 720p HD (1280 x 720 pixels) at 24 frames per second (fps)
- The Nikon DX-format CMOS sensor, which is significantly larger than those used in typical camcorders, and can be expected to produce a far smaller depth of field with a much lower noise level, and therefore higher quality image
- The choice of a huge range of Nikkor lenses from full-frame fisheye to super telephoto, providing a degree of optical versatility and flexibility unknown to the user of traditional video cameras

Note: The 24 fps rate is the common frame rate for motion pictures shot on film and has been the industry standard since its very earliest days. Video is usually shot at 30 fps, which gives it a slightly different look. Therefore, it is very apt that Nikon has called the video recording feature of the D90 "Movie mode."

However, once you begin to peel away at what exactly the D90 does deliver in its so-called Movie mode, it soon becomes apparent that the suggestions made by some Nikon marketing types about being able to leave your camcorder at home and rely entirely upon the D90 to record stills and video are somewhat over inflated. Let me make it quite clear that while the D90 is without doubt a very fine, state-of-the-art, mid-range D-SLR camera, it is not a video camera by any stretch of the imagination.

Even at the lowest end of the consumer camcorder market, the various models available offer considerably more features and functions, including autofocus, stereo sound recording with the ability to attach an external microphone, an articulating LCD monitor, and a powered lens zoom action; the D90 lacks all of these!

Furthermore, once the camera is in its video mode, you relinquish any control over shutter speed, aperture, and ISO level. In effect, the D90 shifts into a fully automated point-and-shoot mode that is akin to the 🔲 shooting mode available when the camera is used to record still pictures. The reason behind this is the way that Nikon has implemented the recording of video in the D90; in essence what the camera designers and engineers have done is take the video feed from the camera's sensor that provides the real-time image displayed on the LCD screen when the camera's Live View function is in operation, and use this for its Movie mode.

Like the Live View mode, the Movie mode is designed to produce the best possible image in terms of exposure. So, when the D90 is in Movie mode, it will make settings automatically to that end, regardless of what manual settings you may have made.

Once the camera is in its Live View mode, the only parameters you can control during video recording are: manual focus (autofocus does not operate in the camera's Movie mode), manual lens zooming, exposure compensation, and white balance.

Prior to entering the Live View mode, from where video recording is activated, it is possible to adjust the lens aperture, plus any of the parameters that can be set within the Picture Control selected currently on the camera. It is important to avoid setting the level of contrast and sharpening too high when recording video, as the former will cause a reduction in the dynamic range the camera can record, and the latter can result in a ghost image, in which a black edge appears to follow any moving elements in the image.

Note: Restrictions do apply to aperture settings because it appears the aperture must be approximately f/8 or bigger for video recording to function properly when using any Nikkor lens with an electronic aperture control. So, the camera will limit the minimum aperture accordingly, regardless of the aperture value set before entering the Movie mode.

Unless you intervene, the D90 will exercise fully automatic control of the exposure during video recording (and Matrix metering will be used exclusively, regardless of the metering pattern selected on the camera) which is problematic for a number of reasons. First, if the level of illumination in the scene being recorded changes (for example, the camera is panned from an area that is lit brightly to an area of deep shadow or the lens is zoomed so the ratio of tones within the frame changes significantly), the camera will adjust shutter speed and ISO accordingly in order to maintain what the camera thinks is an appropriate level of exposure. As a consequence, the noise level in the image can increase perceptibly as the ISO level is increased. Furthermore, as with any automated exposure system, it is likely that if the scene is filled or nearly filled with particularly dark tones, it will be overexposed. Allied to this is the problem of how the camera adjusts exposure changes in a distinctly stepped manner that is manifest in a noticeable shift in the level of illumination in the recorded image.

So, how can you tame the D90 in its Movie mode and exercise some degree of control over the exposure to obtain greater consistency and accuracy? Well, there are two options: First, in the P, S, A, and M shooting modes, it is possible to use the 🔲 exposure compensation feature; and second, you can use the [AE Lock (hold)] option available under CS-f4, which operates in all shooting modes.

Both of these controls must be used after the camera has entered its Live View mode if they are to be effective during video recording, so the following is my suggested sequence for setting up the D90 to achieve a consistent exposure level in its Movie mode:

1. Before activating Live View, select the required aperture value in the camera's normal still-picture shooting mode (remember that the minimum aperture value available in Movie mode when using a Nikkor lens with electronic aperture control is approximately f/8). Also confirm that the [AE Lock (hold)] option is selected under CS-f4 for operation of the AE-L/AF-L button.

2. Activate Live View by pressing the **Lv** button.

3. Point the camera at the subject and focus using either [Wide area], or [Normal area] Live View autofocus mode; if the subject comprises tones that are significantly lighter or darker than average middle grey, use the exposure compensation to set a positive or negative value respectively, and then press the AE-L/AF-L button (remember the exposure compensation function is only available in the P, S, A, and M modes). This approach is suitable in situations where the subject and camera remain static, and the level of illumination remains constant.

4. As an alternative to step 3 above, use a middle tone test target such as an 18% grey card, and after ensuring that it is in the same level of light as the subject, point the camera at the test target and press the AE-L/AF-L button. This approach ensures that the camera will record average tones accurately, while lighter and darker tones will also be rendered accurately, provided they are within the dynamic range of the sensor; plus the lens can be zoomed without the risk that the camera will shift exposure if the scene's tonal range changes significantly.

5. The exposure level calculated by the camera will now be locked until the AE-L/AF-L button is pressed again (the AE Lock can be switched on and off at will during a video recording by pressing the AE-L/AF-L button); when it is active, "AE-L" is displayed on the screen beside the metering pattern icon.

Note: It appears that the application of an exposure compensation value also influences the shutter speed that the D90 will use during video recording. Although no definitive values are available, setting any negative exposure compensation seems to result in the use of a faster shutter speed, while positive exposure compensation values cause a slower shutter speed to be set.

Rolling Shutter Effect

There is one other surprise that awaits the uninitiated user of the D90 in its Movie mode, and it concerns the way the readout from the sensor is handled. The CMOS sensor does not capture each frame of video simultaneously, but records it in a scanning process of horizontal lines that starts from the top edge of the sensor and works toward the bottom. The consequence of this is manifest when the camera and/or the subject move(s) rapidly during recording. This movement can cause vertical lines in static subjects that are skewed in a diagonal direction, or moving subjects that appear to have a cartoon-like, exaggerated lean.

A more pernicious version of this skewing effect occurs with a hand-held camera that, due to a lack of stability, moves laterally left and right during recording, with the result that vertical static lines in the frame, such as the edge of a building, take on a wavy appearance and look as though they are wobbling.

Unfortunately, there is no cure-all remedy for these unwanted effects; therefore, it is a matter of anticipating them in certain situations and attempting to mitigate the worst effects by shooting appropriately. This means panning the camera slowly or following a moving subject carefully. Furthermore, you simply have to accept the inevitable distortion in the foreground and background. The single most effective step you can take is to use a tripod whenever you record in Movie mode on the D90!

Built-In Limitations

There are several limitations built into the Movie mode of the D90:

- The maximum file size for any single video recording is 2GB; this is due to the limit on FAT 32 file sizes.
- The maximum duration for a single video recording made at the 720p HD (1280 x 720 pixels) resolution is five minutes; this is not a technical limitation but one imposed by politics! Within the European Union (EU), any device that can record more than five minutes of HD video is classified as a video recorder and therefore attracts higher import duties than still cameras.
- The maximum duration for the use of the Live View mode is one hour; this is to prevent the camera from overheating and its circuitry being damaged. Provided the ambient temperature is cool it may be possible to reactivate Live View immediately; however, in high ambient temperatures, it is likely the camera will shut down automatically before the 60-minute limit.
- The audio recording of the D90 uses a 16-bit mono channel with a relatively low sampling rate of just 11 kHz (most dedicated video cameras provide stereo channel sound recording and the sampling rate of 48 kHz). The inbuilt microphone picks up sounds made by camera operation, like rotating the rear command dial or zooming the lens. Or, in some instances, manual focus adjustment is recorded with distressing clarity! Probably the worst offender is the rear command dial, however, as it generates a very sharp clicking noise. The ability to record a short interview or to caption details may be helpful to some users, but others will probably wish to invest in an independent, stand-alone audio-recording device, if their purpose is to add the ambient sounds from the scene being recorded, and leave the [Sound] item in the Shooting menu of the D90 set to [Off].
- Supplying sufficient power to the D90 when it is used for recording video can certainly be an issue, since as well as writing data continuously to the memory card, the camera

is performing all its other functions, including Live View and Vibration Reduction (VR), which are the two most demanding functions. Filling a 2GB memory card with video will leave a fully charged EN-EL3e battery heavily depleted if not exhausted, so pack plenty of spare batteries if you anticipate making full use the Movie mode.

Note: Movie mode is just an extension of the Live View function, so the precautions described under "General Notes on Using Live View" still apply in Movie mode. Most importantly, never point the camera at the sun or any other strong light source, when using the Live View mode. Doing so may cause damage to the sensor and/or associated electrical circuitry.

The Recorded Movie

Using its 720p HD (1280 x 720 pixels) resolution, the D90 records at the rate of 1.7Mbps (approximately 100MB/minute), so each Gigabyte (GB) of storage on an SD or SDHC memory card will store about ten minutes (although the maximum clip length is five minutes).

The D90 records moving images in an Open DML JPEG video format, which is known more informally as Motion JPEG (or M-JPEG). In the motion JPEG format, each video frame in the recorded sequence is compressed as a separate JPEG image. These JPEG images are then stored together with any audio recording in what is known as an Audio Video Interleave (.AVI) container file; AVI is the standard container file used by Microsoft Windows applications, but it is also supported by applications like QuickTime, so D90 video is also viewable on computers running Apple operating systems. Editing .AVI files in appropriate applications supported by the Windows operating system should not be an issue; however, using an application such as Final Cut Pro on a Macintosh operating system to edit video clips from the D90 can be somewhat awkward. Therefore, it can be helpful to convert the (.AVI) file into the QuickTime file format (.MOV), which is the standard container file for the ubiquitous QuickTime application. One example of a program that will perform this conversion is MPEG Streamclip (http://www.squared5.com), which is available for both the Macintosh and Windows operating systems. And best of all, it is free!

Using Movie Mode

To use the Movie mode on the D90:

1. Press the [Lv] button to open the Live View function. If there is insufficient space to record a video on the installed memory card, the icon will be displayed in the LCD screen.
2. Compose the opening frame of your video and press the shutter-release button down halfway to activate Live View autofocus.
3. Once focus has been confirmed, press the (OK) button to begin recording. The recording indicator and available recording time are both displayed on the screen. Remember that when recording is active, the autofocus function is disabled; therefore it will be necessary to use manual focus.
4. To end the recording, press the (OK) button again; alternatively, to end the recording and take a still picture in the shooting mode selected currently on the mode dial, press the shutter-release button down all the way. If no action is taken to manually stop recording, it will end automatically as soon as the maximum 2GB file size is reached or the memory card is full.

Movie Mode Conclusions

Results from my initial tests suggest that the D90 is capable of producing good quality video but only in comparison to other still cameras because, given the large size of its sensor, it would (on paper at least) appear to have greater potential. The key issue with the quality of the video recording is the relative softness of the image, which is disappointing given the razor-sharp resolution that is possible when using the camera to shoot still pictures with a high-quality Nikkor lens. In light of the other limitations I have discussed above I would assess the Movie mode of the D90 as an interesting extra feature that is easy to use once you appreciate what it can do, and more importantly, what it cannot do; it is not a camera to be considered if video capabilities are a priority.

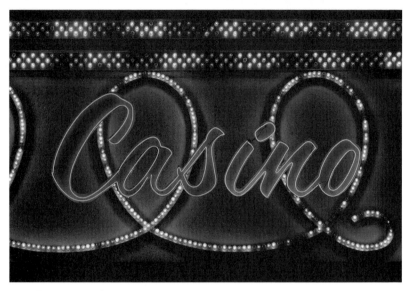

The 3-inch LCD screen on the D90 allows for more decision-making and editing in-camera than did the smaller screens of its predecessors.

Image Review Options

One of the most useful features of a digital camera is the ability to get instant feedback on photographs as you shoot. Using the playback functions on the D90 will allow you to see not only the images you have taken, but also a range of useful information about them.

The 3-inch (7.62 cm) LCD screen of the D90 provides virtually a 100% view of the image file when it is reviewed/played back (remember the viewfinder only provides a 92% view of the scene so you will see more of it in the monitor!). Pictures can be displayed either as single images or in multiples. When used to display a single image, the review function has a zoom facility that enables a [Large] size image to be enlarged by up to 27x.

Assuming [On] is selected for [Image review] in the Playback menu, the most recently taken image in single-frame and self-timer release modes will be displayed on the LCD monitor almost instantaneously. In either of the continuous release modes, the camera must write the image data from the buffer memory to the memory card before they can be viewed, which causes a short delay that becomes cumulative as more images are recorded; the camera displays each image chronologically, as soon as it has been saved. If [Off] is selected for [Image review] in the Playback menu, no image is displayed following an exposure being made. In this case, use single-image playback to evaluate images by pressing the ▶ button.

Full-Frame Playback
To view the last image or video recorded by the camera, press the ▶ button. If you wish to view other images or videos saved on the memory card, press ◀ and ▶ to scroll through them. To display the information pages for a still image, use ▲ and ▼ (see below for full details). To return to the Shooting mode, press the ▶ button again – although the quicker method, if you are in the midst of shooting, is to press the shutter-release button down halfway.

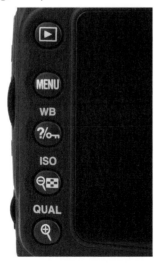

The ▶ button is located near the upper-left-hand corner of the LCD screen, on the back of the D90.

To display any image shot in an upright (vertical) format in the correct orientation, select [On] for the [Auto Image Rotation] item in the Setup menu, and select [On] for the [Rotate tall] item in Playback menu. Although this may seem a convenient method to display an image, the size of the displayed picture is reduced in order to fit the long edge of the image within the short edge of the screen.

The preview image, including those for NEF files, is always derived from a JPEG file, to which in-camera processing (white balance, contrast, saturation, etc.) has been applied. An NEF file will contain more data and have a wider range of tonal values and colors; therefore, an overexposed highlight in the JPEG preview may not be an overexposed highlight when the NEF file is examined in a RAW file converter such as Nikon Capture NX2. Hence, you should treat the highlights warning and histogram that the camera can be set to display with a degree of latitude and not as an absolute definitive that overexposure has occurred.

Information Pages

A very useful feature of the image playback function on the D90 is the wealth of information that can be accessed while viewing the image on the LCD monitor. This information can help ensure that you have achieved a good exposure, as well as give you detailed information about how, when, and where the exposure was made. Depending on the selections made in the [Display Mode] option in the Playback menu, and whether an image file contains data recorded from an attached GPS, there are up to eight different pages of information that can be displayed for each image file viewed on the screen.

To access these information displays, press ▲ to scroll through each page in the following order: File information, RGB and Composite Histograms, Highlights (warning), Shooting Data (1), Shooting Data (2), Shooting Data (3), Shooting Data (4), GPS Data (only displayed if file contains GPS data), and Overview data. Press ▼ to scroll through in the reverse order.

The File information and Overview data pages are always displayed. To display the focus point used, select [Focus point] under the [Basic photo info] option of the [Display Mode] item of the Playback menu. The additional pages for Highlights (warning), RGB and Composite Histograms, and Shooting Data (up to 3 pages) can be selected/deselected through the [Detailed photo info] option of the [Display Mode] item in the Playback menu.

File Information: Displays an unobstructed view of the image while providing the following additional information.

> Protect Status
> Retouch indicator
> Frame number/Total number of frames
> File name
> Image quality
> Image size
> Time of recording
> Date of recording
> Folder name

RGB Histogram: Provides an individual histogram for each of the red, green, and blue channels, together with an RGB composite histogram and a thumbnail of the image. To magnify a part of the image, press the ⊕ button and use the multi selector button to scroll around the full image (a smaller thumbnail image is displayed to assist navigation within the full frame area). The histogram will represent only the enlarged section of the image displayed on the screen. All of the following is displayed:

> Protect status
> Retouch indicator
> White balance /White balance fine-tuning
> Camera name
> Histogram – RGB composite
> Histogram – Red channel
> Histogram – Green channel
> Histogram – Blue channel
> Frame number/Total number of frames

Highlights: Displays an unobstructed view of the image. Any area of the image that may be overexposed is shown with a flashing border. The following information is displayed:

> Protect status
> Retouch indicator
> Image highlights
> Camera name
> Frame number/Total number of frames

Note: When recording NEF files, the highlights warning is taken from an embedded 8-bit JPEG file, which may suggest an area of the image is overexposed when in fact this is often not the case. The histogram display is generally more reliable at indicating whether an image has areas that are overexposed, but should not be taken as perfectly accurate in the case of NEF files, either.

Shooting Data Page 1: A block of information will be displayed, superimposed over the center portion of the screen, obstructing the view of the image. This page is only displayed if [Data] is selected under the [Display mode] item in the Playback menu. This page displays:

> Protect status
> Retouch indicator
> Metering method
> Shutter speed
> Aperture
> Exposure mode
> ISO sensitivity [1]
> Exposure compensation
> Optimal exposure tuning [2]
> Focal length
> Lens data
> Focus mode
> VR lens [3]
> Flash mode
> Flash compensation
> Commander mode / group name / flash control mode

Camera name
Frame number/Total number of frames

1. *Displayed in red if ISO auto control was on*
2. *Displayed if CS-b4 [Fine tune optimal Exposure] is set to value other than zero*
3. *Displayed only if a VR lens is attached*

Note: This screen can be particularly useful if you are trying to achieve certain results, learn about your shooting style, and learn what settings produce particular results.

Shooting Data Page 2: A block of information will be displayed superimposed over the center portion of the screen, obstructing the view of the image. This page is only displayed if [Data] is selected under the [Display mode] item in the Playback menu. This page displays:

Protect status
Retouch indicator
White balance / color temperature / WB fine-tuning / preset
Color space
Picture control
Quick adjust [1]
Original picture control [2]
Sharpening
Contrast
Brightness
Saturation [3]
Filter effects [4]
Hue [3]
Toning
Camera name
Frame number/Total number of frames

1. *[Standard], [Vivid], [Portrait], and [Landscape] Picture Controls only*
2. *[Neutral], [Monochrome], and Custom Picture Controls only*
3. *Not displayed with Monochrome Picture Controls*
4. *Monochrome Picture Controls only*

Note: This screen can help you understand the effects of image settings and adjustments on the appearance of your picture.

Shooting Data Page 3: A block of information will be displayed, superimposed over the center portion of the screen, obstructing the view of the image. This page is only displayed if [Data] is selected under the [Display mode] item in the Playback menu. This page displays:

> Protect status
> Retouch indicator
> High ISO noise reduction/Long exposure noise
>   reduction
> Active D-Lighting
> Retouch history
> Image comment
> Camera name
> Frame number/Total number of frames

GPS Data: A block of information will be displayed, superimposed over the center portion of the screen, obstructing the view of the image. This screen will only be displayed if the camera was connected to a compatible GPS unit that was switched on and active at the time the exposure was recorded. This page displays:

> Protect status
> Retouch indicator
> Latitude
> Longitude
> Altitude
> Coordinated Universal Time (UTC)
> Camera name
> Frame number/Total number of frames

Overview Data: Provides a thumbnail view of the image file with two panels of information. The following information is displayed:

Frame number/Total number of frames
Protect status
Camera name
Retouch indicator
Histogram (composite only)
ISO sensitivity [1]
Focal length
GPS data indicator
Image comment indicator
Flash mode
Flash compensation
Exposure compensation
Metering method
Exposure mode
Shutter speed
Aperture
Picture control
Active D-Lighting
File name
Image quality
Image size
Time of recording
Date of recording
Folder number
White balance / Color temperature / WB fine-tuning / Preset manual
Color space

1. Displayed in red if ISO auto control was on

Viewing Multiple Images

If you wish to view multiple thumbnails of images and videos on the monitor, press the ⊖▦ button to change from single-frame to four, nine, or 72 images, and finally to the Calendar playback, which displays pictures based on the date that they were taken. To return to a single-image view from multiple-image display, press the ⊕ button repeatedly until a single image is displayed.

In a multiple thumbnail display, a yellow border surrounds the currently highlighted image or video; to highlight an alternative thumbnail image, use ⊕ . To view the highlighted image in full-frame view, press ⊛ ; to return to the thumbnail view, press the ⊟ button. The highlighted thumbnail image can be protected by pressing ?/�֊ and deleted by pressing 🗑 ; to return to the Shooting mode, press the ▶ button or press the shutter-release button down halfway.

Calendar Playback
To view an image or video taken on a specific date, press the ⊟ button to display 72 thumbnail images and then press it once more. Once the Calendar playback display is shown, any date on which one or more images or videos was recorded will be indicated by a thumbnail image on that date. Use the ⊟ button to switch back and forth between the calendar of dates [Date list] and the list of thumbnails [Thumbnail list] displayed to the right of the calendar. To highlight a specific date or image in the thumbnail image list, use the multi selector button.

In the [Date list], use ⊕ to exit to the 72-thumbnail display, ⊛ to view the first picture taken on the selected date, ⊕ to highlight a date, or 🗑 to delete all pictures taken on the selected date.

In the [Thumbnail list], use ⊕ to enlarge the highlighted picture, ⊛ to view the highlighted picture, ⊕ to highlight a picture, or 🗑 to delete the highlighted picture; to return to the Shooting mode press the ▶ button or press the shutter-release button down halfway.

Playback Zoom
The image displayed on the screen is usually too small to check its sharpness with any certainty. The playback zoom will allow you to enlarge a [Large] size image by up to 27x

134

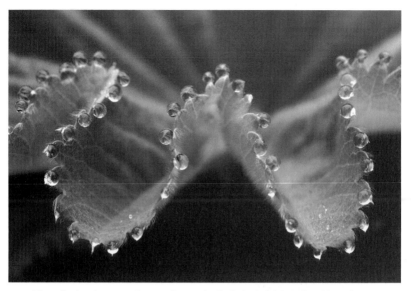

The playback zoom feature is particularly helpful for checking sharpness in shots like this one, where depth of field may be very shallow.

(equivalent to a 400% view on a computer screen), a [Medium] size image up to 20x, and a [Small] size image up to 13x. To see a 100% view (i.e., an actual pixel view) of a [Large] image, press the ⊖▦ button twice from full magnification. At this magnification, it is possible to make a sound assessment of the sharpness and noise level in the image. As far as color and contrast are concerned, any critical analysis should be left until the image is displayed on a computer monitor.

Note: Playback zoom can only be used with still images; if you select a video file and press the ⊕ button a warning message, "Cannot zoom in on this image," is displayed.

To zoom into the image displayed on the screen, press the ⊕ button. The image will be displayed with a yellow frame border inside a navigation window. To increase the degree of magnification, keep pressing the ⊕ button; the size of the yellow frame will reduce to indicate the area of the image that will be enlarged. The selected area, as defined by the yellow frame, is shown on the screen. To view an alternative part of the image at the same magnification, press ⊕ . The same area of another image at the same magnification can be viewed by rotating the main command dial to scroll through the images. This is a useful feature if there are a number of similar images of the same subject on your memory card and you want to check a specific detail, such as a certain person's eyes in a group portrait. To return to the Shooting mode, press the ▶ button or press the shutter-release button down halfway.

The playback zoom buttons are located on the rear of the D90 to the left of the LCD screen.

Protecting Images

To protect an image or video file against inadvertent deletion, either display the image or video file on the monitor in full-frame, single-image playback or highlight it in multiple-thumbnail playback, and then press the **?/o-n** button. A small key icon will appear in the upper-left corner, superimposed over the image. To remove the protection, open or highlight the image or video file and press **?/o‒** again. Check to make sure the key icon is no longer displayed. Any protected image or video will be deleted if the memory card is formatted; however, the protect status is preserved when any image or video file is transferred to another storage device or computer. To remove the protection from all images in a folder or folders currently selected in the [Playback folder] menu, press and hold **?/o‒** and 🗑 simultaneously for approximately two seconds.

Deleting Images

Images can be deleted using one of two methods. The quickest and easiest way to delete a single image or video file is to press the 🗑 button when the image or video file to be deleted is displayed on the monitor. The first press of the button opens a warning dialog box that asks for confirmation of the delete command. To complete the process, simply press the 🗑 button again. To cancel the delete process, press the ▶ button.

Images can also be deleted in multiples via the [Delete] item in the Playback menu. There are three options: [Selected] only those images or video files selected for deletion will be deleted, [Selected date] to delete all images and video files taken on a selected date, or [All] to delete all images and video files in the folder currently selected for playback. If two memory cards are installed in the camera, a slot-selection dialog box will be displayed before the deletion options are displayed.

Hint: Never be in too much of a hurry to delete pictures unless they are obvious failures. I always recommend that it is better to leave the editing process to a later stage – your opinions about a particular picture can and often do change. These days, memory cards are remarkably cheap and come in much larger capacities than just a few years ago, so there is no excuse to skimp on image storage!

Assessing The Histogram Display

The histogram is a graphical display of the tonal values recorded by the camera. The shape and position of the histogram curve indicates the range of tones that has been captured in the picture. The horizontal axis represents 256 different tonal values from pure black at the extreme left end to pure white at the extreme right end; so darker tones will be distributed to the left of the histogram graph and lighter tones to the right. The vertical axis represents the number of pixels that have that specific tonal value.

In a well exposed picture of a scene containing an average distribution of tones that includes a few dark shadows, a sizable number of mid-tones, and a few bright highlights, where no clipping of shadow or highlights has occurred, the curve will extend across much of the horizontal axis; in this case, all tones in the scene will have been recorded.

Obviously, not all scenes contain an even spread of tones; many have a natural predominance of light or dark areas. In these cases, the histogram curve will be biased to the right with scenes containing mainly light tones, or to the left when the scene contains mainly dark tones; this is not an indication of over- or underexposure respectively, but an indication of the limited range of tones in the scene. Hence, there is no single, perfect, or ideal histogram curve for all scenes and subjects; the shape of the histogram curve will vary widely depending on the nature of the scene recorded. Provided the histogram curve stops on the bottom axis before it reaches either end of the graph, the image will contain the full range of tones from the darkest to the lightest in the scene being photographed.

However, if the curve begins at a point partway up the left or right vertical axis of the histogram display (i.e., it does not end on the horizontal axis but the histogram curve looks as though it has been cut off abruptly), the camera will not have recorded some tones. This is often referred to as "clipping." If the curve is stacked up against the left axis, or there is a peak in the histogram against the left axis, some of the darker tones (i.e., shadows areas in the image) will likely be compromised due to

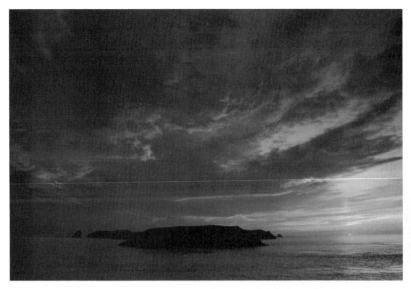

Use the histogram as a guide to make sure that the range of exposure values in your photo doesn't exceed the dynamic range of the camera's sensor, but do not use it as your only guide and don't delete any images until you've seen them on a computer screen, especially in the case of NEF files.

underexposure, whereas if the curve is stacked up against the right axis or there is a peak in the histogram against the right axis, some of the lighter tones (i.e., highlight areas in the image) will likely be compromised due to overexposure. The exception would be in a scene where there were very bright specular highlights, such as the sun reflecting off water or streetlights in a nighttime cityscape – these small areas will almost invariably be much brighter than most of the other light tones in the scene, and therefore, it is of little consequence if they are overexposed. Significant under- or overexposure is to be avoided if possible but especially the latter, as it is unlikely that highlight areas that have been overexposed will be able to render any detail, and nothing can be done to rectify this in post-processing. It is often possible to recover shadow detail lost due to underexposure; however, there is likely to be a penalty of reduced image quality in these areas due to an increased level of noise.

Many photographers adopt a technique known as "expose to the right," in which they adjust the exposure to the point that the histogram curve is as far to the right as it can be without clipping occurring to ensure they capture as wide a tonal range as possible and with as many levels to describe those tones. This is a valid technique, but do not base your exposure on just the composite RGB histogram, but rather look carefully at the histograms for the three individual channels, as it is often possible to encounter a situation where one of the color-channel histograms begins to show clipping before the composite RGB histogram. A common example occurs when photographing a sunrise or sunset, when it is likely the red channel will begin to clip first due to the higher level of red/orange/yellow light in the scene.

As mentioned previously, the "clipping" of the histogram curve is usually an indication of under- or overexposure but do remember that the preview image, including those for NEF files, is always derived from an 8-bit JPEG file to which the camera settings (white balance, contrast, saturation, etc.) have been applied, and it is the tonal distribution of this JPEG file that the histogram describes. An NEF file will contain more data and have a wider range of tonal values; therefore, an overexposed highlight in the JPEG preview may not be an overexposed highlight when the NEF file is examined in a RAW file converter such as Nikon Capture NX 2. Even if an NEF file has been incorrectly exposed, it is possible to apply retrospective exposure compensation using software such as Nikon View NX or Capture NX 2, between about -1.0 Ev and +1.5 Ev; no such flexibility exists with a JPEG file.

Scenes that are low in contrast will have a rather narrow curve that ends before reaching either the left- or right-hand extremity of the bottom axis. You have two choices about how to deal with this situation: (1) Using the Picture Control System to either increase the contrast setting in an existing Nikon Picture Control or create a Custom Picture Control with an increased level of contrast (see pages 85-89); or (2) adjust the contrast level at a later stage using an image-processing software application. I would recommend the latter approach, as it offers a far greater degree of control.

Hint: It is always preferable to err on the side of lower image contrast because it is easier to boost contrast than it is to try to reduce it at any stage after the original exposure.

Two-button Reset: Restore Default Settings

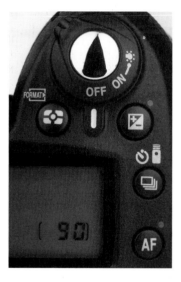

The ⊞ button, together with the AF button, is used to restore a range of default settings on the D90; both are located on the top-right of the camera and each has a green dot beside it.

If you want to restore the settings listed below to their default values, press and hold the ⊞ and AF buttons (they have green dots beside them to help you identify them) for more than two seconds.

Option	Default
Image Quality	JPEG Normal
Image Size	Large
Release mode	Single frame
ISO	
Auto and Scene modes	Auto
P, A, S, M	200
White Balance	Auto
Fine tuning	0
Color temperature	5,000K
Picture Control modifications	None
Autofocus mode	AF-A
Autofocus (Live View)	
[icons]	Face priority
[icons] P, A, S, M	Wide area
[icon]	Normal area
Focus point	Center [1]
Metering	Matrix
AE/ AF Lock hold	Off
Flexible program	Off
Exposure compensation	±0 (Off)
Flash compensation	Off
Bracketing	Off [2]
FV Lock	Off
Flash mode	
[icons]	Auto front-curtain sync
[icon]	Auto slow sync
P, A, S, M	Front-curtain sync
Multiple exposure	Off

1. *Focus point not displayed if Auto-area is selected at CS-a1 [AF area mode]*
2. *Number of shots left to zero, increment to 1 Ev (exposure/flash) or 1 WB (white balance)*

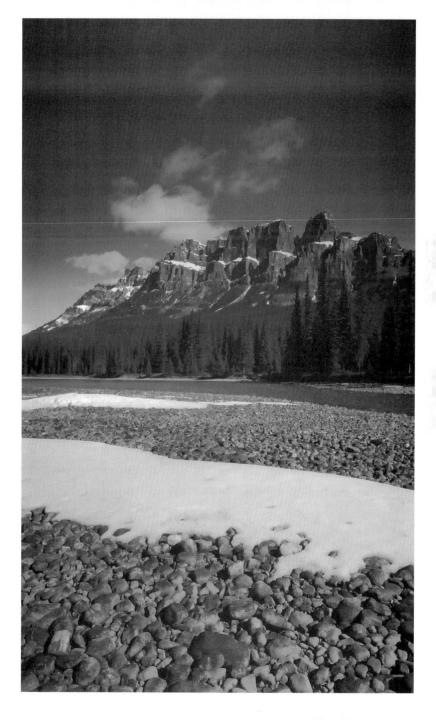

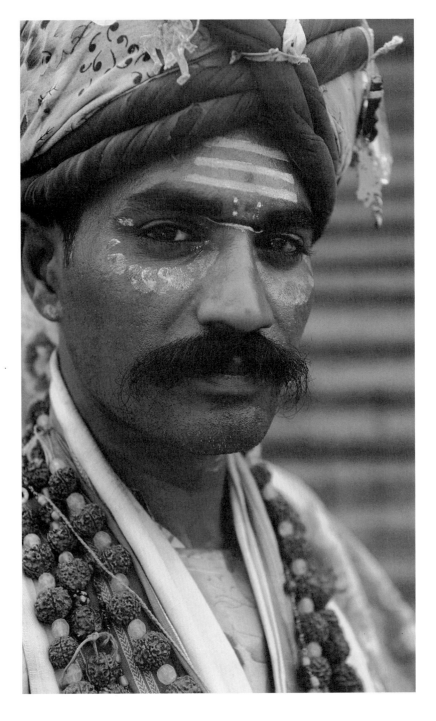

Exposure & The AF System

Regardless of whether you are content to let the D90 make decisions about exposure settings or you prefer to take control of the camera and make them for yourself, it is essential to understand how the camera reads, evaluates, and records light.

ISO Sensitivity

Shooting with film requires you to make a decision about which ISO (sensitivity) rating to choose in order to cope with the prevailing or expected lighting conditions, and the entire roll must be exposed at the same ISO value. One of the great advantages of digital photography is that digital cameras allow you to adjust the ISO sensitivity from picture to picture. The ISO sensitivity rating used by Nikon D-SLR cameras follows the guidelines set by the International Organization for Standardization using the ISO scale; therefore, where the sensitivity setting on a camera complies with these guidelines, it is referred to as being ISO equivalent.

The D90 offers ISO equivalent settings from 200 to 3200 that can be adjusted in steps of 0.3 or 0.5 Ev, plus the option to decrease sensitivity by approximately 1 Ev below ISO 200 (offering ISO equivalents of 100 – 160), or increase it by up to 1 Ev above ISO 3200, in steps of 0.3, 0.7, and 1.0 Ev (offering an ISO equivalent of 6400). The options to shift the sensitivity outside the normal range are referred to as Lo and Hi. For example, a setting of Lo 0.3 corresponds to an ISO sensitivity of 160, while Hi 0.3 is equivalent to an ISO sensitivity of 4000.

↺ *Even if you prefer to use automatic settings, understanding how the autofocus and autoexposure functions on the D90 work will help you take great photos.*

It is easy to assume that using the lowest possible ISO setting would deliver the maximum potential image quality; after all, this applies generally with film. However, digital sensors do not react to light in the same way as film. The standard base ISO sensitivity is where the sensor usually delivers optimal performance, which is ISO 200 in the case of the D90. At settings below this, the dynamic range of the camera is effectively reduced. Although low and midtone values are preserved, there is a tendency for highlight values to become overexposed more quickly. So, unless you really need to reduce the sensitivity, for example to use a wider aperture in bright conditions, I recommend you shoot at ISO 200 to get the best out of your camera.

To adjust the ISO sensitivity, press the ISO button and rotate the main command dial until the required value is displayed in the top control panel and viewfinder. Alternatively, the ISO sensitivity can be adjusted via the [ISO sensitivity] item in the Shooting menu. To set the step value for the adjustment of ISO sensitivity, use CS-b1. The camera also has the ability to adjust the ISO sensitivity automatically according to the light conditions; this feature is also set via the Shooting menu via the [ISO Sensitivity] option.

The ISO button is located on the rear of the D90; it is the second button from the bottom on the left-hand side of the LCD screen.

High ISO Performance

At higher ISO settings, a digital image will show an increasing amount of electronic noise. Generally, as the ISO value is hiked higher and higher, other unwanted effects also appear increasingly: Dynamic range is reduced (by about one stop of dynamic range for each full stop increase in ISO), plus the saturation of color and tonal separation are reduced, which leads to a flat and dull looking image.

Provided exposure accuracy is correct, the high ISO performance of the D90 is remarkably good. For the absolute optimum image quality, keep ISO sensitivity set to 200, where the D90 is easily capable of producing a dynamic range of no less than nine stops. That said, unless you really ramp up the level of contrast and sharpening in-camera, or photograph a scene with excessively high contrast, separating shots taken at an ISO 200, 400, or 800 is an exercise in splitting hairs; the ISO performance of the D90 is so good up to ISO 800 that it is possible to shoot at just about any combination of camera settings (e.g., compression, contrast, color saturation, sharpening) with virtually no detrimental effect on image quality. However, you can still expect to see noise in any image, regardless of the ISO setting, if you shoot using a long exposure (i.e., one second or longer); use the feature for Long Exposure Noise Reduction found in the Shooting menu in such circumstances.

Even at more elevated ISO levels, the dynamic range, color saturation, and noise levels are remarkably good, making ISO 1600 perfectly usable and ISO 3200 a practical solution provided other camera settings are appropriate in respect to controlling contrast and saturation (i.e., do not set these too high, as it is far better to adjust these parameters at a later stage in post-processing). Furthermore, the noise at ISO 1600 to 3200 can be used for creative purposes, and is particularly effective with the black-and-white options available on the D90, emulating the qualities of high-speed, grainy, black-and-white film.

When you move beyond the normal ISO range to the range of Hi settings, you will find a noticeable change in ISO performance, especially by ISO 6400, where there is a significant loss in dynamic range and increase in noise and contrast. I would consider these as a last resort; however, for those situations where any picture is better than no picture, these Hi ISO settings provide a valuable solution that was previously unavailable in a camera of this class.

To help reduce the effects of noise at higher ISO settings, there is a specific [High ISO NR] feature available via the Shooting menu (see pages 210-211, for more details). While this can be effective, it will result in some loss of definition in very fine detail, especially at the [High] setting. It is usually preferable to use either the noise reduction feature of an NEF file converter, or a dedicated noise reduction application, such as Noise Ninja (www.picturecode.com) or Neat Image (www.neatimage.com).

ISO Sensitivity Auto Control
Although Nikon has improved the functionality of this feature compared with previous models, it is still important to understand how it works since it may not be quite what you expect.

In P (Programmed-auto) and A (aperture-priority) exposure modes, the ISO sensitivity will not be altered unless underexposure would occur at the value specified for [Minimum shutter speed] option under the [ISO sensitivity auto control] item in the Shooting menu. The range of shutter speeds for [Minimum shutter speed] extends from one second to 1/2000 second.

However, if the camera cannot achieve a proper exposure at the ISO specified as the [Maximum sensitivity] value, which covers the range from ISO 400 to Hi 1 (ISO 6400), the D90 will begin to select slower shutter speeds.

In Shutter-priority mode, the ISO sensitivity is shifted when the exposure reaches the maximum aperture available on the lens. Indeed, this is probably the exposure mode that is most useful with this feature because it will raise the sensitivity setting and thus maintain the pre-selected shutter speed, which is usually critical to the success of the picture.

Again, the [Maximum sensitivity] option for the ISO can be specified under the [ISO sensitivity auto control] item. In Manual exposure mode, the sensitivity is shifted if the selected shutter speed and aperture cannot attain a correct exposure (as indicated by the display in the viewfinder). When the [ISO sensitivity auto control] feature is active, ISO-AUTO is displayed in the control panel and the viewfinder; if the ISO sensitivity is altered from the value set by the user, the ISO-AUTO icon will blink and the adjusted ISO sensitivity value is shown in the viewfinder.

TTL Metering

The D90 has options for three metering patterns that will be familiar if you have used a Nikon AF camera before: Matrix, center-weighted, and spot. To select a metering mode, press the 🔅 button and rotate the main command dial. The appropriate icon will be displayed in the control panel.

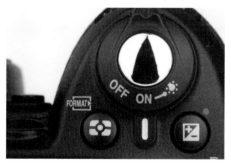

The metering pattern is selected using the metering mode button 🔅 , which is located on the top of the camera, to the right of the control panel.

🔅 Matrix Metering

The metering pattern for this mode covers virtually the entire frame area with each of the segments on the 420-segment RGB metering sensor (located in the viewfinder head of the camera just above the eyepiece) acting as a sampling point. This is the same sensor as used in the D80, the predecessor to the D90, except it has been enhanced by the addition of a small diffraction grating placed immediately in front of it. This forms the core of Nikon's innovative Scene Recognition

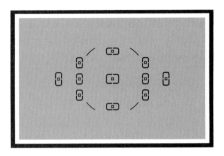

The coverage of the Matrix metering pattern extends virtually to the edges of the full frame area.

System, which helps to separate the light falling on the sensor into its component colors, thus improving the efficiency and accuracy with which the camera assesses both the color and contrast of the light from the scene being photographed. The D90 uses this enhanced information to improve metering accuracy, especially for skin tones.

It is necessary to use a D- or G-type Nikkor lens to derive the most from the Matrix metering capabilities of the D90, since these provide additional focus distance information that assists the camera in estimating how far away the subject is located. The metering system also knows which AF point is selected and uses this information to estimate the position of the subject within the frame. Nikon calls the system 3D Color Matrix Metering II. If an AF Nikkor lens that does not communicate distance information to the camera is used, the system defaults to standard color Matrix metering II (i.e., the distance information is not integrated in the exposure computations). This also applies to use of a non-CPU type lens, provided the focal length and maximum aperture value are specified using the [Non-CPU lens data] item in the Setup menu.

In Matrix metering (and i-TTL flash control), the D90 benefits from the enhanced analysis of highlights within the frame achieved by the Scene Recognition System feature, which is combined with its assessment of color, as well as brightness and contrast, and then compared against databases containing a total of over 30,000 sample images that cover an enormous range of lighting conditions. The

150

result is Nikon's most advanced TTL metering available to date in a camera of this class. Matrix metering uses four principal factors when calculating an exposure value:

• The overall brightness level in a scene
• The ratio of brightness between the 420 segments
• The focused distance, provided by the lens (D- or G-type only)
• The location of the active AF point

When shooting an evenly illuminated scene with moderate contrast, where the active AF point covers a midtone value, the D90 produces consistently good exposures via its Matrix metering. Also, the Matrix metering system is remarkably accurate when shooting a scene filled with very light tones; the D90 will usually cope extremely well and not require any exposure compensation to be applied, unlike previous Nikon models in this class that usually need some positive exposure compensation in such situations.

However, the Matrix metering does appear to produce greater variability in results when the active AF point covers a very light or very dark tone (i.e., the camera's metering seems to pay more attention to the tone under the active AF point compared with some Nikon camera models)—when shooting in a strongly backlit situation, for example. In these situations, it is advisable to check the histogram display to monitor both highlight and shadow levels.

⊡ Center-Weighted Metering

Available in P, S, A, and M exposure (shooting) modes, only the center-weighted metering pattern harkens back to the TTL metering systems used by early Nikon SLR film cameras. In these cameras, the frame area was usually divided in a 60:40 ratio, with the bias placed on the central portion of the frame. The D90 uses a higher ratio of 75:25, with 75% of the exposure reading based on the central area of the frame and the remaining 25% based on the outer area. Unlike Matrix metering, no color information is assessed when the center-weighted pattern is selected, so metering is performed using a grayscale.

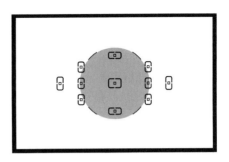

The default coverage of the center-weighted metering pattern covers an 0.31-inch (8-mm) diameter circle.

Hint: At the default setting, a 0.31-inch (8-mm) circle in the middle of the frame represents the center-weighted metering area; the diameter of this circle can be adjusted using the options available at CS-b3 [Center-weighted area].

Hint: Center-weighted metering offers nowhere near the level of sophistication of Matrix metering, but for some subjects, its simplicity can be an advantage for photographers who like to control exposure and understand how it works.

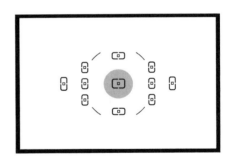

The coverage of the spot-metering pattern covers a circle centered on the active AF point that represents about 2% of the total frame area.

⊡ Spot Metering

Available in P, S, A, and M shooting modes, spot metering is extremely useful for metering from a highly specific area of a scene. For example, faced with a subject against a virtually black background, which might cause the Matrix metering system to overexpose the subject, the spot meter allows a reading to be taken from the subject without being influenced by the background. The sensing area for the spot-metering pattern is a

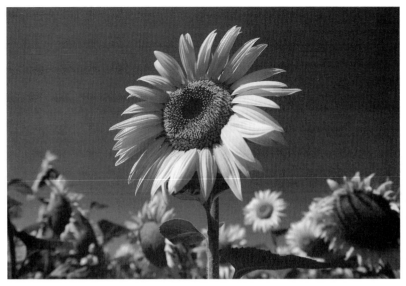

The D90's center-weighted metering considers the light in the entire scene, but places priority (75%) on the central part of the frame.

circle approximately 0.14 inch (3.5 mm) in diameter, which represents about 2% of the total frame area. This circle is centered on the active AF point, unless Auto-area AF is selected, in which case, the central AF point is the only area to perform metering. Again, as with the center-weighted pattern, no color information is assessed when the spot-metering pattern is selected, so metering is performed using a grayscale.

Also be aware that in Dynamic-area AF, the D90 will attempt to follow a moving subject by shifting focus control between different AF points. If this occurs, the spot metering also shifts, following the active AF point.

Hint: The TTL metering system measures reflected light in center-weighted and spot metering modes, and is calibrated to give a correct exposure for midtones. When using either of these two metering patterns, you must make sure that the part of the scene you meter from represents a midtone, otherwise you will need to compensate the exposure value.

AUTO and the Scene Modes

The AUTO and dedicated scene modes represent the most automated level of control available on the D90. The camera manages many key features, providing you with no option to intervene and override them. For example, the metering pattern, white balance, exposure compensation, and Picture Controls cannot be adjusted from their default settings. This is unlikely to be of any concern for those who are content to let the D90 make decisions on their behalf. But I recommend avoiding these modes for photographers who want a certain level of control, and suggest working in Aperture-priority, Shutter-priority, or Manual shooting mode.

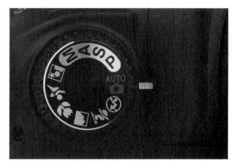

For the simplest form of fully automated point and shoot, select AUTO *on the mode dial.*

AUTO AUTO

The AUTO mode is designed as a universal point-and-shoot mode. The camera attempts to select a combination of shutter speed and aperture that will be appropriate for the current scene. It does this by using information from the through-the-lens (TTL) metering system in the camera, which assesses the overall level of illumination, contrast, and color quality of the prevailing light, together with information from the autofocus system used to estimate the location of the subject in the frame area and its distance from the camera. This mode is most effective for general-purpose snapshot photography, such as family events or vacations.

Auto (Flash off)

This mode is essentially the same as the AUTO mode, with the exception that the built-in flash is turned off and will not

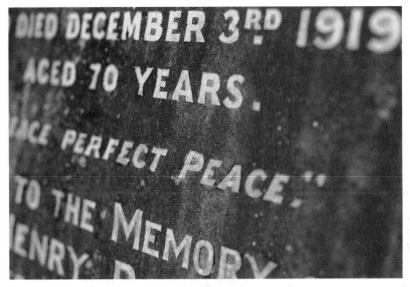

You may encounter situations where the camera's metering system determines that flash is necessary, but you know it isn't appropriate for the particular scene you are trying to photograph. In these situations, use the ⚡ *mode.*

operate regardless of the level of ambient illumination, even if it is very low.

⚡ is useful when shooting in such situations as a museum, where flash may be prohibited, or in natural low-light conditions where you do not want to spoil the atmosphere by using flash. Although the operation of the built-in flash is cancelled, the AF-assist illuminator lamp will still function to assist autofocus operation in poor lighting conditions.

Hint: Since the camera can set slow shutter speeds in this mode, always check the viewfinder information to ensure that the selected shutter speed will allow the camera to be held without risk of camera shake affecting the picture. At slow shutter speeds, consider using a camera support such as a tripod.

⅀ Portrait

The ⅀ mode is designed to select a wide aperture (low f/number) in order to produce a picture with a shallow depth of field. Generally this renders the background out of focus so it does not detract from the subject, although the effect is also dependent on the distance between the subject and the background, and the focal length of the lens used. This mode is most effective with focal lengths of 100mm or more, and when the subject is relatively far away from the background.

Hint: Best results for portraits are often achieved when the subject nearly fills the frame. Since the autofocus area is set automatically to Auto-area mode, there is no guarantee that the camera will focus on at least one of the subject's eyes. Therefore I strongly recommend that you override the default option and use Single-point AF [ı] , and choose a focus area that covers one of the subject's eyes to ensure it is focused sharply.

⛰ Landscape

The ⛰ mode is designed to select a small aperture in order to produce a picture with an extended depth of field. Generally, this renders everything from the foreground to the horizon in focus, although this will depend to some degree on how close the lens is to the nearest subject. This mode is most effective with wide-angle or wide-angle zoom lenses, and when the scene is well lit.

It is important to ensure the main area of interest in your composition is in sharp focus. Since selection of the focusing area is fully automatic at the default setting, the camera may not focus where you expect it to. Consequently, you may prefer to override the default option by selecting Single-point AF [ı] in this mode to ensure you know which part of the scene the camera is focusing on.

Hint: When using a wide-angle focal length (i.e., a focal length less than 35mm), try to include an element of interest in the foreground of the scene, as well as the middle distance, to help produce a balanced composition and a way of leading the viewer's eye into the picture.

🌷 Close Up

The 🌷 mode is for taking pictures at short shooting distances of subjects such as flowers, insects, and other small objects. It is designed to select a small aperture (high f/number) in order to produce a picture with an extended depth of field. Generally, depth of field is limited when working at very short focus distances, even when using small apertures, so this program tries to render as much of the subject in focus as possible. The final effect will also be dependent on how close the camera is to the subject and the focal length of the lens used. This mode is most effective with lenses that have a close-focusing feature, or with a dedicated Micro-Nikkor lense.

Hint: Due to the emphasis this mode places on using a small aperture, the shutter speed can often be relatively slow. To prevent image blur caused by camera shake, use a tripod or some other form of camera support.

🏃 Sports

The 🏃 mode is designed to select a wide aperture in order to maintain the highest possible shutter-speed to "freeze" motion in fast-paced action, such as sports or children on the go. It also has a beneficial side effect: This aperture/shutter speed combination produces a picture with a very shallow depth of field that helps to isolate the subject from the background. This mode is most effective with telephoto or telephoto-zoom lenses, and when there are no obstructions between the camera and the subject that may cause the autofocus function to focus on something other than the subject.

Hint: There is always a slight delay between pressing the shutter-release button and the shutter opening; therefore, it is important to anticipate the peak moment of the action and press the shutter just before it occurs. The decisive moment will be missed if you wait to see it in the viewfinder before pressing the shutter release.

⭐ Night Portrait

The ⭐ mode is designed to capture properly exposed pictures of people against a background that is dimly lit. It is useful when you want to include background detail in the photo, such as a cityscape or sunset, and is most effective when the background is in low light, as opposed to near dark or totally dark conditions. The built-in Speedlight will activate automatically in low light; alternatively, an external Speedlight such as the SB-400 or SB-600 can be used to supplement the ambient light.

Hint: It is important to ensure the main area of interest in your composition is in sharp focus. Since focus area selection is fully automatic at the default setting, there is no guarantee that the camera will focus where you expect it to in ⭐ mode; therefore, I recommend that you override the default option and use Single-point AF [⚬] , and choose a focus area that covers the subject to ensure it is focused sharply.

Common Settings in AUTO Exposure and Scene Modes

The following apply in ⚙AUTO mode and the six Scene modes at default settings:

Image quality	JPEG Normal	White balance	Auto
Image size	Large (4288 x 2848 pixels)	Long exposure noise reduction	Off
Release mode	Single	High ISO noise reduction	Normal
Autofocus mode	AF-A (Auto select)	Active D-Lighting	Auto
ISO	Auto	Function button	AF-area mode
Metering pattern	Matrix	AE-L/AF-L button	AE Lock (hold)
Exposure compensation	Not available	Color space	sRGB
Exposure/flash bracketing	Not available	Multiple exposure	Not available

General notes on using the $\overset{AUTO}{\square}$ and Scene shooting modes:

- Metering, Active D-Lighting, and white balance can only be used at their default settings. The other parameters listed in the chart above can be altered in AUTO and the Scene modes.
- If you alter the default setting for either the AF mode or AF-area mode, the selected options are only retained while the camera remains in the current shooting mode. If you turn the mode dial to another shooting mode, the default settings for autofocus operation (AF mode and AF-area mode) are restored.
- The Picture Controls are applied at default settings and cannot be modified; contrast and sharpening are applied automatically.
- For details of the various flash modes, see pages 293-294. For the effective maximum flash shooting range based on the Guide Number of the built-in Speedlight and ISO sensitivity setting, see page 301.
- In $\overset{AUTO}{\square}$ AUTO and the six Scene modes at default settings, the Picture Control, flash mode, and AF-area mode vary as follows:

	Picture Control	Flash	AF-area mode
AUTO	Standard	Auto	Auto-area
Flash off	Standard	Flash off	Auto-area
Portrait	Portrait	Auto	Auto-area
Landscape	Landscape	Flash off	Auto-area
Close-up	Standard	Auto	Single-point
Sport	Standard	Flash off	Dynamic-area
Night Portrait	Portrait	Auto slow	Auto-area

P, S, A, & M Shooting Modes

The D90 offers four further shooting modes that are also set via the mode dial.

Pictured here is the mode dial with Programmed-auto mode selected. The Program exposure mode provides most of the automatic settings of a point-and-shoot mode, but allows more manual control than does the AUTO mode.

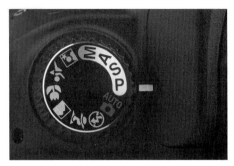

If you use a CPU type lens with an aperture ring while shooting in any of these, ensure that it is set and locked to the minimum aperture value (i.e., the highest f/number).

Programmed-Auto (P)

Programmed-auto mode automatically adjusts both the shutter speed and lens aperture to produce a properly exposed image, as determined by the selected metering mode. If you decide that a particular combination of the shutter speed and aperture chosen by the camera is not suitable, you can override the P mode settings by turning the main command dial when the camera meter is activated. This is called Flexible Program mode, and P * appears in the control panel; there is no indication in the viewfinder that you have overridden the exposure other than the altered shutter speed and aperture values. The two values change in tandem, so the overall exposure level remains the same (i.e., increasing the shutter speed decreases the aperture); rotating the command dial to the right sets a larger aperture (smaller f/number)/faster shutter speed, while rotating the command dial to the left sets a smaller aperture (larger f/number)/slower shutter speed.

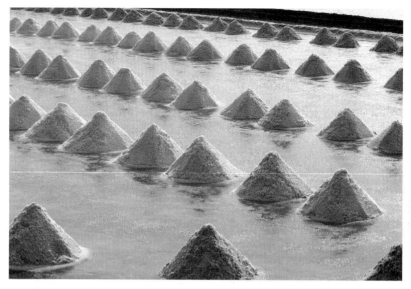

Aperture-priority offers automatic exposure with the ability to maintain manual control over depth of field.

Note: If you override the Program mode, it will remain locked to its new settings for shutter speed and aperture even if the meter auto-powers off and is then switched on again by pressing the shutter release halfway. To cancel the override, you must do one of the following: Rotate the main command dial until the asterisk * next to the P is no longer displayed; change the exposure mode; turn the power off; or perform a two-button reset.

In my opinion, Program mode is not all that different from the point-and-shoot exposure control options of 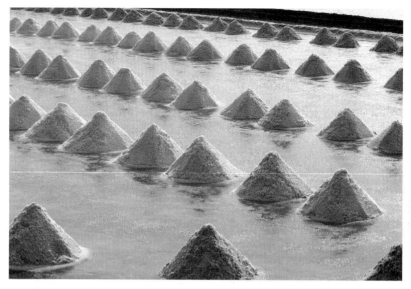 and the Scene modes. since you effectively relinquish control of exposure to the camera. If you want to make informed decisions about shutter speed and aperture for creative photography, do not use Programmed-auto mode!

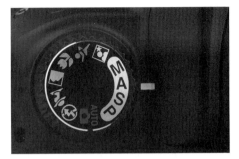

The mode dial is pictured here, with Aperture-priority auto mode selected. Aperture-priority does set exposure for you automatically, but allows you to control how the scene is rendered in terms of depth of field.

Aperture-Priority Auto (A)

In this mode, the photographer selects an aperture value and the D90 will choose a shutter speed to produce an appropriate exposure, as determined by the selected metering mode. The aperture is controlled by the sub-command dial (default) and is changed in increments of 1/3 Ev (default). The shutter speed the D90 selects will also change in increments of 1/3 stop (default). The Ev step level can be adjusted using CS-b1 [EV steps for exposure cntrl].

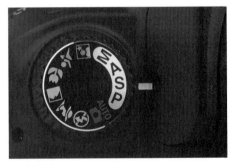

The mode dial can be seen here, with Shutter-priority auto mode selected. Shutter-priority exposure mode also sets exposure automatically but allows you to control how movement is rendered.

Shutter-Priority Auto (S)

In this mode, you select a shutter speed between 30 seconds and 1/4000 second and the D90 will choose an aperture value to produce an appropriate exposure, as determined by the selected metering mode. The shutter speed is controlled by the main command dial (default) and is changed in increments of 1/3 stop (default). The aperture value the D90 selects will also change in increments of 1/3 stop (default). The EV step level can be adjusted using CS-b1 [EV steps for exposure cntrl].

Hint: If you use the D90 remotely when you make an exposure (i.e., your eye is not to the viewfinder eyepiece), you must ensure the viewfinder eyepiece is covered (the DK-5 cap is supplied for this purpose). The 420-segment RGB metering sensor of the D90 is located within the viewfinder-head; therefore, light entering via the viewfinder eyepiece will influence exposure calculations made in P, A, and S modes.

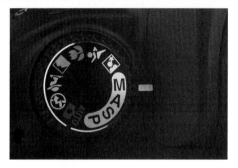

The Manual mode leaves exposure control completely up to you. An exposure scale, indicating what the correct exposure is, helps you make the right aperture and shutter speed settings.

Manual (M)

Manual mode offers the photographer total control over exposure, and is probably the most useful if you want to learn more about the relationship between shutter speed and aperture and how they affect the final appearance of your pictures. You choose and control both the shutter speed, via the main command dial (default), and lens aperture, via the sub-command dial (default). If required, the roles of the two command dials can be changed via CS-f5 [Customize command dials].

An analog display shown in the control panel and viewfinder indicates the level of exposure your settings would produce. If the camera determines the exposure values are set for a proper exposure, a single indent mark appears below the central 0 point of the scale. At the default setting for CS-f7 [Reverse indicators], if the camera determines that the settings would produce an underexposed result, the degree of underexposure is indicated by the number of indent marks that appear to the right (minus) side of the central 0. Conversely, if the chosen settings would create an overexposed result, the degree of overexposure is indicated by the number of indent marks to the left (plus) side of the central 0. The more indent marks that appear, the greater the degree of deviance from the "correct" exposure, as calculated by the camera.

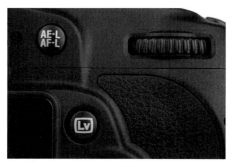

The AE-L/AF-L button is located on the rear of the camera above the Live View button.

Autoexposure Lock (AE-L)

If you take a meter reading in any of the three autoexposure modes (P, A, or S) and recompose, it is likely—particularly with spot metering—that the newly metered area will now fall on a different part of the scene and probably produce a different exposure value. The D90 allows you to lock the initial exposure reading in center-weighted or spot metering before you reframe and shoot (note that this feature is less effective for Matrix metering, because Matrix metering assess the entire frame area and the range of contrast within it as well as the level of brightness to produce the most balanced exposure).

Start by positioning the part of the scene you want to meter within the appropriate metering area. Next, press the shutter release halfway to acquire focus and an exposure reading, then press and hold the AE-L/AF-L button to lock the exposure (and focus, except in manual-focus mode). You can now recompose and take the picture at the metered value. AE-L will appear in the viewfinder display while this function is active. When using AE Lock, it is possible to alter the shutter speed and/or aperture value in P, A, and S modes without altering the metered exposure level. In P mode, shutter speed and aperture can be changed; in S mode, the shutter speed can be changed; in A mode, the aperture can be changed, but the overall exposure level always remains the same.

Hint: It is possible to use the shutter-release button to perform the autoexposure lock function; select [On] at CS-c1 [Shutter-release button AE-L] the exposure will lock while the shutter-release button is held down halfway. The function of the AE-L/AF-L button can be set via CS-f4 [Assign AE-L/AF-L button].

Exposure Compensation

Exposure compensation can be applied regardless of the TTL metering pattern in use, but the most consistent results are achieved with either center-weighted or spot metering. As mentioned previously, in these latter two TTL metering patterns, the D90 uses simple grayscale metering with no color information or influence of the Scene Recognition System to affect the metered reading. Working on the assumption that the camera is pointed at a scene with a reflectivity that averages out to that of a midtone, it appears Nikon has calibrated the TTL metering against a reference that has a reflectivity value of approximately 12% to 13%. Hence, if you use an 18% gray photographic card to estimate exposure, you will find your results will be approximately 1/3 to 1/2 stop underexposed.

Many scenes you encounter will not reflect 12% to 13% of the light falling on them. For example, a landscape under a blanket of fresh snowfall is going to reflect far more light, while an animal with a very dark coat will reflect far less than an average midtone. Unless you compensate your exposure accordingly for these extremes, the camera will attempted to render them as midtones, causing a light one to appear underexposed and a dark tone to be overexposed.

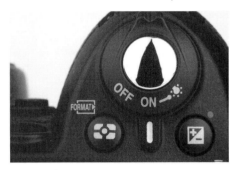

The exposure com-pensation button ![EV] is located just behind the shutter-release button, on the top of the camera.

To set an exposure compensation factor in P, S, A, and M exposure modes (it is disabled in AUTO and Scene shooting modes), hold down the exposure compensation button, located to the rear and right of the shutter-release button. Turn the main command dial until the required value is shown in the top control panel. Compensation can be set to values between -5 Ev and +5 Ev, in increments of 0.3 Ev. The value is also displayed in the viewfinder while the button is held down. The degree of compensation will change in steps of 1/3 or 1/2 Ev, depending on which step size is selected at CS-b1 [EV steps for exposure comp].

In Manual exposure mode, the exposure is set according to the value suggested by the camera's TTL meter if the ana-log display shows no deviance to either side of the 0 mid-point. If an exposure compensation factor is applied in this mode, the display shifts either to the left (positive compensa-tion) or right (negative compensation) of the 0 midpoint by the amount of compensation applied, while the numerical value of the compensation amount is displayed and the 0 blinks. As you dial in the compensation, will see a small + or – icon displayed to the right of the analog scale (the exposure compensation button must be depressed to see this). As soon as you release the exposure compensation button, ⚡ appears in its place (it is also shown in the control panel), and the numerical value of the compensation amount is no longer displayed.

To put the exposure compensation into effect, you must now adjust the shutter speed and/or aperture, so the analog scale display is shifted back to where no indent marks are shown on either side of the 0 midpoint on the scale. Once you have made these adjustments and the analog scale is centered on 0 again, if you press the exposure compensation button, the analog scale shifts to show the amount of compensation applied and the icon at the bottom of the scale indicates whether it is a + or − value. This is a quick and useful way to check how much compensation you have applied.

Note: Although exposure compensation can be applied in Manual exposure mode, as described, it is often quicker to simply adjust the shutter speed and/or aperture so the required level of exposure adjustment is displayed on the analog exposure scale.

The exposure compensation icon ⚡ remains visible in the viewfinder and control panel, regardless of the exposure mode in use, as a reminder that you have an exposure compensation value applied. Once you have set a compensation factor, it will remain locked until you hold down the exposure compensation button and reset the compensation value to 0.0.

Bracketing Exposure

It is important when shooting digital pictures to expose as accurately as you can, since overexposure will lose highlight detail and underexposure tends to degrade image quality due to electronic noise as well as blocked shadow detail. In exposure bracketing, the D90 varies the exposure compensation with each exposure in a sequence of a set number; while in

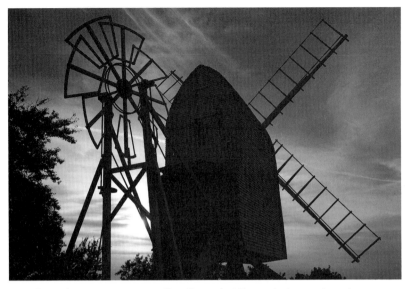

Sometimes an exposure other than what the metering system deems "correct" can produce a better image. In these situations, try the exposure bracketing feature to take a few images with different exposure values so that you can choose the best one.

flash bracketing, the flash level is adjusted with each exposure in i-TTL flash control (it also works with Auto-Aperture flash control available with the SB-900 and SB-800 only). Such bracketing of exposures can be useful in difficult lighting conditions, when there is insufficient time to check exposures and/or adjust camera settings appropriately.

Bracketing is also a very useful feature for any photographer shooting High Dynamic Range (HDR) pictures, which is a technique that uses software to combine a number of shots of the same scene taken at different exposure levels to produce a single image with an extended dynamic range (i.e., a dynamic range beyond a level the camera could record in a single exposure). For more information, check out the Lark Books publication Complete Guide to High Dynamic Range Digital Photography, by Ferrell McCollough.

The bracketing system in the D90 allows you to take a sequence of either two or three exposures varied in steps of 0.3 Ev, 0.5 Ev, 0.7 Ev, or 1 Ev, subject to the setting selected at CS-b1 [EV steps for exposure cntrl]. The bracketing sequence can be selected to affect the exposure [AE only], flash output [Flash only], or a combination of the two [AE & Flash], by selecting the appropriate option at CS-e4 [Auto bracketing set]. The combinations of number of exposures and exposure compensation level are shown in the following table:

Number of shots	Progress indicator	Description
3F	+◀■▶−	3 shots: unmodified, negative, positive
+2F	+◀■	2 shots: unmodified, positive
−−2F	■▶−	2 shots: unmodified, negative

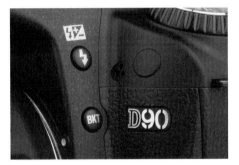

The **BKT** button is located on the front of the camera below the flash mode button ⚡ .

The bracketing function is set by pressing the **BKT** button and rotating the main command dial to select the number of exposures to be made in the bracketing sequence, while pressing the **BKT** button and rotating the sub-command dial is used to select the exposure increment to be applied. Once set, **BKT** is displayed in the control panel/viewfinder.

While bracketing is active, a progress indicator that shows the number of exposures in the sequence is displayed in the control panel; as each exposure is made, one indent mark will disappear from this display. The ■ icon will disappear when the unmodified exposure is made, the ▶— icon will disappear when the negative increment exposure is made, and the ✚◀ icon will disappear when the positive increment exposure is made.

To cancel bracketing, press the **BKT** button and rotate the main command dial until the number of shots in the bracketing sequence is set to zero; **BKT** is no longer displayed in the control panel/viewfinder.

Notes on Exposure Bracketing

- Using ⓢ single-frame release mode, the shutter-release button must be depressed to make each exposure in the bracketing sequence.
- If you set the D90 to one of the continuous-frame modes (⛛L or ⛛H), then press and hold the shutter-release button down, the camera will only take the number of frames specified in the bracket sequence. The camera stops regardless of whether the shutter release continues to be depressed.
- If you turn the D90 off, or have to change the memory card during a bracketing sequence, the camera remembers which exposure values are outstanding, so when you turn the camera on or insert a new memory card, the sequence will resume from where it stopped.
- You can combine a bracketing sequence with a fixed exposure compensation factor. For example, if you apply an exposure compensation of +1.0 Ev to deal with a scene containing predominantly light tones, and then set a bracket sequence with an increment of 1 Ev, for a three-frame sequence at +1.0 Ev, 0, and -1.0 Ev, the actual exposures made will be at 0, +1.0 Ev, and +2.0 Ev.

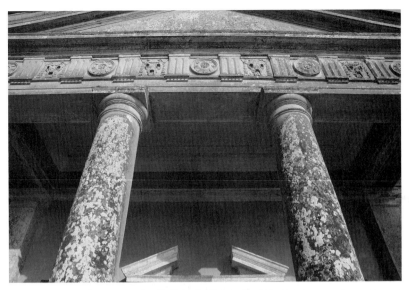

It is more important in digital photography to expose your images precisely than it is with color negative film because the dynamic range, or latitude, of a sensor is significantly less than that of negative film. This is especially true if you shoot JPEG files rather than NEF (RAW) files.

Exposure Considerations

If the D90 is your first digital SLR camera and your previous photography has been with color negative film, you may find controlling exposure with the D90 more demanding. Color negative (print) film is very tolerant to exposure errors, particularly overexposure, and the automated processing machines used to produce your prints are capable of correcting exposure errors over a range of –2 to +3 stops while adjusting color balance at the same time. Chances are that you will never have noticed your exposure errors when looking at the finished prints!

Controlling exposure with a digital SLR is analogous to shooting on transparency (slide) film; there is virtually no margin for error. Even moderate overexposure will blow out highlight detail, leaving no usable image data in these areas. Underexposure is little better since it soon gives rise to digital noise, which will degrade image quality, particularly in areas of dark tone. Make sure you check the histogram display and pay attention to all three color channels (see pages 138-141, for more information).

There are other aspects to the selection of shutter speed and lens aperture that should be kept in mind beyond just the control of exposure level, such as attaining acceptable image sharpness when shooting with a handheld camera or photographing a moving subject (see page 342 for more information), and the effect of aperture setting on depth of field (see pages 377-341 for more information).

Digital Infrared and UV Photography

Many digital cameras have the ability to record light beyond the limits of the spectrum visible to the human eye, particularly in the region of near-infrared (IR), around a wavelength of 780 nm (one nanometer = one millionth of a millimeter). Designers of digital cameras work hard to exclude IR light from digital cameras because it adversely affects apparent sharpness, reduces the contrast in skies, and can reveal unappealing features of skin that would otherwise not be visible. Similar adverse effects occur due to ultra-violet (UV) light. The low-pass filter array in front of the CMOS sensor in the D90 includes a layer designed to reduce the transmission of IR and UV light. It is very effective, and therefore the D90 cannot be recommended for either digital IR or UV photography.

The D90 Autofocus System

The autofocus (AF) system of the D90 is essentially the same as its predecessor, the D80, except it also includes a 3D-tracking capability made possible by the innovative Scene Recognition System (SRS) that has won wide acclaim in the

D300, D700, and D3. However, the implementation of the 3D-tracking in the D90 is rather different from that of those other models: There are far fewer AF points (11 instead of 51); therefore, less of the autofocus area (the total area of the frame covered the AF points) provides focus information; the Multi-CAM1000 AF module has less than one third the number of sensing points as the Multi-CAM3500 AF module used in its more highly specified siblings; and finally, the processing power of the D90 is considerably lower than that of these other models. Hence, Nikon promotes the abilities of the 3D-tracking (11 points) in the D90 as being best-suited to rapid changes of composition with relatively static subjects (i.e., the camera-to-subject distance does not alter significantly between consecutive exposures), rather than keeping pace with a subject that is moving rapidly toward or away from the camera.

The Autofocus Sensor

The D90 uses the Multi-Cam 1000 FX autofocus module. As its name implies, the sensor has a total of 1000 photodiodes distributed between the 11 AF points. The 11 points are sub-divided into one cross-type sensor at the center of the frame and ten line-type sensors; the latter are oriented parallel to the short edge of the frame.

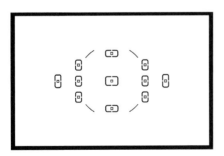

The distribution of the 11 AF points within the full frame is very cen-tralized.

When normal autofocus operation is initiated, the D90 uses a phase-detection focusing method (as opposed to the contrast-detection system employed in the Live View autofocus); the system uses a beam splitter comprising two optical prisms in a small semi-transparent area of the main reflex mirror that captures the light rays coming from the opposite sides of the lens. The prisms are coupled with a small secondary mirror located behind the main mirror that directs their light to the Multi-Cam 1000 module, which is located in the base of the mirror box at the bottom of the camera. The double image projected onto the AF module is then analyzed for patterns of light intensity, and the phase difference between them is then calculated to determine whether the subject is in front of or behind the current plane of focus. This not only informs the AF system which way the focus must be adjusted, but also by how much. The focus point is adjusted immediately and the phase difference checked; provided it is within the tolerances of the AF system, it will not be altered again, as the camera has determined that focus has been acquired.

The central AF point is cross-type, meaning it is sensitive to detail in both a horizontal and vertical orientation; therefore, it is the most reliable. The remaining 10 AF points are line-types; these are only sensitive to detail in a direction that is perpendicular to their orientation, therefore, they only detect detail aligned with the long edge of the viewfinder frame.

The area covered by the central AF point can be adjusted; here it is shown set to [Wide zone] via CS-a2 [Center focus point].

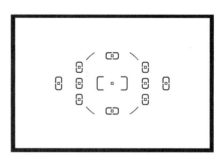

The size of the central AF point can be adjusted; there are two settings available via CS-a2 [Center focus point]: [Normal zone] and [Wide zone]. The [Normal zone] option is best-suited to static subjects that can be framed with a degree of precision and predictability, whereas [Wide zone]

174

should be consider for moving subjects; however, it is not available if [Auto area] is selected at CS-a1 [AF-area mode]. I recommend using the [Wide zone] in combination with [Dynamic-area AF] and AF-C (continuous-servo AF) focus mode when photographing a moving subject.

Hint: Sometimes when using one of the line-type sensing areas, the autofocus system of the D90 will hunt (i.e., the camera will drive the focus of the lens back and forth, but is unable to attain focus). This indicates that the detail in the subject is aligned in the same orientation as the focus sensing area under the active AF point, and thus there is insufficient contrast in the subject for the AF system to acquire focus. If this occurs, try twisting the camera slightly (10 – 15°). This slight adjustment is often enough to allow the camera to acquire focus, as the focus sensing area can detect more contrast in the detail of the subject. Once focus is confirmed, lock it (see Focus Lock section on pages 187-189) and recompose the picture before releasing the shutter.

The AF point, selected in either Single-point AF or Dynamic-area AF, can have a profound effect on the ability of the camera to achieve autofocus; depending on whether it is a cross or line type. The single, central, cross type is far more reliable in low-light or low-contrast conditions and will work with any Nikkor AF lens that has a maximum aperture of f/5.6 or larger.

Scene Recognition System

The autofocus system of the D90 also benefits from the capabilities of Nikon's Scene Recognition System (SRS). This has enhanced the abilities of the 420-pixel RGB metering sensor, by using a small diffraction grating located in front of it; this separates light into its component colors, enabling the sensor to work more effectively and efficiently. The 420-pixel sensor is now able to recognize a subject by its shape, size, and color. To employ the benefits of the SRS, it is necessary to use a D- or G-type Nikkor lens. The SRS requires the focus distance information these lenses provide to perform the necessary calculations in order for its two principle features, subject identification and subject tracking, to function. The pioneering system brings significant benefits to the performance of the autofocus system, as well as improving the autoexposure and auto white balance functions.

The SRS is optimized to recognize skin tones, particularly in any area on the 420-segment RGB sensor that relates to the average size of a human face; this is why the focus data from a D- or G-type lens is essential, as the camera calculates the size of the area on the 420-segment RGB sensor based on the distance information supplied by the lens. To the human eye, the range of skin tones can look noticeably different; however, a metering system that uses a red / green / blue sensor does not see in the same way, and skin tones appear very similar to one another in such a system.

An example of how this improves the autofocusing can be seen in how the subject identification information is used in the Auto-area AF mode to assist the D90 in focusing on people in a scene. The subject identification is also used in the 3D-tracking (11 points) mode to enhance tracking of a subject laterally across the frame. In very simple terms, once the camera has acquired focus initially, it monitors the location of the pattern of pixels on the 420-segment RGB sensor created by the shape and color distribution of the subject (i.e., the subject identification information based on subject color and contrast) to determine the position of the subject in the frame. This mapping of the subject by the 420-segment RGB sensor is combined with the focus tracking information from the Multi-CAM 1000 autofocus sensor, enabling the AF system to predict with speed and precision which AF point(s) to use to maintain focus.

Remarkably, the subject mapping by the 420-segment RGB sensor continues to operate if the subject moves momentarily outside the area covered by the 11 AF points; as soon as the subject returns to the area within the AF points, autofocusing resumes, even if the subject is at a different location within the area covered by the 11 AF points from the one it occupied immediately before it left the area. This combined tracking of the subject by the AF sensor and the 420-segment RGB metering sensor is only used in the Auto-area and 3D-tracking (11-point) AF-area modes. Although not foolproof (the Auto-area tends to be more reliable than 11-point 3D-tracking), these autofocus modes can produce quite amazing results and certainly offer the most advanced form of focus tracking available in any Nikon AF camera of this class to date.

The 3D-tracking (11-point) mode differs from other Dynamic-area AF modes because the camera automatically selects the active focus point as soon as focus is acquired, even if the camera and/or subject move relative to one another. This enables focus to be maintained while rapid and significant changes in composition are made because it is no longer necessary to maintain tracking by keeping the selected AF point over the subject, which is necessary except for brief lapses in the Dynamic-area AF option.

However, when Dynamic-area AF is selected, the D90 uses only its Multi-CAM 1000 AF sensor to perform focus tracking. Essentially, the camera reverts to the established AF system used by previous Nikon D-SLR cameras. This can be an advantage in some situations since the camera has far fewer computations to perform compared with the 3D-tracking (11-points) option, making the AF response faster. These options will be more reliable when shooting some types of moving subjects under artificial light, where the light source is non-white (e.g., some types of fluorescent and mercury-vapor lighting) as this affects the ability of the 420-segment RGB sensor to detect skin tones and thus the SRS is less effective, which in turn will impinge on the performance of the Auto-area AF and 3D-tracking (11-point) AF.

Focus Modes

The D90 has three principal methods of focusing, known as focusing modes: AF-S (single-servo AF), AF-C (continuous-servo AF), and manual focus (M). A fourth option, AF-A (Auto select), which is the default setting, leaves the D90 to automatically select either AF-S (if it detects the subject is stationary) or AF-C (if the camera determines the subject is moving). To select the focusing mode, rotate the AF mode lever (located on the left side of the lens mount below the lens release button) until the white index mark is aligned with either AF or M. To select one of the three autofocus modes, press the AF button and rotate the rear command dial until the appropriate mode is displayed in the control panel or Shooting Information Display.

The focus-mode selector switch is shown here set to AF; autofocus modes are selected via the AF button, located on the top of the camera, to the right of the control panel screen.

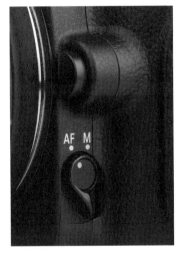

AF-A (Auto select—default setting)

In an attempt to remove the burden of choosing which of the two principal autofocus modes (AF-S and AF-C) you should use, Nikon developed this option. It was first introduced in the D50 and is the default AF mode on the D90. In AF-A mode, the D90 assesses the focus information and selects either AF-S or AF-C mode, depending on whether the camera determines that the subject is stationary or moving. More

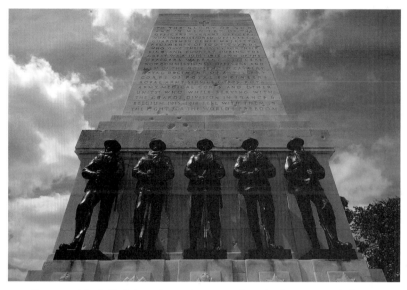

For a subject that is not moving, use the single-servo autofocus mode.

often than not, the AF-A option will select the appropriate AF mode, but if it makes the wrong choice, the result can spell disaster for your photos! In my opinion, the fully automated nature of the AF-A option simply does not provide sufficient reliability for correct autofocus mode selection. I recommend you select the specific AF mode you require, based on the nature of the subject being photographed.

AF-S (Single-Servo AF)

As soon as the shutter-release button is pressed down halfway, the D90 focuses the lens. The shutter can only be released once focus has been acquired and the in-focus indicator ● is displayed in the viewfinder. Focus will remain locked while the shutter-release button is depressed halfway. No form of focus tracking is performed when the camera is set to AF-S; therefore, this mode should be used when the camera-to-subject distance will remain constant.

AF-C (Continuous-Servo AF)

The D90 focuses the lens continuously while the shutter-release button is pressed down halfway. If the camera-to-subject distance changes (i.e., the subject begins to move) the camera will initiate predictive focus tracking in order to shift focus as it follows the subject. It does not matter whether the subject continues to move or stops and starts periodically; the camera will continue to focus until either the shutter is released or you remove your finger from the shutter-release button.

M (Manual Focus)

You must rotate the focusing ring of the lens to achieve focus. There is no restriction on when the shutter can be released. When using a lens with a maximum aperture of f/5.6 or larger, the electronic rangefinder feature will display the in-focus confirmation signal ● when focus is achieved. This confirmation can be particularly useful in low-light or low-contrast conditions.

Note: The focus mode selector lever on the camera must be set to M to manually focus with most AF-Nikkor lenses. However, if the lens you are using has a switch that allows you to select an M/A (manual/autofocus) mode on the lens, you need only to touch the focusing ring and the lens can be focused manually. As soon as you release the focusing ring and press the shutter-release button down halfway, the camera will resume autofocus operation. If the lens attached to the camera has an M/A mode option, the focus mode selector lever on the D90 can be left at AF.

Hint: The profile and position of the AF mode lever makes it quite easy to move inadvertently with potentially serious consequences. I recommend you get into the habit of checking the position of the lever regularly.

Single-Servo vs. Continuous-Servo

It is important that you appreciate the fundamental difference between the single-servo AF (S) and continuous-servo AF (C) modes. In single-servo AF, the shutter cannot be released until focus has been acquired; Nikon refers to this mode as having "focus priority." Once focus is acquired in this mode, the focus distance is locked as long as the shutter-release button is pressed down halfway, or if the AE-L/AF-L button, when set to perform as the AF-ON button **AF-ON** via CS-f4 [Assign AE-L/AF-L button], is depressed. In most shooting conditions, particularly in good light, the delay in acquiring focus is so brief that it is not perceptible and it is has no practical consequence. However, under certain conditions, such as low light or subjects with low contrast, there can be a discernable lag between pressing the shutter-release button and the shutter opening. This is because it generally takes longer for the camera to establish focus in these circumstances, particularly if one of the outer line-type sensing areas is used. Conversely, in continuous-servo AF, the shutter will operate immediately upon pressing the shutter-release button all the way down, regardless of whether focus has been achieved; Nikon refers to this mode as having "release priority."

Some photographers mistakenly assume that if the shutter is released before the camera has attained focus in the AF-C, that the picture will always be out-of-focus. In fact, the combination of constant focus monitoring and predictive focus tracking in this mode (engaged when the camera detects a moving subject—see details to follow), is normally successful in causing the focus point to be shifted within the split-second delay between the reflex mirror lifting and the shutter opening, resulting in a sharp picture. Even if the camera's calculations are slightly off, the depth of field of the image often masks minor focusing errors. To maximize AF performance, while using continuous-servo AF mode to photograph a moving subject, it is imperative that the camera is given sufficient time to assimilate information to perform the focusing action. To achieve this, either press and hold the shutter-release button halfway down or press and hold the AE-L/AF-L button when set to perform the [AF-ON] role as described above.

Predictive Focus Tracking

Whenever the shutter release is pressed all the way down to activate the shutter mechanism, there is a short delay between the reflex mirror lifting out of the light path to the camera's sensor and the shutter actually opening. If a subject is moving toward or away from the camera, the camera-to-subject distance will change during this delay. In continuous-servo AF mode, the D90 uses its predictive tracking system to shift the point of focus on the lens to compensate for this change in camera-to-subject distance, regardless of whether the subject is moving at a constant speed, is accelerating, or decelerating. Predictive focus tracking is always initiated when the camera detects the camera-to-subject distance is changing (i.e., the subject is moving toward or way from the camera), when the shutter release is held down halfway or when the AE-L/AF-L button set is perform the [AF-ON] role. In continuous-servo AF mode, predictive focus tracking is initiated as soon as the camera detects the subject movement, regardless of whether this occurs while the camera is establishing focus, or if it detects the subject moves after focus is first acquired. The camera monitors focus constantly before the shutter is released. The best results are achieved with AF-S type lenses, which have an internal focusing motor that provides faster focusing.

Using Trap Focus

It is possible to use the functionality of the focus system in the D90 to perform the trap focus technique. Trap focus allows the camera to be pre-focused at a specific point and have the shutter released automatically, as soon as a subject passes through the area. If you can accurately predict the path of the subject, this technique can be very effective. The following steps will enable you to set up the D90 for trap focusing:

- Set [AF-ON] **AF-ON** via CS-f4 [Assign AE-L/AF-L button], so that focusing is only performed when the AE-L/AF-L button is pressed, not when the shutter-release button is pressed down halfway.
- Select AF-S (single-servo AF) focus mode, via CS-a1 [AF-area mode]
- Select Single-point as the autofocus area mode. If the lens you are using has a focus mode switch, set it to A or M/A.

Pre-focus the lens on a point that is the same distance from the camera as the point through which the subject will pass, by aligning it with the selected autofocus sensing area and pushing the AE-L/AF-L button. Once focus is acquired, release the AE-L/AF-L button (focus is now locked at that distance). Re-compose the picture so the selected AF point covers the point you expect the subject to pass through. Now, fully depress the shutter-release button (this is necessary to keep the camera activated and enable the shutter to be released as soon as focus is detected). I recommend using the MC-DC2 remote shutter release, as it has a lock facility. When the subject enters the space covered by the selected AF point, the camera will detect focus and the shutter will automatically be released.

Autofocus Area Modes

The D90 has four autofocusing area modes (not to be confused with the three autofocusing modes described above) that determine how the 11 AF points will be used: Single-point AF, Dynamic-area AF, Auto-area AF, and 3D-tracking (11 points). The autofocus area mode is selected via CS-a1 [AF-area mode]. Unlike some other Nikon camera models, there is no external switch on the D90 that enables selection of the AF-area mode. Since this is a fundamental control for autofocus, I recommend that CS-a1 be added to the customized menu [My menu] as the top item so that it can be accessed quickly and efficiently. The four available options operate as follows:

[ᴛ] Single-Point AF

The D90 uses only the single AF point that you selected for focusing via the multi selector button. The camera takes no part in choosing which AF point is used. The selected AF point is highlighted in the control panel display and the Shooting Information Display.

[ᴏ] Dynamic-Area AF

In AF-A and AF-C, the D90 uses the AF point that you selected for focusing. However, if the subject leaves the area covered by this AF point briefly, the camera immediately evaluates information from the other surrounding AF points and will attempt to maintain focus using these AF points as needed until the AF point that you originally selected covers the subject. The selected area is highlighted in the control panel display and the Shooting Information Display where it remains highlighted, even if another AF point is used to momentarily maintain focus. In AF-S mode, the camera only uses the single AF point that you selected for autofocus.

[■] Auto-Area AF

The D90 selects the AF point(s) automatically using information from the Multi-CAM 1000 autofocus module. If a D- or G-type Nikkor lens is used, the subject identification information based on the color and contrast pattern of the subject, as established by the Scene Recognition System using the 420-segment RGB sensor, will also be used to map the position of the subject within the frame. This system is particularly adept at identifying skin tones and is therefore very useful when photographing people. The active AF point(s) are highlighted for approximately one second.

[3D] 3D-Tracking (11 points)

In AF-A and AF-C, the D90 uses the AF point that you selected for focusing. Operation is similar to the Auto-area AF mode insomuch as when shooting with a D- or G-type Nikkor lens, the subject identification information based on the color and contrast pattern of the subject, as determined by the Scene Recognition System, will also be used to map and track the position of the subject as its position shifts within the frame, selecting an alternative AF point to maintain focus, even if there is a significant change from the original composition.

In AF-S mode, the camera uses the AF point that you selected for autofocus, but differs from 3D-tracking in AF-A and AF-C in that it will only use that AF point. If the subject and/or camera moves, the camera will still maintain focus at the selected AF-point.

Unlike the 51-point AF system used in the D300, the D90 has a much lower density of AF points, with far larger gaps between them; consequently, the D90 is not nearly as reliable at maintaining focus on a subject that is moving toward or away from the camera. Nikon acknowledges this and recommends that the 3D-tracking (11 points) AF area mode is most appropriate for relatively static subjects that remain at a near-constant distance from the camera. If a subject moves outside of the frame area while trying to follow it with the D90, it will be necessary to let go of the shutter-release button before recomposing the picture with the selected AF point covering the subject.

Selecting an Autofocus Point

To manually select the AF point that the D90 will initially use to attain focus in Single-point AF, Dynamic-area AF, or 3D-tracking (11 points) AF:

- Rotate the focus selector lock lever (located immediately below the multi selector button) counter-clockwise so its white index mark is aligned with the white dot.
- If the camera is not already active, press the shutter-release button down halfway and release it.
- Press ✤ to select the required AF point (at the default setting of CS-f2 [OK button] (shooting mode) you can select the central AF point by pressing the ⊛ button at the center of the multi selector).

- To prevent unintentional selection of an alternative AF point, rotate the focus selector lock lever clockwise so the "L" is positioned against its white index mark.

Focus Mode and AF-Area Mode Overview

It will probably take a while to get used to the functionality of the Focus Mode and Focus Area Mode options of the D90 if you are new to Nikon's AF system. Therefore, you may wish to re-read the sections above and refer to the following table that summarizes the various autofocus operations.

AF Mode	AF-Area Mode	Selection of Focus Area
Manual	Single-point AF	User
AF-S (single-servo)	Single-point AF	User
AF-S (single-servo)	Dynamic-area AF	User
AF-S (single-servo)	Auto-area AF	Camera [1]
AF-S (single-servo)	3D-tracking (11 point)	User [2]
AF-C (continuous-servo)	Single-point AF	User
AF-C (continuous-servo)	Dynamic-area AF	User [3]
AF-C (continuous-servo)	Auto-area AF	Camera [4]
AF-C (continuous-servo)	3D-tracking (11 point)	User [2]

1. Active AF point(s) are highlighted for approximately one-second.
2. Camera will shift focus to an alternative AF point if the composition is altered; the subject is tracked automatically, based on color and contrast pattern information.
3. Camera will use an alternative AF point if the subject momentarily leaves the selected AF point.
4. Active focus point(s) is not displayed.

Hint: As you change from Single-point to Dynamic-area to Auto-area to 3D-tracking AF, you relinquish more control to the camera in the selection of the AF point. Therefore, consider the most appropriate option based on the nature of the subject you are photographing and whether or not it is moving. For static subjects, use AF-S (single-servo) with Single-point AF-area mode. For subjects that move in a predictable direction, use AF-C (continuous-servo) with Dynamic-area AF. And when photographing a subject that moves in an unpredictable manner, or when you need to recompose the picture rapidly while maintaining focus, use AF-C (continuous-servo) with 3D-tracking. Finally, for point-and-shoot style photography, especially with people in the scene, consider using AF-C (continuous-servo) with Auto-area AF. Remember, a D- or G-type Nikkor lens is necessary to make the most of the 3D-tracking and Auto-area options.

Focus Lock

It is possible to lock the autofocus system once the D90 has acquired focus, so the shot can be re-composed and the original focus distance will be retained, even if an AF point no longer covers the subject.

In single-servo AF autofocus, pressing the shutter-release button halfway will activate autofocus. As soon as focus is acquired, the in-focus indicator ● is displayed in the viewfinder and focus is locked and will remain locked while the shutter-release button is held halfway down. Alternatively, press and hold the AE-L/AF-L button to lock focus (and exposure at the default setting of CS-f4), or consider selecting the [AF lock only] option under CS-f4; once focus is locked using the AE-L/AF-L button, there is no necessity to use the shutter-release button to lock focus.

In continuous-servo AF autofocus, the autofocus system remains active while the shutter-release button is held halfway down, constantly adjusting focus as necessary. Therefore, if the picture is recomposed so that the selected

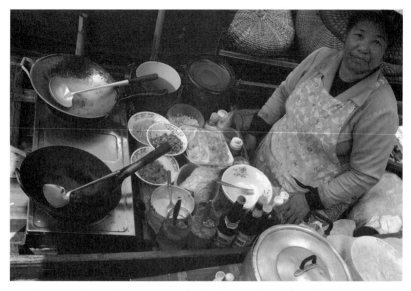

For a subject whose location in the image frame is not covered by one of the AF points, use the AF Lock feature to set the focus, and then recompose the image as desired.

AF point no longer covers the subject, the focus will shift to the point now covered by the selected AF point. To lock focus in this focus mode, press and hold the AE-L/AF-L button; consider the options available as CS-f4 [Assign AE-L/AF-L button], as described above. Alternatively, in AF-C mode, which is most useful for photographing a moving subject, it is possible to lock focus by assigning activation of the AF system to the AE-L/AF-L button, using the [AF-ON] option under CS-f4. Pressing the shutter-release button down halfway no longer activates Autofocus; the AE-L/AF-L button is used instead. Press and hold the button down until focus is achieved, and then release the button to lock the focus distance. Now the picture can be recomposed and the shutter-release button pressed to make the exposure without having any effect on the focus.

Note: If CS-f4 [Assign AE-L/AF-L button] is set to [AF-ON], the Vibration Reduction (VR) feature, available on some Nikkor lenses, will not operate when the AE-L/AF-L button is pressed; VR is only activated by pressing the shutter-release button. If you use the technique of locking focus by controlling autofocus operation via the AE-L/AF-L button, press the shutter-release button and pause briefly when it is depressed halfway—to allow the VR system to activate and settle—before pressing it all the way down to operate the shutter when taking a picture.

Once focus has been locked in either AF-S or AF-C focus mode, ensure the camera-to-subject distance does not change. If it does, re-activate autofocus and re-focus the lens at the new distance before using the autofocus lock options.

AF Assist Illuminator

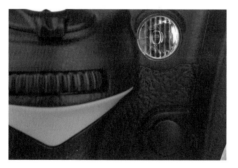

The AF-assist lamp of the D90 is useful for low-light conditions. However, there may be some situations in which you'll choose to disable it.

The D90 has a small, built-in AF-assist illuminator that is designed to facilitate autofocusing in low light conditions. It is located on the front of the camera between the finger grip and the viewfinder head. This feature can be useful in extremely low-light conditions, but you may not always want to have it activated. Here are a few reasons why I suggest using CS-a3 [Built-in AF-assist illuminator] to cancel its operation:

• The lamp only works if you have an autofocus lens attached to the camera, the focus area mode is set to either Single-point AF or Dynamic-area AF with the center focus point selected, or Auto-area AF is active.

- It is only usable with focal lengths of 24mm – 200mm.
- The operating range is restricted to 1'8" – 9'10" (0.5 – 3.0m).
- Due to its location, many lenses obstruct its output, particularly if they have a lens hood attached.
- The lamp overheats quite quickly (6 to 8 exposures in rapid succession is usually sufficient) and will automatically shut down to cool. Plus, at this level of use, it also drains battery power faster.

The D90 can also use the built-in AF-Assist Illuminator lamp of either the SB-900, SB-800, or SB-600 Speedlight, or SU-800 Speedlight commander unit (operation of the camera's lamp is disabled in these circumstances). The wider coverage provided by the AF-assist illuminators of the external units is particularly useful with cameras such as the D90, with its relatively wide array of 11 AF points that cover a large proportion of the frame area. In addition, these illuminators on the external flash units are located farther off the lens axis, reducing the risk that the lens will obstruct their light. The AF-assist function can be used in isolation on the SB-900 and SB-800 by canceling flash firing via the Custom Settings menu of the Speedlight.

When used with AF lenses with focal lengths of 17 – 135 mm, the SB-900 provides AF-assist for autofocus with the following AF points:

When used with AF lenses and focal lengths of 24 –105 mm, the SB-800, SB-600, and SU-800 provide AF-assist for autofocus with the following AF points:

24-34mm	
35-105mm	

If you want to use the SB-600, SB-800, or SB-900 off camera, the SC-29 TTL flash cord has a built-in AF-assist lamp that attaches to the camera's accessory shoe.

Limitations of the AF System

Although the autofocus system of the D90 is quite capable, there are some circumstances or conditions that can impair or limit its performance:

• Low light
• Low contrast
• Highly reflective surfaces
• Subject too small within the autofocus sensing area
• The AF point covers a subject comprising fine detail
• The AF point covers a regular geometric pattern
• The AF point covers a region of high contrast
• The AF point covers objects at different distances from the camera

If any of these conditions prevent the camera from acquiring focus, either switch to Manual focus mode or focus on another object at the same distance from the camera as the subject, then use the AF Lock feature to lock focus before recomposing the picture.

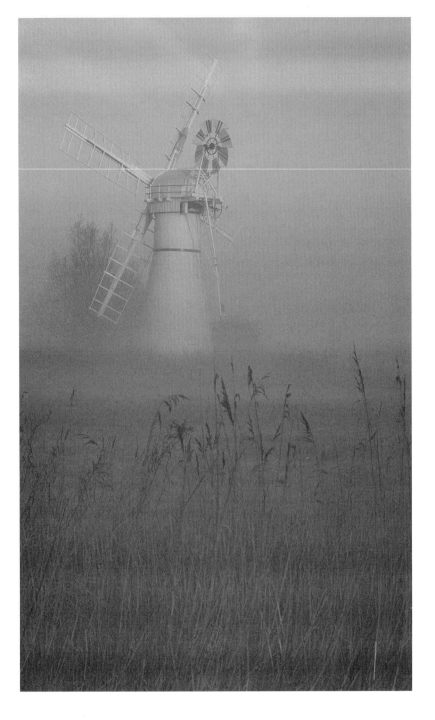

The Menu System

Control of many of the features and functions on the D90 relies on an extensive and comprehensive menu system that is displayed on the LCD monitor. It is divided into six main sections:

- **Playback menu:** This menu is used to review, edit, and manage the pictures stored on the inserted memory card.
- **Shooting menu:** Here, you can select more sophisticated camera controls that have a direct influence on the quality and appearance of your pictures. This menu also contains several special features such as the Picture Control settings, Active D-Lighting, and configuration of multiple exposures.
- **Custom Settings menu:** As the title of this menu suggests, the options available here allow you to select and set a wide range of controls to fine-tune camera operation to match your preferences. The menu is sub-divided into six setting groups that each deal with a specific area of camera operation: (a) Autofocus, (b) Metering/Exposure, (c) Timers/AE lock, (d) Shooting/Display, (e) Bracketing/ Flash, and (f) Controls.
- **Setup menu:** This menu is used to establish the basic configuration of the camera. Once the items in this menu are set, they generally are not changed very frequently.
- **Retouch menu:** This menu is only available when a memory card containing picture files is inserted in the camera. It offers a range of items that enable you to crop, enhance, and add effects to a picture and save it as a separate copy without affecting the integrity of the original picture file. With the D90, you can even process and convert NEF (RAW) files in-camera and save the new files as JPEGs.

The D90 offers seemingly endless options for capturing, viewing, and manipulating your photos. Learning to navigate the menu system will not only give you more control in those respects, but also in how the camera operates.

193

• **Recent Settings / My menu:** With [My menu], you can create your own fully customized menu from any variety of the items contained in the Setup, Shooting, Custom Settings, Playback, and Retouch menus. This improves the efficiency of camera operation because it saves you from having to navigate through the full menu system to access frequently used items. You can edit and reorder the menu items at any time. As an alternative to the [My menu] display, the [Recent settings] item can be selected to show up to twenty recently used menu settings; the most recently used item will be at the top of the list.

The menu system of the D90 is even more complex than that of previous Nikon D-SLR cameras due to the incorporation of more features and functions. For this reason, the [My menu] and [Recent settings] selections are especially helpful. There are a total of 95 main menu items, many of which have numerous sub-options. Since each page in the menu system can only display eight items, a lot of time can be spent scrolling through pages and options to reach a desired setting. Unfortunately, with the exception of [My menu], it is not possible to rearrange the order of the items in the menus. This compounds the amount of navigation required as, in many cases, the items you are most likely to want access are located beyond the first page of the menu displays. That said, it is only possible to add a maximum of four items to the display in [My menu] before it becomes necessary to start scrolling to a subsequent page. Finally, as far as navigating the menu system is concerned the Quick Settings Display, which is part of the Shooting Information Display, can be used to access a limited number of menu items directly (see pages 40-41 for more details).

In short, the menu system has become cumbersome and over-extended. Many of the options within the menu system can be set using buttons and dials located on the camera body. Where such an alternative route is available, I would recommend using it, as this will improve the efficiency of camera handling with the benefit of reduced battery power consumption by avoiding use of the LCD screen.

Accessing Menus

To access any of the menus, push the **MENU** button and press ◀ to highlight one of the six tabs used to identify each menu (top to bottom): ▶ Playback menu, 📷 Shooting menu, 🖉 Custom Settings menu, ⚑ Setup menu, ☑ Retouch menu, and either 📄 Recent Settings, or 🖾 My menu.

When you have highlighted the required menu tab using ⊕ , the chosen menu will be displayed to the right of the six tabs. Press ⊕ to enter the selected menu and highlight an option. To navigate to a specific menu item, press ⊕ on the multi selector. To display the sub-options available for a selected menu item, press ⊕ . Again, use ⊕ to highlighted the desired sub-option and press the ⊛ button to confirm the selection. To exit the menu system, press the shutter release button halfway or press the **MENU** button twice.

Note: Most menus have multiple pages. Scrolling up or down using ⊕ to view all the options.

Note: Pressing ⊕ generally has the same effect as pressing the ⊛ button. However, there are some menu options that can only be selected by pressing ⊛ .

Note: If a menu option is displayed in gray, it cannot be accessed. This can be for one of a number of reasons, including the current camera settings, state of the memory card, or condition of the battery.

In the following sections of this chapter, we will cover the features and functions controlled by the various menu options. Some of these will be outlined fully in this chapter, while others are discussed in full detail elsewhere in the book; please refer to the relevant pages as referenced.

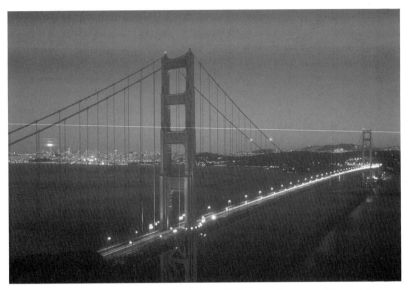

The D90's Playback menu includes all the functions you'll need to review your images, along with some controls that allow you to manage your photos while they're still in the camera.

▶ Playback Menu

The Playback Menu will only be displayed if a memory card is currently installed in the camera.

Delete Images

By using the [Delete] option in the Playback menu, you can choose to erase individual images, a group of images, or all of the images on the card. The D90 introduces a new option to select images and video files by the date they were recorded.

Note: Deleting all of the images on the card in this manner does not have the same effect as formatting the memory card, which should be done regularly to avoid card error. (See pages 277-278 for details.)

Hint: To delete images one by one, it is quicker and easier to use the 🗑 button on the back of the camera. However, to erase a group of images, using the Delete function in the Playback menu will probably save a lot of time. To delete a group of images:

1. Highlight the [Delete] option in the Playback menu and press ⊙ .
2. Highlight ▦ [Selected] and press ⊙ .
3. Thumbnails of all of the images on the inserted memory card will be displayed, regardless of whether they are stored in different folders. Scroll through the images using ⊕ ; a yellow frame will be displayed around the selected image. To see an enlarged view of the selected image, press and hold the ⊕ button.
4. To select the highlighted image for deletion, press the ⊕ button. A small icon of a trashcan will appear in the upper right corner of the thumbnail image.
5. Once all the files to be deleted have been selected, press the ⊛ button.
6. The total number of images to be deleted will be displayed, along with two options: [No] or [Yes]. Highlight the required option and press the ⊛ button to complete the process.

To delete a group of images taken on a selected date:

1. Highlight the [Delete] option in the Playback menu and press ⊙ .
2. Highlight DATE [Select date] and press ⊙ .
3. A list of all the dates on which images and video files have been recorded will be displayed. Highlight the required date, and then press ⊙ to place a checkmark against the date. Repeat this process for each date where images are to be deleted.
4. Once the date(s) have been selected, press the ⊛ button.
5. A warning message will be displayed, "Delete all images taken on selected date?" along with two options: [No] or [Yes]. Highlight the required option and press the ⊛ button to complete the process.

To delete all images:

1. Highlight the [Delete] option in the Playback menu and press ⊙ .
2. Highlight **ALL** [All] and press ⊙ .
3. Highlight either [No] or [Yes] as required.
4. Press the ⊛ button to complete the process.

Note: It is not possible to delete pictures that have been protected.

Note: Images that have been hidden will not be displayed and, therefore, cannot be selected for deletion.

Playback Folder

The [Playback folder] item in the Playback menu allows you to determine which images will be displayed during playback. There are two options available:

• **[Current] (default):** Only the images in the folder currently selected for [Active Folder] in the Shooting menu will be displayed during playback.
• **[All]:** All of the images on the memory card can be displayed, regardless of the camera used to record them (provided it conforms to the Design rule for Camera File system, or DCF). All Nikon digital cameras and most other current digital cameras are DCF compatible.

To select the [Playback folder] option:

1. Highlight the [Playback folder] item in the Playback menu and press ⊙ .
2. Highlight the desired option using ⊙ .
3. Press ⊛ to confirm the selection.

Hide Image

The [Hide image] option of the Playback menu enables the user to hide or reveal selected images. Images that are hidden cannot be viewed during normal image playback. Hidden images can only be viewed using the [Hide image] item in the menu. They are also protected against deletion; they will only be "deleted" from the memory card if it is formatted. To use [Hide image]:

1. Highlight the [Hide image] option in the Playback menu and press ⊕ .
2. Highlight ⊞ [Select/set] and press ⊕ .
3. Thumbnails of all of the images on the memory card will be displayed, regardless of whether they are stored in different folders. Scroll through the images using ⊕ ; a yellow frame will be displayed around the selected image. To see an enlarged view of the selected image, press and hold the ⊕ button.
4. To select the highlighted image to be hidden, press the ⊟ button. A small icon of a frame with a diagonal line through it will appear in the upper right corner of the thumbnail image.
5. Once you have selected all images to be hidden, press the ⊗ button to finalize your selection and hide all selected images.

To reveal selected hidden images:

1. Highlight the [Hide image] option in the Playback menu and press ⊕ .
2. Highlight [Select/set] and press ⊕ .
3. Thumbnails of all of the images will be displayed, whether or not they are hidden and regardless of whether they are stored in different folders. Scroll through the images using ⊕ ; a yellow frame will be displayed around the selected image. To see an enlarged view of the selected image, press and hold the ⊕ button.
4. To select a highlighted hidden image and allow it to be seen during playback, press the ⊟ button. The small icon of a frame with a diagonal line through it that denotes a hidden image will disappear.
5. Once you have selected all hidden images that are to be revealed, press the ⊗ button.

To hide all images taken on a specific date:

1. Highlight the [Hide image] option in the Playback menu and press ⊙ .
2. Highlight ⟨DATE⟩ [Select date] and press ⊙ .
3. A list of all the dates on which images and video files have been recorded will be displayed. Highlight the required date, and then press ⊙ to place a check-mark against the date. Repeat this process for each date where images are to be hidden.
4. To confirm the selection, press the ⊕ button and the selected images will be displayed; to resume the process, press the ⊕ button again.
5. Once the date(s) have been selected, press the ⟨OK⟩ button.

To reveal all hidden images:

1. Highlight the [Hide image] option in the Playback menu and press ⊙ .
2. Highlight **ALL** [Deselect All?] and press ⊙ .
3. "Reveal all hidden images?" is displayed on the screen. Highlight [Yes] or [No] as required.
4. Press the ⟨OK⟩ button to confirm the action.

Display Mode
The [Display mode] option determines which pages of image information in addition to the File Information and Overview Data pages are available during single-image playback. This option allows you to choose whether or not to display [Highlights], [RGB Histogram], and [Data] (a range of pages, depending on camera settings and use of a GPS device, which show information about the image). To select options for [Display mode]:

1. Highlight the [Display mode] option in the Playback menu and press ⊙ .
2. Highlight the desired option using ⟨⊕⟩ , and then press ⊙ ; a checkmark will appear in the box to the left of the option title.
3. Repeat step 2 for any other desired options.

4. Finally, highlight [Done] and press ⊛ to confirm the selection and return to the Playback menu.

Image Review

The [Image review] option in the Playback menu determines if an image will be displayed on the monitor immediately after it is recorded. There are situations when reviewing every image recorded by the camera immediately is undesirable, such as when shooting in low-light conditions where the light from the screen is a distraction. When weighing the necessity of immediate image review, you should consider that the LCD monitor consumes a relatively large amount of power, increasing the drain on the battery. I recommend switching this option off and using the ▶ button whenever you wish to review an image. To set your [Image review] preference:

1. Highlight the [Image review] option in the Playback menu and press ⊛ .
2. Highlight [On], or [Off] (default).
3. Press ⊛ to confirm the selection.

Rotate Tall

The [Rotate tall] option determines whether pictures shot in the vertical (portrait) format are displayed automatically in that orientation, or displayed in the horizontal (landscape) format in image playback. Displaying an image in the vertical orientation on the screen will decrease the overall size of the image to about two-thirds the size of an image displayed horizontally; a horizontally displayed image uses the full viewing area of the screen.

Note: The [Auto Image Rotation] option in the Setup menu must be set to [On] for the [Rotate tall] function to operate.

To select [Rotate tall]:

1. Highlight the [Rotate tall] option in the Playback menu and press ⊛ .
2. Highlight [On] or [Off].
3. Press ⊛ to confirm the selection.

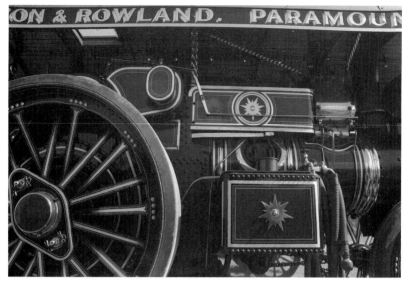

To create slideshows of your pictures in-camera, use the Pictmotion function. You can even add sound!

Note: Images will not be rotated automatically during the automated image review directly after shooting even when [On] is selected for [Rotate tall]; images will be rotated automatically during image playback.

Pictmotion

The [Pictmotion] item in the Playback menu is used to create and view slideshows. Only images and video files stored in the folder currently selected under the [Active folder] in the Shooting menu can be selected. The transition between individual images can be selected from a range of effects, and the D90 can be set to play pre-recorded music stored on the camera to accompany the slideshow. To set [Pictmotion]:

202

1. Highlight the [Pictmotion] option in the Playback menu and press ⊚ .
2. The four options displayed on the next page are used to create and play the Pictmotion slideshow. Highlight [Select pictures] and press ⊚ to reveal three further options.
3. Highlight ▣▣▣ [Selected] to select individual images and press ⊚ .
4. Thumbnails of all of the images stored on the inserted memory card will be displayed, regardless of whether they are stored in different folders. Scroll through the images using ⊚ ; a yellow frame will be displayed around the selected image. To see an enlarged view of the selected image, press and hold the ⊕ button.
5. To select the highlighted image press the ⊞ button. A small checkmark will appear in the upper right corner of the thumbnail image.
6. Once you have chosen all the images for the slideshow, press the ⊛ button to finalize your selection.

To select images by date, repeat steps 1 and 2 above then:

3. Highlight DATE [Select date] and press ⊚ .
4. A list of all the dates on which images and video files have been recorded will be displayed. Highlight the required date, and then press ⊚ to place a checkmark on the date. Repeat this process for each date with images you would like to include in the slideshow.
5. To confirm the selection press the ⊞ button and the selected images will be displayed; to resume the process, press the ⊞ button again.
6. Once the date(s) have been selected, press the ⊛ button.

To select all images, repeat steps 1 and 2 above then:

3. Highlight ALL [All] and press ⊚ .

To select background music:

1. Highlight the [Pictmotion] option in the Playback menu and press ⊚⏵ .
2. Highlight [Background music] and press ⊚⏵ to reveal five further options.
3. Highlight the required option and press ⊚⏵ .

To select the transition effect between images in the slideshow:

1. Highlight the [Pictmotion] option in the Playback menu and press ⊚⏵ .
2. Highlight [Effects] and press ⊚⏵ to reveal five further options.
3. Highlight the required option and press ⊚⏵ .

   To play the slideshow, highlight [Start] in the [Pictmotion] menu and press ⊛ . To pause the slideshow press the ⊛ button; to raise the volume press ⊕ ; to lower the volume press ⊜ . To return to the Playback menu, press **MENU**; to return to basic playback mode, press ▶ ; to resume shooting, press the shutter release button halfway. Once the Pictmotion slideshow has finished, or the ⊛ button is pressed to pause the show, select either [Restart] to restart the show, or [Exit] to return to the Playback menu.

Slideshow

Different than the [Pictmotion] selection, which allows you to select specific images to be displayed in a slideshow for-mat, the [Slideshow] option allows you to view all of the images stored on the current memory card in sequential order. This can be a useful and enjoyable feature, especially if the camera is connected to view the images on a televi-sion. To use [Slideshow]:

1. Highlight the [Slideshow] option in the Playback menu and press ⊚⏵ .
2. [Start] will be highlighted. To commence the slideshow immediately, press the ⊛ button.

204

3. To select the display duration for each image, highlight [Frame interval] and press ⊚ to display four options: 2, 3, 5, or 10 seconds. Highlight the desired interval, and press ⊛ to confirm the selection and return to the main Slideshow page. Repeat step 2 to start the slideshow.

There are a variety of controls available when the Slideshow function is active:

• To return to previous image, press ◄ .
• To skip to next image, press ► .
• To display and scroll the photo information pages, press ⊚ .
• To pause the display, press the ⊛ button. A submenu with three options will be displayed: [Restart], [Frame Interval], and [Exit]. Highlight the desired option and press ⊛ .
• To stop the display and return to the Playback menu, press the **MENU** button.
• To stop the display and return to regular image playback (full frame or thumbnail view), press ▶ .
• To stop the display and return to shooting; press the shutter release button halfway.

At the end of the slideshow, a menu will be displayed with the following options: [Restart], [Frame Interval], and [Exit]. This is the same menu that is displayed when the slideshow is paused by pressing the ⊛ button. Highlight the required option and press ⊛ .

Note: Images that have been hidden will not appear during the slideshow display.

Hint: Due to the protracted use of the LCD screen, the slideshow function can consume a significant amount of battery power, especially if a large number of images are stored on the memory card. Either use a fully charged battery or, preferably, plug the camera into AC power using the EH-5 / EH-5a AC adapter.

Print Set (DPOF)

The [Print Set (DPOF)] item in the Playback menu enables you to create and save instructions that allow a set of images to be automatically printed by a DPOF compatible printing device. (See pages 355-358 for more details.)

◙ Shooting Menu

The following are the various options available in the Shooting menu of the D90.

Set Picture Control

The new Picture Control System in the D90 replaces the Optimize Image system used in previous Nikon D-SLR cameras. It allows you to set specific controls that determine how the camera performs image processing. The D90 has six basic Nikon Picture Controls: Standard, Neutral, Vivid, Monochrome, Portrait, and Landscape. (See page 80 for more details.)

Manage Picture Control

This setting allows you to create and save custom Picture Controls. These custom Picture Controls can be copied to a memory card and applied in another D90 camera or used in compatible Nikon software. Picture Controls created in compatible Nikon software using the Picture Control utility can also be uploaded to a D90. (See page 90 for more details.)

Image Quality

The [Image Quality] option allows you to select the file format for images recorded by the camera. The D90 can record images in JPEG or NEF (RAW). (See pages 279-289 for more details.)

Image Size

The [Image Size] selection determines the file size, or resolution, of an image. Image size is expressed as the number of pixels per inch in the image file. Image size adjustments will only apply to images saved using the JPEG format. NEF (RAW) files are always saved at the camera's highest resolution. (See pages 279-289 for more details.)

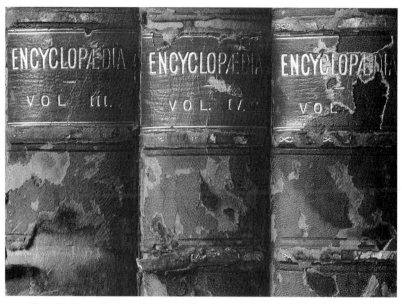

The Picture Control System offers several options for how your images will be rendered including Neutral, Vivid, and Monochrome. Try the sepia tone in the Monochrome Picture control to give an antique look to a black-and-white photo.

White Balance

The [White Balance] option allows you to select the color temperature to which the images you are shooting will be balanced and processed. (See pages 59-75 for more details.)

ISO Sensitivity

ISO sensitivity in the D90 emulates the sensitivity to light of film bearing the same ISO number. The higher the ISO number, the greater the camera's light-sensitive response. (See pages 145-146 for more details.)

Active D-Lighting

The [Active D-Lighting] feature (not to be confused with the [D-Lighting] item in the Retouch menu) can be used to optimize exposure settings when using Matrix metering. Since the effects of Active D-Lighting are applied during the processing of an image file, it is not possible to reverse them when recording JPEG files. The effects of Active D-Lighting on an image recorded in the NEF (RAW) format can be altered in post-processing using appropriate Nikon software. (See pages 92-93 for more details.)

Color Space
The range of colors capable of being displayed in an image recorded by the D90 is determined by the [Color Space] setting. The D90 provides two options for color space: [Adobe RGB] and [sRGB]. The color space determines the range (gamut) of colors that will be available in an image file for color reproduction and should be chosen according to how the image will be processed after it has been exported from the camera. (See pages 91-92 for more details.)

Long Exposure Noise Reduction
Images taken at shutter speeds of eight seconds or longer with the D90 will often exhibit a high level of electronic noise. Noise is the result of amplification processes that are applied to the data captured by the sensor, which is then compounded by the higher internal temperature of the camera due to the extended shutter speed. Noise manifests as irregularly placed, bright, colored pixels that disrupt the appearance of an image, particularly in areas of even tonality. The [Long Exp. NR] feature helps to reduce the appearance of noise when using long exposures. To set [Long Exp NR]:

1. Highlight the [Long Exp. NR] option in the Shooting menu and press ⊚ .
2. Highlight [On] or [Off] (default) as required.
3. Press the ⊛ button, to confirm the selection and return to the Shooting menu.

If [On] is selected, the processing time for each recorded image will equal the duration of the shutter speed used for the exposure. While the image data is being processed "Job nr" will appear, blinking in place of the shutter speed and aperture value displays in the control panel. No other pic-

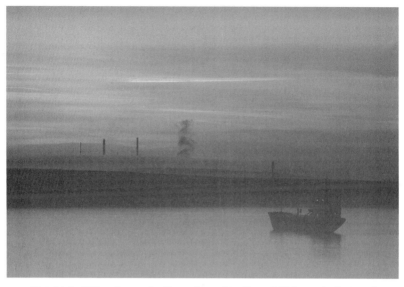

Use high ISO noise reduction when shooting at ISO equivalents of 800 and higher. This will help to reduce the "grainy" effect caused by the amplified electronic signal that accompanies the use of those higher sensitivity levels.

ture can be recorded while "Job nr" is displayed and image processing is in progress.

The process used by the D90 to perform long exposure noise reduction involves the camera making a second exposure, known as a "dark frame exposure," during which the shutter remains closed but the camera maps the sensor and records the values of each photodiode (pixel). Sometimes, a photodiode can "lock-up" and retain a value that is erroneous; this often occurs if the sensor gets hot due to prolonged usage (such as during a long exposure) or high ambient temperature. After mapping the sensor for "hot" (overly bright) photodiodes, the camera subtracts the dark frame photodiode values from the values of the main exposure in an effort to reduce the effect of noise in the final image.

Hint: Nikon states that when the long exposure noise reduction feature of the D90 is on, it will operate whenever the shutter speed exceeds eight seconds. In testing, I have found the D90 to be remarkably noise free, even at exposure durations of several minutes, which is something that the D80 did not achieve. Even so, however, I recommend very strongly that the long exposure noise reduction feature be used whenever shutter speed duration becomes protracted.

High ISO Noise Reduction

At high ISO sensitivity settings, the presence of electronic noise in an image increases due to the greater degree of signal amplification that takes place during in-camera processing (analogous to the more visible grain structure of higher ISO film). The [High ISO NR] feature helps reduce the amount of noise in images taken at ISO sensitivities of 800 and higher. To set [High ISO NR]:

1. Highlight [High ISO NR] option in the Shooting menu and press ⊕ .
2. Highlight the required option: [High], [Normal], [Low], or [Off]. (See the table below for details).
3. Press the ⊛ button to confirm the selection and return to the Shooting menu.

Option	Effect
High	Noise reduction is applied at ISO sensitivities
Normal (default)	of ISO 800 or higher. Select the level of noise
Low	reduction from one of the three options.
Off	Noise reduction is only applied at ISO sensitivities of HI 0.3 (ISO 4000) and higher. The level applied is lower than the amount applied when [Low] is selected for [High ISO NR].

Noise reduction will affect the resolution of fine detail and, at high levels, the brightness of colors. The ISO noise performance of the D90 is extremely good, with very clean images being produced at ISO settings up to and including ISO 800. The random, almost film-like grain quality caused by noise in D90 images from around ISO 1000 on up is not, for the most part, troublesome until the sensitivity is pushed beyond ISO 3200.

Note: The in-camera noise reduction for higher ISO sensitivities does not offer the same level of control as found in dedicated noise reduction software. Unless you must use the in-camera options, I recommend applying noise reduction during post-processing.

Active Folder

The D90 uses a folder system to organize images on the installed memory card. The [Active folder] option in the Shooting menu allows you to select which folder the images you are currently recording will be saved in and enables you to create new folders. If you do not use any of the folder options, the camera will automatically create a folder named 100NCD90 in which the first 999 pictures recorded by the camera will be stored. If you exceed 999 pictures, the camera will create a second new folder, named 101NCD90. A new folder will be created for each set of 999 pictures. The three-digit prefix is only displayed when the memory card is connected to a computer, either directly from the camera, or via a card reader.

You can also create your own folders and name them for easy reference. A three digit number between 100 and 999 always prefixes the folder title, but you can then assign a five-character folder name. If you use multiple folders on a single memory card, you must select one "active" folder to which all images will be stored until an alternative folder is chosen. If the maximum capacity of 999 pictures is exceeded in the active folder, the D90 will create a new folder using the same five-character suffix you have selected, but assigning a new three-digit prefix with an incremental increase of one (i.e., folder 100NCD90 becomes 101NCD90).

Note: If the folder that has reached full capacity (999 images) is folder number 999NCD90, the camera will disable the shutter release button and prevent you from making an exposure. You will have to create a new folder with a lower number or choose another folder on the memory card that still has space for new images. Likewise, the shutter release button will be disabled if the active folder contains a picture numbered 999.

To create a new folder:

1. Highlight the [Active folder] option in the Shooting menu and press ⊕ .
2. Highlight the [New] option from the [Active folder] options list and press ⊕ .
3. Designate the name/number of the new folder by using the keypad of letters and numbers that are displayed on the monitor. Use ⊕ to select the required character and press ℚ to input it. To move the cursor press and hold ⊜ , and then press ⊕ .
4. To delete a character at the current cursor position press the 🗑 button.
5. Press ⊛ to confirm the action and return to the Shooting menu, or press **MENU** to exit without creating a new folder.

To select an existing folder:

1. Highlight the [Active folder] option in the Shooting menu and press ⊕ .
2. Highlight the [Select folder] option from the [Active folder] options list and press ⊕ .
3. A list of the folders currently stored on the memory card is displayed; highlight the folder you wish to use by pressing ⊕ .
4. Press ⊛ to confirm the selection and return to the Shooting menu.

Creating folders may be useful if you expect to take pictures of a variety of subjects (i.e., various different locations on a vacation), but with the relatively low cost of memory cards, it is probably easier and more efficient to simply use multiple cards. Personally, I believe using multiple folders to be time consuming and potentially confusing. Plus, if you have more than one Nikon digital camera and move cards between them, the different cameras will not be able to display images stored in folders created by another camera. If the second camera then creates a new folder, it will have a higher prefix number than the folder created by the first camera. Even multiple folders created by the D90 can present problems in other cameras, as new images will be saved to the currently selected folder with the highest prefix number. I would rather use a browser application, such as Nikon View NX, to organize my image files.

Multiple Exposure

The [Multiple Exposure] feature enables the camera to take up to three different exposures to be combined into a single image. The individual files must be shot in consecutive order and are not saved as separate files. (See pages 104-105 for more details.)

Movie Settings

This item is used to select and set the frame size and sound options for the D90's movie mode (video recording). There are three options for the frame size:

The D90 records at the rate of 24 frames per second regardless of frame size. To achieve the highest quality, select the ⊞¹²⁸⁰₇₂₀ 1280 x 720 option. Sound recording is either switched [On] or [Off].

Frame Size	Description
⊞¹²⁸⁰₇₂₀ 1280 x 720 (16:9)	Each frame is 1280 x 720 pixels
⊞⁶⁴⁰₄₂₄ 640 x 424 (3:2) (default)	Each frame is 640 x 424 pixels
⊞³²⁰₂₁₆ 320 x 216 (3:2)	Each frame is 320 x 216 pixels

1. Highlight the [Movie setting] item in the Shooting menu and press ⊕ to display the two sub-options: [Quality] and [Sound].
2. Highlight [Quality] and press ⊕ . Select the required option (see the chart on page 213) and press ⊛ .
3. Next, highlight [Sound] and press ⊕ .
4. Select [On] or [Off] and press ⊛ .

✐ Custom Settings Menu

The Custom Settings menu allows you to fine-tune the performance of the D90 to suit your preferences and adapt the camera to meet the demands of specific shooting situations. It contains a comprehensive set of items, each with a range of options that covers virtually every aspect of camera operation. The items are grouped logically by the nature of their function, as set out in the table below:

Group		Custom Settings
a	Auto focus	a1 – a7
b	Metering / Exposure	b1 – b4
c	Timers / AE&AF Lock	c1 – c5
d	Shooting / Display	d1 – d12
e	Bracketing / Flash	e1 – e6
f	Controls	f1 – f7

Selecting Custom Settings Options

Highlight the Custom Settings menu tab ✐ to display the list of the six Custom Settings groups, plus [R: Reset Custom Settings]. Press ⊕ and highlight the required group, then press ⊕ again to display a full list of the items in that group. Use ⊕ to highlight the desired item, and press ⊕ to display the options available for that item. Use ⊕ to select the desired option and use ⊛ to confirm the selection and return to the main list of items in the group.

R: Menu Reset

To reset to the defaults used in the Custom Settings menu, use the [R: Menu Reset] option.

1. Highlight [R: Menu Reset] and press ⊕ to display the options.
2. Select [No] or [Yes] and press ⊗ .

The default custom settings are outlined in the table below:

Option	Default
a1: AF area mode	Auto area
a2: Center focus point	Normal zone
a3: Built in AF assist illuminator	On
a4: AF point illumination	Auto
a5: Focus point wrap around	No wrap
a6: AE LIAF LforMB D80	AE/AF lock
a7: Live view autofocus	Wide area
b1: EV steps for exposure cntrl.	1/3 step
b2: Easy exposure compensation	Off
b3: Center weighted area	8 mm
b4: Fine tune optimal exposure	No
c1: Shutter release button AE L	Off
c2: Auto _meter off delay	6s
c3: Self timer	
Self timer delay	10s
Number of shots	1
c4: Monitor off delay	
Playback	10s
Menus	20s
Shooting info display	10s
Image review	4s
c5: Remote on duration	1 min

Option		Default
d1:	Beep	On
d2:	Viewfinder grid display	Off
d3:	ISO display and adjustment	Show frame count
d4:	Viewfinder warning display	On
d5:	Screen tips	On
d6:	CL mode shooting speed	3 fps
d7:	File number sequence	Off
d8:	Shooting info display	Auto
d9:	LCD illumination	Off
d10:	Exposure delay mode	Off
d11:	Flash warning	On
d12:	MB D80 battery type	LR6 (AA alkaline)
e1:	Flash shutter speed	1/60s
e2:	Flash cntrl for built in flash	TTL
e3:	Modeling flash	Off
e4:	Auto bracketing set	AE & flash
e5:	Auto FP	Off
e6:	Bracketing order	MTR> under > over
f1:	D switch	LCD backlight
f2:	OK button (shooting mode)	Select center focus point
f3:	Assign FUNC. button	FV lock
f4:	Assign AE L/AF L button	AE/AF lock
f5:	Customize command dials	
	Reverse rotation	No
	Change main/sub	Off
	Menus and playback	On
f6:	No memory card?	Release locked
f7:	Reverse indicators	

Autofocus

a1: AF-Area Mode: This item determines how the autofocus point is selected. The options are:

- **[⟨⟩]** **[Single point]:** You select the AF point manually using the multi selector. The D90 will only use the selected AF point, so this option is most applicable with subjects that are stationary. Single point AF is the default AF-area mode for the 🌷 scene mode.

- **[⟨⟩]** **[Dynamic area]:** In AF-A and AF-C autofocus modes, you select the AF point manually using the multi selector. The D90 will use the selected AF point unless the subject leaves its coverage area; then, the camera will use surrounding AF points to try and maintain focus. This option is most applicable with subjects that move errati-cally. In AF-S autofocus mode, the camera will only use the selected AF point. Dynamic area AF is the default mode for the 🏃 scene mode.

- **[■]** **[Auto area]:** The D90 selects the focus point(s) automatically based on information processed by the Scene Recognition System and the integrated Face Recog-nition System. (See pages 175-177.) Auto area AF is the default mode for all exposure modes and scene modes except 🏃 and 🌷 .

- **[3D]** **[3D tracking (11 points)]:** Using Nikon's innova-tive Scene Recognition System (SRS), the D90 is able to identify a subject by its distribution of color/contrast. In AF-A and AF-C autofocus modes, you select the AF point using the multi selector. Once focus has been acquired, you can make significant changes to the composition provided you keep the shutter release pressed down halfway; the camera will use 3D tracking to select a new AF point to try and ensure that the subject remains in focus. This AF area mode is intended for changing the composition with a relatively static subject. If the subject leaves viewfinder coverage, it will be necessary to reac-quire focus by selecting a new AF point. In AF-S autofo-cus mode, the camera will only focus using the selected AF point.

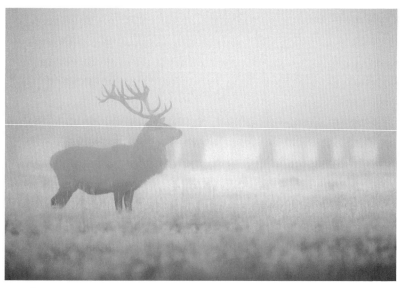

For a moving subject, or one that may potentially move while you are composing the picture, set the AF-area mode to 3D tracking.

a2: Center Focus Point: This item is used to determine the size of the central AF point. Options are:

- **[ꞏꞏ]** **[Normal zone] (default):** This option is best for focusing on stationary subjects that can be framed easily under the center AF point.
- **[ꞏ ꞏ]** **[Wide zone]:** This option is best for moving subjects, but is not available when [Auto-area] **[■]** is selected at CS-1a (AF-area mode).

a3: Built-In AF-Assist Illuminator: The D90 has a built-in lamp that activates to assist autofocus operation in low-light shooting situations. This menu item determines whether that lamp operates or not. It requires the following conditions: single-servo AF must be selected for the focus mode, and either [Single point], [Auto-area], or [3D-tracking (11 points)] must be selected for CS-a1 [AF-area mode], or

[Dynamic-area] is selected and the center AF point is used. The options are for this menu selection are:

- **[ON] (default):** The built-in lamp activates to assist auto-focus operation in low-light shooting situations.
- **[Off]:** The lamp does not light, regardless of the level of ambient illumination.

a4: AF Point Illumination: To facilitate the identification of the active AF point, particularly in low-light situations, this menu selection can be set to highlight the AF point in red. The options are:

- **[Auto] (default):** The selected AF point is highlighted in red if required, depending on the level of ambient illumination.
- **[On]:** The selected AF point is always highlighted in red, regardless of the level of ambient illumination.
- **[Off]:** The selected AF point is not highlighted.

Hint: The default option of Auto is probably the best for most shooting situations. However, you may wish to consider setting the [Off] option for this item if you expect to shoot rapid sequences of frames, as displaying the active AF point does introduce a very slight delay in shutter operation.

a5: Focus Point Wrap-Around: This menu item controls how the selection of an autofocus sensing area is performed. The options are:

- **[Wrap]:** This allows the selection of AF points to "wrap around" the autofocus area from top to bottom, bottom to top, left to right, and right to left.
- **[No Wrap] (default):** If the selected AF point is at the edge of the autofocus area, pressing the multi selector in the direction of the edge has no effect.

Hint: I recommend setting the [Wrap] option for this item; it helps to speed up selection of an AF point.

a6: AE-L/AF-L for MB-D80: This item determines the function assigned to the AE-L/AF-L button on the MB-D80 battery pack when fitted to the D90. The options are:

- 🔒 **[AE/AF lock] (default):** While pressed and held, the button locks focus and exposure.
- 🔒 **[AE lock only]:** While pressed and held, the button locks exposure only.
- 🔒 **[AF lock only]:** While pressed and held, the button locks focus only.
- 🔒 **[AE lock (Hold)]:** Pressing the button locks the exposure, which remains locked until the button is pressed a second time or the exposure meter is turned off.
- **AF-ON** **[AF-ON] (default):** Pressing the button activates the autofocus system.
- **FL** **[FV lock]:** The flash output value for the built-in Speedlight and external SB-900, SB-800, SB-600, SB-400, and SB-R200 Speedlights is locked when the button is pressed. It remains locked until the button is pressed again, or the meters turn off.
- **[⊡]** **[Focus point selection]:** The focus point can be selected by pressing the button and rotating the sub-command dial.

Note: Pressing ▶ when [AE/AF lock], [AE lock only], or [AF lock only] is selected displays the [Focus point selection] submenu. If [On] is selected the focus point can be selected by pressing the AE-L/AF-L button and rotating the sub-command dial

a7: Live View Autofocus: This item determines how the focus point for autofocus in Live View is selected. Options are:

- 😊 **[Face priority]:** The camera uses its Scene Recognition and integrated Face Recognition system to identify up to five people's faces. The camera will focus automatically on the detected face(s). This is the default setting for the 🖼 and 👤 scene modes.

- ⬚ **[Wide area] (default):** The focus point is selected manually. This setting is best for handheld pictures of landscapes or other scenes that do not included a person's face. This is the default setting for all exposure modes except the 🏔 , 🏃 , and 🌷 scene modes.

- ⬚ **[Normal area]:** Use this selection for precision focus on a defined point in the frame. It is best if the camera is supported on a stable platform such as a tripod. This is the default setting for the 🌷 scene mode.

Metering / Exposure

b1: EV Steps for Exposure Control: Use this item to select the size of the step when adjusting shutter speed, lens aperture, exposure/flash compensation, and bracketing. The options are:

- **[1/3 Step] (default):** Shutter speed and aperture change in steps of 0.3EV. Bracketing steps can be selected from 0.3, 0.7, and 1.0EV.

- **[1/2 Step]:** Shutter speed and aperture change in steps of 0.5EV. Bracketing steps can be selected from 0.5 and 1.0EV

Hint: I recommend using the [1/3 Step] option to provide the finest degree of exposure control.

b2: Easy Exposure Compensation: This item controls whether the exposure compensation button is required to set an exposure compensation value in P, S, A, or M exposure modes. The options are:

- **[On]:** Exposure compensation is set by rotating one of the command dials without pressing the exposure compensation button. Compensation selected using this method is not reset when the camera or exposure meter is turned off, or [Off] is selected for CS-b2.

- **[Off] (default):** Exposure compensation is set by pressing the 🔲 exposure compensation button, and rotating the main command dial. Compensation is reset when the camera or exposure meter is turned off.

221

The choice of which command dial will control exposure compensation when [On] selected for CS-b2 depends on the exposure mode and the option selected at CS-f5: [Customize command dials]. Options do not apply to manual exposure mode.

Exposure mode	CS-f5	Command dial
P	Off	Sub-command dial
A	Off	Main command dial
S	Off	Sub-command dial
A	On	Sub-command dial
P	On	Sub-command dial
S	On	Main command dial

Hint: This menu item introduces additional complexity to the D90, especially if you have other Nikon cameras that do not offer this level of control. Most modern Nikon cameras use a combination of pressing a button and turning a command dial to set exposure compensation. I suggest leaving this item set to the default option of [Off], especially if you are used to working with other Nikon camera models.

b3: Center-Weighted Area: In center-weighted exposure metering, the D90 assigns approximately 75% of the metering influence to a circular area in the center of the frame. This menu option allows you to change the diameter of the circular metering area used in P, S, A, and M exposure modes. Options are:

- **[6 mm]**
- **[8 mm]**
- **[10 mm]**

Hint: This is definitively a personal preference item. I use center-weighted metering very rarely, so I leave it set to the default 8-mm circle. Using a smaller circle will enable you to meter from a more precise area of the frame.

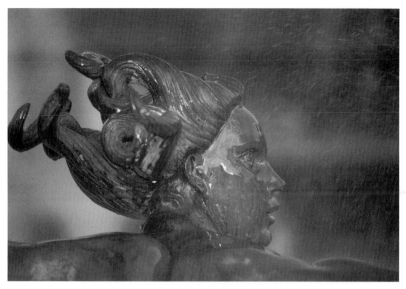

You can use CS-b3 to change the size of the center of the frame, where the metering system assigns 75% of the priority when determining how to expose a given scene when it is in the center-weighted metering mode. The center circle's size can be made smaller or larger than the default diameter of 8 mm.

b4: Fine Tune Optimal Exposure: This option enables you to fine-tune exposure measurement. It can be set independently for each metering method over a range of +/- 1 Ev in steps of 1/6 Ev. Highlight CS-b4 and press ⊚ to display the options [No] and [Yes].

- **[No]:** Use this option to exit the item without adjusting exposure.
- **[Yes]:** Highlight [Yes] and press ⊚ to open a submenu that displays the three metering modes. Highlight the required metering mode and press ⊚ to open the next menu page that displays the exposure adjustment value. Use ⊚ to selected an adjustment level and press ⊛ to save the setting.

Hint: I recommend you avoid using this item if you use Matrix metering, as it will adjust exposure by unknown amounts based on each individual subject or scene. However, if you use the spot meter to take a meter reading from a known test target, this item is useful to ensure that the meter reading suggested by the camera actually matches the reflectivity of the test target. For example, if you use an 18% gray card as a test target, you will probably want to set a fine-tune value of +2/6EV or +3/6EV due to the way the camera meter is calibrated. The key to using this menu option successfully is to test your equipment with care and precision and only make an adjustment when you are positive it is necessary.

Timers / AE Lock

c-1: Shutter-Release Button AE-L: This menu selection determines how exposure value can be locked. This is a matter of personal preference, but if you wish to recompose the picture after taking a meter reading, having the exposure locked by simply pressing the shutter release button can be convenient. The options are:

- **[Off] (default):** The exposure is only locked by pressing the AE-L/AF-L button.
- [**On**]: The exposure can be locked by either pressing the AE-L/AF-L button or by pressing the shutter release button down half way.

c2: Auto Meter-Off Delay: This item determines how long the camera's exposure meter will remain active when no camera operation is performed. Options are:

- **[4 s]**
- **[6 s]** (default)
- **[8 s]**
- **[16]**
- **[30]**
- **[1 min]**
- **[5 min]**
- **[10 min]**
- **[30 min]**

Hint: To prevent undue drain on the battery, I recommend using either the default setting or the [8 s] option. These provide a good compromise between having sufficient time to read and assess the meter reading and conserving battery power.

Note: If the camera is powered by the EH-5 / EH-5a AC adapter, the exposure meter will not turn off automatically.

c3: Self-Timer: This item controls the duration of the shutter release delay in the self-timer mode, as well as the number of exposures that will be made when the shutter release button is pressed in self-timer mode. (When more than one exposure is made, they will be made at the rate selected for 🖳L continuous-low at CS-d6 [CL mode shooting speed].) Selecting the [Number of shots] item will bring up a list from which you can select a number from one to nine. The options for duration are:

- **[2 s]**
- **[5 s]**
- **[10 s]** (default)
- **[20 s]**

Hint: Set the duration of the delay to match the shooting situation; using a duration that is unnecessarily long will just increase the drain on battery power.

Note: Unfortunately, it is not possible to apply any exposure bracketing to the sequence of pictures taken with this option, which would have made it a more practical choice.

c4: Monitor-Off Delay: This option determines how long the LCD screen on the back of the camera will remain on, if no other camera operation is performed. Use the shortest possible duration to prevent undue drain on the battery power. Options are:

- **[4 s]** (default for image review)
- **[10 s]** (default for playback and shooting information)
- **[20 s]** (default for menus)
- **[1 min]**
- **[5 min]**
- **[10 min]**

Note: If the EH-5 / EH-5a AC adapter is used, the LCD monitor will switch off after ten minutes regardless of the option selected at CS-c4.

c5: Remote On Duration: Use this item to set the duration of time the camera will wait to receive the signal from the ML-L3 IR remote release before it cancels Delayed or Quick-response remote modes. Use the shortest possible duration to prevent undue drain on the battery power.

- **[1 min]**
- **[5 min]**
- **[10 min]**
- **[15 min]**

Shooting / Display
d1: Beep: This item controls the audible warning that sounds when the release timer is counting down in self-timer mode, Delayed remote mode, when the camera attains focus in AF-S (single-servo) autofocus, or when a photograph is taken in Quick response mode. Select [On] (default) or [Off].

Hint: This is a matter of personal preference, but the audible warning can be a distraction in many shooting situations. For that reason, I recommend selecting [Off] for this item; will be displayed in the control panel to confirm that the beep is switched off.

d2: Viewfinder Grid Display: This menu item determines whether a pattern of grid lines is displayed in the viewfinder. Select [On] or [Off] (default).

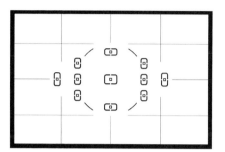

The grid lines available under CS-d2 [Viewfinder grid display] can help ensure proper alignment of the camera to the scene being photographed.

Hint: Although useful for any photography that requires precise alignment of elements in the picture (such as the horizon, or other defined edges), this feature is somewhat limited, as the grid pattern does not extend inside the area of the frame covered by the AF points.

d3: ISO Display and Adjustment: The ISO value can be set to be displayed in the viewfinder and control panel in place of the remaining exposures counter, plus it is possible to adjust the ISO value using the command dials in P, S, and A exposure modes. There are three options:

- **[Show ISO sensitivity]:** The ISO value is displayed in place of the frame count display.
- **[Show ISO/Easy ISO]:** ISO sensitivity can be adjusted by rotating the sub-command dial in P and S modes, or the main command dial in A mode. The ISO value is displayed in place of the frame count display.
- **[Show frame count] (default):** The number of remaining exposures is displayed in the control panel and viewfinder.

d4: Viewfinder Warning Display: Selecting [On] for this menu item enables display of the following warnings in the viewfinder.

- **B/W** : Displayed when the Monochrome picture control is selected
- **▭** : Displayed to warn of a low battery
- **☒** : Displayed to warn that no memory card is installed in the camera

The viewfinder warnings for the D90 are activated via CS-d4.

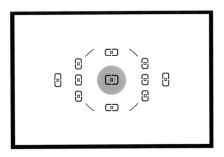

d5: Screen Tips: This setting controls whether the camera displays tips fir items selected in the Quick Settings Display. Select [On] (Default) or [Off]. When [On] is selected, a text field or diagram is displayed to identify the item highlighted in the Quick Settings Display when the **info** button is pressed twice.

d6: CL Mode Shooting Speed: This item determines the frame rate of the camera when the shooting mode is set to continuous low (CL). Select a frame rate between one and four frames per second (fps); the default setting is [3 fps].

Hint: I never use the CL shooting mode, as I prefer to have the camera shoot at its fastest rate when necessary, or control shooting by taking individual frames in rapid succession in continuous high shooting mode. Your own specific shooting requirements will determine the choice you make for this item.

Note: The effective frame rate can be influenced by the shutter speed and capacity of the buffer memory. The D90's top frame rate in CL shooting mode is 4 fps.

d7: File Number Sequence: This menu selection controls whether file numbering continues in a consecutive sequence from the last number used when a memory card is formatted, a new folder is created, or a new memory card is inserted in the camera, or if it is reset to 0001. The options are:

- **[On] (default):** Whenever a memory card is formatted, or a new memory card is inserted in the camera, file numbering continues consecutively from the last number used or the largest number in the current folder, whichever is higher. If the current folder contains a photograph numbered 9999, a new folder will be automatically created, and numbering will be reset to 0001.
- **[Off]:** File numbering is reset to 0001 whenever a memory card is formatted, a new folder is created, or a new memory card is inserted in the camera.
- **[Reset]:** The same as the [On] option, except that the file number for the next picture that is taken is assigned by adding one to the largest file number in the current folder. If that folder is empty, file numbering is reset to 0001.

Hint: If you expect to shoot pictures using more than one memory card, I strongly suggest that you use the [On] option. Otherwise you will potentially end up with duplicate file numbers and names, which could become very confusing once images are saved to your computer.

d8: Shooting Info Display: The item determines the nature of the shooting info display that is shown when the [info] button is pressed in shooting mode. Options are:

- **[Auto] (default):** The display will change automatically from black on white to white on black to maintain the best contrast with the background.
- **[Manual]:** Select [B] for dark characters on a light background, or [W] for white characters on a dark background. The monitor brightness adjusts automatically for maximum contrast.

Hint: This option is very much a personal preference. I have found the manual [W] setting useful when shooting in low light, as the screen emits far less light compared with the [B] option, making it less distracting. Conversely, the [W] setting is probably easier to read in bright conditions.

d9: LCD Illumination: This selection controls the operation of the backlight in the LCD display of the control panels. The options are:

- **[On]:** The backlight remains on while the exposure meter is active.
- **[Off] (default):** The backlight only illuminates when the power switch it rotated past the [On] position to ☀ and released.

Hint: Since the use of the backlight will increase drain on the battery power, I recommend leaving this item set to [Off], its default option.

d10: Exposure Delay Mode: This item enables the camera to delay the release of the shutter by approximately one second after the shutter release button is pressed and the reflex mirror has been raised. Its purpose is to help reduce the risk of camera vibration, which might affect the sharpness of the picture. Select [On] or [Off] (default).

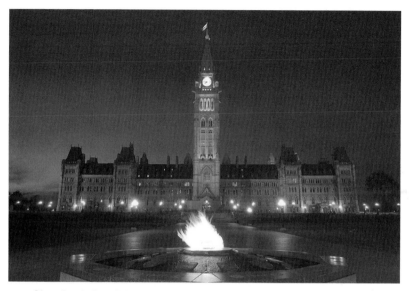

Shooting in low light is likely to cause blurriness in your pictures due to camera shake. To offset this effect, use a tripod and set the Exposure Delay Mode at CS-d10 to [On].

Hint: Since the D90 lacks a proper mirror lock-up setting to be used in conjunction with remote shutter release, this option can be worthwhile when you need to ensure maximum sharpness when working with long focal length lenses or at high magnifications.

d11: Flash Warning: Only available in the P, S, A, and M exposure modes, this item enables the D90 to display a warning in low-light conditions to recommend the use of flash. When [On] is selected (default), in low light, the ⚡ flash ready light will blink in the viewfinder when the shutter release is pressed down halfway to warn that additional illumination is required. When [Off] is selected, no warning is displayed.

d12: MB-D80 Battery Type: To ensure efficient and proper operation of the MB-D80 battery pack when fitted with AA size batteries, use this item to select the type of battery inserted:

- **[LR6 (AA Alkaline)]**
- **[HR6 (AA NiMH)]**
- **[FR6 (AA Lithium)]**
- **[ZR6 (AA NiMn)]**

Hint: Although I would suggest that use of AA batteries in the MB-D80 battery pack should only be considered as an emergency measure, if you have to resort to using such batteries, ensure the correct type is selected for this item.

Bracketing/Flash
e1: Flash Shutter Speed: Use this item to select the slowest possible flash synchronization speed in A (Aperture-priority) and P (Programmed-auto) exposure modes when using front or rear-curtain sync, or red-eye correction. The options are:

- **Shutter speeds** between [1/60 s] (1/60 second) and [30 s] (30 seconds) can be selected.

Hint: I recommend using a shutter speed at which you are confident you can hold the camera steady, otherwise there is a risk that any part of the picture illuminated by ambient light will not be sharp due to the effects of camera shake. For most practical purposes with a short focal length lens (i.e., < 50mm) this will be around 1/30 to 1/15 second. At longer shutter speeds, use a tripod or some other form of camera support.

Note: Regardless of the option selected at CS-e1, shutter speeds as slow as 30 seconds can be selected in Shutter-priority and Manual exposure modes, or at flash settings of slow sync, slow rear-curtain sync, or red-eye correction with slow sync.

e2: Flash Control for Built-in Flash: Use this item to select the flash mode for the built-in Speedlight of the D90.

- **TTL⚡ TTL (default):** The camera uses its 420-segment RGB sensor (the same sensor used for Matrix metering) to control flash output automatically; it performs iTTL balanced fill-flash (monitor pre-flashes are used) and distance information is included with D- or G-type lenses. Standard TTL flash is used if the camera is set to spot metering; alternatively, it can be selected on an external Speedlight.

- **M⚡ Manual:** The flash can be set to deliver a specific amount of light between its maximum output and 1/128 of its maximum output. The Guide Number (in Manual flash mode) is 59/18 (ft/m, ISO200).

- **RPT⚡ Repeating flash:** The flash can be set to emit a sequence of outputs during a single exposure to produce a strobe-light effect. This item has three options: Output—similarly to manual flash, the output of the flash is set to a specific level between 1/4 and 1/128; Times—choose the number of times the flash fires (this is dependent on the shutter speed used and frequency for flash outputs); and Frequency—used to set the frequency of flash outputs.

- **C⚡ Commander mode:** The built-in Speedlight is used as a master flash to control one or more remote Speedlight(s), in up to two separate groups. All Speedlights must be compatible with the Advanced Wireless Lighting system (at the time of writing the only external Speedlights that support this are the SB-900, SB-800, SB-600, and SB-R200).

The options available within this item provide a variety of ways for using the built-in Speedlight (see pages 291-327 for a full explanation of the flash modes available here).

Hint: If the SB-400 Speedlight is attached to the D90 and activated, CS-e2 changes to Optional flash, which allows the flash control mode for the SB-400 to be selected only from TTL and Manual.

e3: Modeling Flash: Pressing the Depth-of-Field Preview button will cause either the built-in flash or an external flash unit (currently only the SB-900, SB-800, SB-600, or SB-R200) to emit a rapid series of low intensity light pulses that acts as a modeling light so you can assess the effect of the flash illumination. It is only available in P, S, A, and M exposure modes.

- **[On]:** The modeling light function operates when the Depth-of-Field Preview button is pressed.
- **[Off] (default):** No light will be emitted when the Depth-of-Field Preview button is pressed.

Hint: Due to the low intensity and brevity of the light pulses emitted, this item is only really useful at short flash shooting distances. However, if you take an external Speedlight off the camera using a dedicated TTL flash cord such as the SC-28, it can be helpful in assessing the position and nature of shadows cast by the flash.

e4:Auto Bracketing Set: This item allows you to decide which settings are affected when the automatic bracketing feature is used.

- **[AE & flash] (default):** The camera brackets the exposure for both ambient light and flash output.
- **[AE only]:** The camera only brackets the ambient light exposure.
- **[Flash only]:** The camera only brackets the flash output level.
- **[WB bracketing]:** The camera brackets the white balance value when recording pictures in the JPEG format (this feature is not available for NEF or NEF + JPEG options).
- **[ADL bracketing]:** The camera takes two pictures, one with and the other without Active D-Lighting.

White balance bracketing affects only the color temperature value (i.e., only the amber-blue values in the white balance fine tuning display shift; it causes no change to the color balance values of the green-magenta). Only one exposure is made in white balance bracketing, and the camera then processes the required number of pictures by altering the color balance of the original exposure (see pages 73-75 for full details).

Active D-Lighting (ADL) bracketing is set by highlighting the [ADL bracketing] option and pressing ⊚ . Next, press the **BKT** button and rotate the main command dial to display the bracketing icon **BKT** and the bracketing progress indicators ■ and ▶— in the control panel. The camera will take two exposures in the ADL bracket sequence; the first at the unmodified level (i.e., Active D-lighting is off) and the second at the level of Active D-Lighting selected currently in the Shooting menu. The ■ segment of the bracket progress indicator will disappear when the first exposure is made and the ▶— segment when the second exposure is made.

To cancel the ADL bracketing, press the **BKT** button and rotate the main command dial so the bracketing progress indicator is no longer displayed in the control panel.

e5: Auto FP: This enables Auto FP flash sync, allowing compatible external Speedlight flash units (SB-900, SB-800, SB-600 and SB-R200) to be used with camera shutter speeds between 1/200 and 1/4000 second (see pages 317-318 for full details) in P,S, A, and M exposure modes.

• **[On]:** Auto FP flash sync is enabled.
• **[Off] (default):** Auto FP flash sync is disabled.

e6: Bracketing Order: This option allows you to select the order in which the camera makes exposures in a bracketing sequence (it is only available in P, S, A, and M exposure modes). It applies to exposure, flash exposure, and white balance bracketing.

• **[MTR>Under>Over] (default):** The "correct" exposure is followed by underexposed and then overexposed frames. The order for white balance would be no modification, A (amber), and then B (blue).

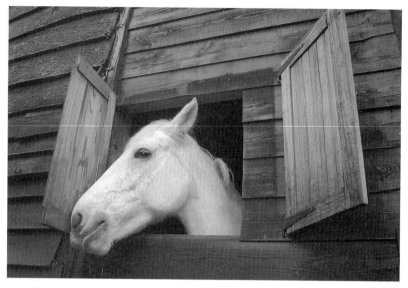

For a subtle fill-flash effect (especially outside on a sunny day), try using Auto FP flash sync. Using a faster shutter speed than normal will help to prevent overexposure caused by the light from the flash combining with the ambient light. CS-e5 must be set to [On] and a compatible Speedlight must be connected for Auto FP to be functional.

- **[Under>MTR>Over]:** The underexposed frame is taken first, followed by the "correct" and then overexposed frames. White balance order is A (amber), no modification, and then B (blue).

Hint: Choice of the options available within this item will be a matter of personal preference based on the prevailing shooting conditions; however, I recommend you use one option consistently; you can assess exposure quickly as you always know which frame is which in the sequence.

Controls

f1: :☀: **Switch:** This item determines the function of the power switch when it is rotated to the :☀: position.

- :☀: **[LCD backlight] (default):** The control panel back-light will illuminate for 6 seconds.
- :☀: **[Info] [Both]:** The control panel backlight will illuminate and the shooting information is displayed on the monitor.

f2: OK button (Shooting mode): The ⊗ button can be used to select several camera operations in both the Shooting mode and the Playback mode. Use CS-f2 to determine its function while the camera is in Shooting mode.

- **[Select center AF point] (default):** Pressing the ⊗ button will select the center AF point.
- **[Highlight active focus point]:** Pressing the ⊗ button will illuminate the active AF point.
- **[Not used]:** Pressing the ⊗ button has no effect when the camera is in the Shooting mode.

f3: Assign FUNC Button: The Function (Fn) button, located on the front of the camera below the AF-assist lamp, can be assigned a variety of different functions using this item.

- ⊞ **[Framing grid]:** Press the Fn button and rotate the main command dial to display the viewfinder grid lines.
- [+] **[AF-area mode]:** Press the Fn button and rotate the main command dial to select the AF-area mode.
- "¡⁺¡ **[Center focus point]:** Press the Fn button and rotate the main command dial to toggle between normal and wide center focus points.
- 🔒 **[FV lock] (default):** Press the Fn button to lock flash value (only supported by SB-900, SB-800, SB-600, and SB-R200). Press again to cancel FV Lock.
- ⚡ **[Flash off]:** Press and hold the Fn button to cancel flash firing.
- 🔳 **[Matrix metering]:** Press the Fn button to activate Matrix metering.

237

- $\boxed{\bullet}$ **[Center-weighted metering]:** Press the Fn button to activate center-weighted metering.
- $\boxed{\cdot}$ **[Spot metering]:** Press the Fn button to activate spot metering.
- ◫ **[Access top item in My Menu]:** Press the Fn button to go directly to the top item in [My Menu].
- **[RAW+NEF (RAW)]:** If image quality is set to JPEG Fine, Normal, or Basic, an NEF (RAW) file will be recorded with the next exposure made after the Fn button is pressed. To cancel the process, press the Fn button again.

Hint: Choice of the options available within this item will be a matter of personal preference based on the specific shooting situation. When using flash, the FV Lock is useful; and when shooting in ambient light, I find it beneficial to be able to switch to spot metering from Matrix metering at the press of this button. One other potentially useful option is [AF-area mode] because, unlike some other Nikon D-SLR cameras that have an external switch to select the AF-area mode, there is no way to alter this on the D90 other than to navigate the menu system, which is time consuming.

f4: Assign AE-L/AF-L button: The AE-L/AF-L button, located on the rear of the camera to the right of the viewfinder eyepiece, can be assigned a variety of different functions with this option.

- ◫ **[AE/AF lock] (default):** Focus and exposure are locked when the AE-L/AF-L button is pressed.
- ◫ **[AE lock only]:** Exposure is locked when the AE-L/AF-L button is pressed.
- ◫ **[AF lock only]:** Focus is locked when the AE-L/AF-L button is pressed.
- ◫ **[AE lock (hold)]:** Exposure is locked when the AE-L/AF-L button is pressed and remains locked until the button is pressed again or the exposure meter turns off automatically.
- **AF-ON** **[AF-ON]:** Autofocus is initiated when the AE-L/AF-L button is pressed. Pressing the shutter-release button will not activate autofocus.

238

- **🔒** **[FV lock]**: Press the AE-L/AF-L button to lock the flash output level (see pages 319-320 for full details). Press the button again to cancel FV Lock.

Note: If this option is set to [AF-ON], the Vibration Reduction (VR) feature, available on some Nikkor lenses, will not operate when the AE-L/AF-L button is pressed; VR is only activated by pressing the shutter-release button. If you use the technique of locking focus by controlling autofocus operation via the AE-L/AF-L button, press the shutter-release button and pause briefly when it is depressed halfway, allowing the VR system to activate and settle down, before pressing it all the way to record a picture.

f5: Customize Command Dials: This item provides additional functionality to the main and sub-command dials.

- **[Reverse rotation]**: Select [No] (default) to have the command dials operate as described in this book and the Nikon manual. Select [Yes] if you wish to have the command dials operate in the reverse direction. This option also affects the command dials of the MB-D80.
- **[Change Main/sub]**: Select [Off] (default) to have the main command dial control the shutter speed and the sub-command dial control the aperture. Set [On] to reverse these controls.
- **[Menus and playback]**: Select [On] (default) to use the main command dial to select images for full-frame playback, move the highlight cursor left or right during thumbnail playback, and move the highlight cursor when navigating through menus. Use the sub-command dial to show additional image information pages in full-frame playback and move the highlight cursor up or down during thumbnail playback. When a menu is displayed, rotating the sub-command dial to the right displays the sub-menu for the selected menu item, while rotating the sub-command dial to the left displays the previous menu. To select an option, press either ▶ or ⓞⓚ . Selecting [On (image review excluded)] has the same effect as [On], except the command dials are disabled during

image review. If [Off] is selected, the multi selector can be used to choose the picture displayed during full-frame playback, highlight thumbnail images, and navigate menus.

Hint: Choice of the options available within this item will be a matter of personal preference. Personally, I leave each option set to its default to avoid confusion when I use other Nikon camera models that do not offer the alternatives that can be set here. If you use other Nikon camera models, I recommend you do the same.

f6: No Memory Card?: This item allows the shutter to operate without a memory card being installed in the camera.

- **[Release locked] (default):** The shutter release is disabled if no memory card is installed in the camera.
- **[Enable release]:** The shutter release operates if no memory card is installed in the camera. The camera stores no images; however, the last recorded image is displayed on the monitor.

Hint: Disaster potentially looms with this item if it is set to the [Enable release] option—you do not want the camera to operate as though it is recording pictures when in fact there is no memory card installed!

Note: If pictures are recorded directly to a computer using Camera Control Pro 2 software, they will not be recorded to a memory card installed in the camera, and the shutter will be enabled regardless of the setting chosen for this item.

f7: Reverse indicators: At the default setting, the exposure indicator display shown in the control panel, viewfinder, and shooting information display has positive values to the left and negative values to the right. The display can be reversed using this item.

- **[+ 0 -] (default):** Positive values are shown to the left and negative values to the right.

- **[- 0 +]:** The exposure indicator display is reversed; positive values are shown to the right and negative values to the left.

Hint: If you are familiar with previous Nikon SLR cameras, film or digital, you will probably already be familiar with the default exposure display; therefore, it is probably best to leave this option set to the default.

⚊ Setup Menu

The Setup menu is used to establish the basic configuration of the camera. Once the settings for most of the items in this menu are made, it is unlikely they will be changed very frequently.

Format Memory Card

A new memory card should always be formatted when it is first placed into the D90. It is also a good idea to format any memory card you insert into the camera, even if the card has been formatted using a computer. This is particularly important if you use your memory cards between different camera bodies. Ensure that any image files stored on the card have been saved to another storage device before you format the memory card (see pages 277-278 for more details).

LCD Brightness

The brightness of the LCD monitor on the back of the camera is set to a default value. However, this can be adjusted to help improve the visibility of any displayed image or page of information. This feature can be particularly helpful when trying to read file information in bright outdoor light, but attempting to assess the image quality under such conditions will most likely be a fruitless exercise. To adjust LCD brightness:

1. Highlight the [LCD brightness] option from the Setup menu and press ⊙ .
2. Adjust the brightness value up or down by pressing ▲ or ▼ .
3. Press the ⊛ button to confirm the screen brightness value.

A negative value reduces screen brightness, while a positive value increases screen brightness. The screen displays a grayscale to help you judge the effect of the brightness level on the full tonal range present in your images.

Hint: I consider the default value for the screen brightness level to be too high. For a more accurate assessment of images, I suggest setting screen brightness to -1.

Clean Image Sensor
This option is used to automatically clean the optical low-pass filter by vibrating it (see pages 364-366 for more details).

Lock Mirror Up for Cleaning
This option is used to manually clean or inspect the optical low-pass filter (see pages 366-369 for more details).

Video Mode
The Video mode option allows you to select the type of signal used by any video equipment, such as a DVD player or television, to which your camera may be connected. This option should be set before connecting your camera to the device with the supplied A/V cord (see pages 348-349 for more details).

HDMI
The D90 has an HDMI (High Definition Media Interface) connector located under the large rubber connector cover on the left side of the camera. This connection port allows pictures to be played back on high definition televisions and monitors using a type-C HDMI cable. The [HDMI] option in the Setup menu allows you to select one of five HDMI formats. Ensure you select the correct format before connecting the camera to the HDMI device. The camera monitor will turn off automatically when an HDMI device is connected.

Option	Description
Auto	The D90 selects the appropriate format automatically
480p (progressive)	640 x 480 (progressive) format
576p (progressive)	720 x 576 (progressive) format
720p (progressive)	1280 x 720 (progressive) format
1080i (interlaced)	1920 x 1080 (interlaced) format

World Time

World Time enables you to set and change the date and time recorded by the camera's internal clock and how it is displayed. To set the internal clock, highlight the [World time] item in the Setup menu. Press ⊕ to display the menu options and use ⊕ to highlight [Time zone]: Pressing the multi selector to the right displays a map of world time zones. Use ⊕ to select the appropriate time zone and press ⊛ to confirm the selection and return to the World Time menu.

Now, use ⊕ to highlight the [Date and time] option, and press ⊕ to display the date/time clock. Use ⊕ to select each item in turn, adjusting as needed by using ⊕ until the full date and time have been entered. Press ⊛ to confirm the settings and return to the World Time menu.

Next, use ⊕ to highlight the [Date format] option and press ⊕ to display the list of choices. To determine the order in which the date and time are displayed, use ⊕ to highlight the desired date format and press ⊛ to confirm the selection.

Finally, use ⊕ to highlight the [Daylight saving time] option and press ⊕ to display the two choices; the default setting for [Daylight saving time] is [Off]. If Daylight Saving Time is in effect, highlight [On] and press ⊛ to confirm the selection. To exit the menu system and return the camera to its Shooting mode, press the shutter-release button halfway down.

Hint: If you travel to a different time zone, it is only necessary to adjust the [Time Zone] option in the World Time menu; the date and time will be automatically adjusted for the selected time zone. The only other option that may need to be adjusted is the [Daylight saving time] option.

The internal clock is not as accurate as many wristwatches or domestic clocks, so it is important to check it regularly. You may wish to consider connecting a GPS device to the D90 (see pages 249-251 for details) if recording accurate time and date information for each image is essential to your photography.

Language

The [Language] option in the Setup menu of the D90 allows you to select one of 17 languages when displaying menus and messages. To select the language, press the **MENU** button and highlight the required [Language] option using ▲ or ▼ . Finally, press the ⊛ button to confirm and lock your selection. If you wish to change the language at any time after the initial setup, repeat the procedure.

Image Comment

The Image Comment feature of the Setup menu allows you to attach a short note or reference to an image file. Comments can be up to 36 characters long and may contain letters and/or numbers. Since the process requires each character to be input individually, this is not a feature you will use for every picture you take. However, as a way of assigning a general comment (i.e., the name of a location / venue / event) or attaching notice of authorship / copyright, it is very useful. To attach an image comment:

1. Highlight the [Image comment] option from the Setup menu and press ⊙▸ .
2. Highlight [Input comment] from the options list and press ⊙▸ .
3. To enter your comment, highlight the character you wish to input by using ⊕ and press ⊕ to select it. If you accidentally enter the wrong character, use the

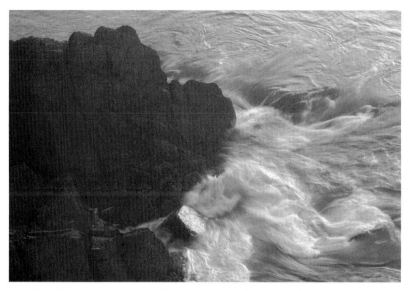

Use the image comment feature in the Setup menu to add text to a photo file, in order to recall where the picture was taken or other details that are not recorded in the EXIF data.

⊖▦ button in combination with ⊕ to move the cursor over the unwanted character and press the 🗑 button to erase it.

4. Press the ⊛ button to save the comment and return to the [Image comment] options list.

5. To actually attach the comment to your photographs, highlight the [Attach comment] option, and then press ⊕ . A small check mark will appear in the box to the left of the option.

6. Finally, highlight [Done] and press the ⊛ button to confirm the selection.

If you wish to exit this process at any time without attaching the comment prior to step 5, simply press the **MENU** button. When the check mark is present in the [Attach comment] option of the [Image comment] item, the saved comment will be attached to all subsequent images shot on the D90. To prevent the comment from being attached to an image, simply return to the [Image comment] menu and uncheck the [Attach comment] box by highlighting the option and pressing ⊕ . The image comment will remain stored in the camera's memory and can be attached to future images simply by rechecking the [Attach comment] box. The comment will be displayed on the third page of the photo information display, available via in single-image playback. It can also be viewed in Nikon View NX or Capture NX2 software.

Auto Image Rotation
The D90 automatically recognizes the orientation of the camera as it records an image: horizontal, vertical (with camera rotated 90° clockwise), or vertical (camera rotated 90° counter-clockwise). At its default setting, the camera stores this information so the image can be automatically rotated during image playback. It will also be displayed in the correct orientation on a computer with compatible software. If you do not want the camera to record the shooting orientation, the Auto Image Rotation feature can be switched off. To set Auto Image Rotation:

1. Highlight the [Auto image rotation] item from the Setup menu and press ⊕ .
2. Highlight [On] or [Off] as required.
3. Press ⊛ to confirm the selection.

Note: The [Rotate tall] item in the Playback menu must also be turned on for images to be displayed in the orientation in which they were originally taken during image playback on the camera. However, if the [Image review] item in the Playback menu is set to [On], images will not be rotated for image review since the camera will already be in the correct orientation.

Image Dust Off Reference Photo
The [Dust Off ref photo] item of the D90 is designed specifically for use with the Image Dust Off function in Nikon Capture NX2. The image file created by this function creates a mask that is electronically "overlaid" on an

NEF file to enable the software to reduce or remove the effects of shadows that are cast by dust particles on the surface of the optical low-pass filter. To obtain a reference image for the Dust Off Ref Photo function you must use a CPU-type lens (Nikon recommends use of a lens with a focal length of 50mm or more). This function can only be used with NEF files; it is not available for JPEG or TIFF files. To use Dust Off Ref Photo:

1. Highlight the [Dust Off Ref Photo] option from the Setup menu and press 	⊙▸ .
2. [Start] will be highlighted on the monitor. Press 	⊛	 to begin the process. The message, "Take photo of bright featureless white object 10cm from lens. Focus will be set to infinity." will be displayed in the monitor.
3. Point your camera at a white, featureless subject positioned approximately 4 inches (10 cm) from the front of the lens.
4. Press the shutter-release button all the way down (focus will be set automatically to infinity).

Once you have recorded the Image Dust Off Reference data file, it can be displayed in the camera during image playback. It appears as a grid pattern with Image Dust Off Data displayed within the image area. A Dust Off Reference data file can be identified by its file extension, which is NDF. These files cannot be viewed using a computer.

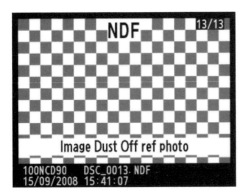

Use Image Dust Off Reference Photo periodically while you're shooting so that Capture NX2 can remove spots caused by dust particles on the sensor or low-pass filter.

Note: If the reference target is too bright or too dark, the camera will probably not be able to acquire Dust Off Reference data. In this case, a warning will be displayed on the monitor: "Exposure settings are not appropriate. Change exposure settings and try again." Either use an alternative target or change the level of illumination.

Hint: This feature is reasonably effective, but the dust particles can be dislodged and may shift between shots, providing no guarantee that this technique will be completely successful if you save only one reference file. The best approach is to shoot several reference files during the course of a shoot and use the one that was made closest to the time of the exposure you need to correct.

This is the graphic display you will see when the D90 is powered by an EN-EL3e rechargeable battery.

Battery info

Bat. meter   87%
Pic. meter   12

Battery age   0
(0 - 4)

OK Done

Battery Info
The EN-EL3e rechargeable battery has an electronic chip in its circuitry that allows the D90 to report detailed information regarding the status of the battery. To access this information, select [Battery info] from the Setup menu; when the camera is powered by the EN-EL3e, three parameters concerning the battery will be displayed on the screen (see the chart below).

Parameter	Description
Bat. Meter	Current level of battery charge, expressed as a percentage
Pic. Meter	Number of times the shutter has been released with the current battery since it was last charged. This number will include shutter release actions when no picture is recorded (e.g., to record an Image Dust Off Reference frame or to measure color temperature for a preset white balance value).
Battery age	Displays the condition of the battery as one of five levels (0 – 4); level 0 indicates the battery is new, and level 4 indicates the battery has reached the end of its charging life and should be replaced. Batteries charged at temperatures below 41° F (5° C) might show a reduced charge life; this will return to normal once charged at a temperature of 68° F (20° C) or higher.

Note: If the MB-D80 battery pack is fitted to the D90, the Battery Info display will show information for each battery slot separately, as per the chart above. If the MB-D80 contains AA batteries, only the battery level is displayed using the [Battery Info] item; in the control panel, only one of three icons will be displayed when powering the camera with AA batteries: ▰▰▰ fresh batteries, ▭▱ battery level is low, or ▭ (blinks) batteries exhausted.

Press the **info** button to open the Shooting Information Display and the battery type (EN-EL3e or AA), charge status; and if two EN-EL3e batteries are installed in the MB-D80, the battery currently in use will be highlighted.

GPS

Nikon announced the GP-1 Global Positioning System (GPS) unit at the same time as the D90 camera. The GP-1 connects to the remote accessory terminal of the camera, which is located beneath the small rubber cover on the left side of the D90.

Turn the D90 off before connecting the GP-1, which can be attached to the camera's accessory shoe. Switch the camera on (the GP-1 draws its power from the camera battery); as soon as the camera confirms communication with the GP-1 device, **GPS** will be displayed in the control panel. The information recorded when an exposure is made with the GPS connected includes current latitude, longitude, altitude, and time. The time provided by the GPS device uses Coordinated Universal Time (UTC) and is independent of the camera's internal clock. To view GPS data, open an image in single-image playback and use ⊛ to scroll through the photo information pages until the GPS Data page is displayed. GPS has two options: [Auto meter off] and [Position].

- **[Auto meter off]:** Choose whether or not the exposure meters will turn off automatically after a period of non-use when the GP-1 unit is attached. Highlight [Auto meter off] and press ⊛ to display the two sub-options:

  [Enable] (default): If no camera operation is performed for the period selected at CS-c2 [Auto meter off delay], the exposure meter will turn off automatically. While this reduces drain on the camera's battery, it will prevent GPS data from being recorded because if the camera's meter is turned off, the GPS device is also switched off. If the shutter release is then pressed all the way without pausing to read an exposure value, there may be insufficient time for the GPS device to reactivate.

  [Disable]: The camera's exposure meter will not turn off automatically while the GP-1 device is connected. GPS data will always be recorded, as the GP-1 device also remains powered and active.

Note: Given the excellent performance of the EN-EL3e and efficient power management of the D90, there is no reason why the [Disable] option should not be set, as it will have little impact on the battery performance when the D90 is used with the GP-1. However, if you expect to be shooting for a long period of time, it would be prudent to make sure you carry a spare EN-EL3e.

- **[Position]:** Only available if a GP-1 device is connected and GPS communication is confirmed; if not, the [Position] item is grayed out in the menu. When GPS communication is established, the camera displays current latitude, longitude, altitude, and time (UTC) as reported by the GP-1 device.

Eye-Fi Upload

Eye-fi is a technology that allows you to automatically and wirelessly upload your photos either to your computer via a home wireless network, or to the web via Wi-Fi hotspots.

At the time of publication, the wireless Eye-fi system is only available in the United States and requires a dedicated 2GB Eye-fi memory card to be used in the D90 to upload JPEG files directly from the camera to the predetermined destination [Enabled]. If the Wi-Fi signal is not sufficiently strong, image upload will not take place. In areas where Wi-Fi is unavailable or wireless devices are prohibited, ensure the [Disable] option is selected.

Firmware Version

When [Firmware version] is selected from the Setup menu, the current version of the installed firmware is displayed on the monitor. Highlight the [Firmware version] option from the Setup menu and press ⊚ . The details of the firmware are displayed on the next page. Press ⊛ button to return to the Setup menu.

Firmware updates can be downloaded from any of the Nikon technical support websites. To check for current updates visit: www.nikon.com.

☑ Retouch Menu

The Retouch menu enables you to create retouched (modified), trimmed (cropped), or resized versions of the image files saved on a memory card that is installed in the camera. When the features in this menu are applied to an image, a new copy of the file is created and stored on the same memory card. The original image file remains on the card in its unmodified form.

While I feel options available in the Retouch menu are a useful aspect of camera control, I believe it is important to keep them in perspective. The items available in this menu cannot be considered anywhere near as sophisticated as their counterpart adjustments in any good digital imaging software. They are intended to provide a quick, convenient, and largely automated method of producing a modified version of the original image without the use of a computer. As such, they offer an unprecedented level of control when using in-camera processing to produce a finished picture directly from the camera.

Selecting Images
To select an image, open the Retouch menu, highlight the desired function, and press ⊙ to select it and display up to six thumbnail images on the screen. Depending on the item selected, a further menu of options may be displayed before the thumbnail images; if so, highlight the required option and press ⊙ again. Use ✪ to scroll through the thumbnail images; a yellow border will frame the currently selected picture. To view an image full frame, press and hold the ⌕ button. Once you have selected the picture to be modified and copied, press the ⊛ button to display the retouch options (see details below for each Retouch menu item). To cancel the process, press the **MENU** button. To apply the retouch option and save the new copy image, press the ⊛ button.

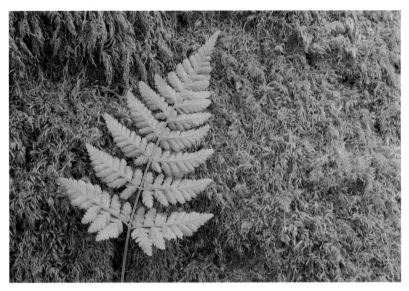

The Retouch menu in the D90 allows an unprecedented amount of in-camera post-processing. I recommend, however, that these controls be used sparingly because the tools in image editing software are much more powerful and precise. Furthermore, it is far easier to manipulate an image when you can look at it on a computer screen, rather than on the camera's 3-inch LCD.

Alternatively, it is possible to access the Retouch menu directly from full-frame playback. Display the picture to be modified and press the ⓄⓀ button. The Retouch menu item will be displayed; select the required item by using ⊕ and press ⊕ to open the options for that item. To return to the full-frame playback, press the ▶ button. Press ⓄⓀ to create the retouched copy. An ☑ icon identifies the retouched copy file.

Image Quality and Size

The image quality and size of the copy image created by the Retouch menu will depend on the quality and size of the original image file(s). The selected option within the Retouch menu may also affect image size and quality. The following applies except in the case of [Trim], [Small picture], and [Image overlay]:

1. Copies created from JPEG images are the same size and quality as the original file.
2. Copies of NEF (RAW) files are saved as a JPEG files with [Large] and [Fine] selected for size and quality, respectively.
3. The copy created by the [Image Overlay] option is always saved at the image quality and size currently set on the camera, regardless of the fact that this option is only available with NEF images. If you wish to save the copy image as an NEF file, ensure the image quality on the camera is set to NEF before you apply this option.

Note: Copies created using the [Trim] and [Small picture] items cannot be modified further. [Quick retouch] is disabled with copy files created using [D-Lighting], and vice versa. All of the Retouch menu items can also be applied once to a copy image that was previously created using the Retouch menu. [D-Lighting], [Red-eye correction], [Filter effects] (except [Cross screen]), [Quick retouch], and [Color balance] cannot be applied to monochrome copies. Except for [Cross screen], [Filter effects] cannot be applied to copy files with filters other than [Cross screen]. [Image overlay] can be applied multiple times, while all other options in the Retouch menu can only be applied once to an existing copy file. Depending on the option used, such further retouching may result in a loss of image quality.

Retouch Menu Options

D-Lighting: The D-Lighting feature of the Retouch menu brightens shadow areas to reveal more detail. It is not an overall brightness control; its application is selective. By modifying the tone curve applied to the image, it only affects the shadow areas of the recorded image and preserves the mid- and highlight tones.

Select the image (as described above) and press the   button to display two thumbnail images; one unmodified (left) and the other modified (right). You can select three levels of D-Lighting: low, normal, or high, using ⊛ . To view the preview image full frame, press and hold the ⊕ button. Once you have decided which level is most appropriate, press the ⊛ button to apply the change and create the copy image. You can press the **MENU** button to cancel the function without making any changes.

⊙ **Red-Eye Correction:** This option is only available with pictures taken using either the built-in Speedlight of the D90 or an external Nikon Speedlight. Select the image (as described above) and press the ⊛ button. If no flash was used for the chosen exposure, a small yellow box containing a cross is displayed over the thumbnail image, and the image cannot be selected. If flash was used but the camera cannot detect the presence of red-eye, a message stating "Unable to detect red-eye in selected image." will be displayed.

If the D90 detects what it considers to be a red-eye effect, the image will be displayed with a small navigation window; press and hold the ⊕ button to zoom in on the image. You can navigate around the image to view other areas of the picture by pressing the multi selector ⊛ ; the area currently displayed on the monitor is shown with a yellow border in a navigation window. Press and hold the multi selector down to scroll rapidly to another area of the picture.

If you can see the effects of red-eye in the selected picture, press the ⊛ button to cancel the zoom control and return to the full-frame playback and then press ⊛ again. The D90 will then create a copy image automatically, using processed image data, to reduce the red-eye effect.

✂   **Trim:** The [Trim] option enables you to crop (trim) the original image to exclude unwanted areas. Highlight the [Trim] option in the Retouch menu and press ⊙ to display a set of six thumbnails images. Select the image (as described above) and press the ⊗ button.

The selected image is displayed on the LCD monitor, along with a yellow frame to show the crop area; you can move the crop frame around the image using ⊕ . Press the ⊖▨ button to reduce the size of crop area. Use the ⊕ button to increase the size of the crop area; the crop size is displayed in the top left corner of the image in pixel dimensions (width x height). It is also possible to adjust the aspect ratio of the cropped area; rotating the main command dial allows you to switch between 3:2, 4:3, and 5:4. To preview the crop, press the ⊗ button.

Once you have decided on the location, size, and aspect ratio of the crop area, press the ⊗ button to create the cropped copy. The new copy image will be displayed on the LCD monitor. Press the **MENU** button to return to the Retouch menu display.

The size of the copy file varies with the selected crop size and aspect ratio as follows:

Aspect ratio	Range of image sizes available
3:2	3424 x 2280, 2560 x 1704, 1920 x 1280, 1280 x 856, 960 x 640, 640 x 424.
4:3	3424 x 2568, 2560 x 1920, 1920 x 1440, 1280 x 960, 960 x 720, 640 x 480.
5:4	3216 x 2568, 2400 x 1920, 1808 x 1440, 1200 x 960, 896 x 720, 608 x 480.

■■ **Monochrome:** This item allows you to save the copied image in one of three monochrome effects: [Black-and-white] (grayscale), [Sepia] (brown tones), or [Cyanotype] (blue-and-white tones). In all three cases, the image data is converted to black and white using an algorithm dedicated to this feature; it is a different algorithm than the one used for the [Monochrome] option in the Picture Controls. The image data for the black-and-white copy is still saved as an RGB file (i.e., it retains its color information).

Select the image as described above. You must select the option before the thumbnail images are displayed. If you select either the [Sepia] or the [Cyanotype] option, the appropriate color shift is applied after the copy picture is converted to black and white. The degree of the color shift can be adjusted using ⊛ to increase or decrease the effect. Once you are satisfied with the preview image, press the ⊛ button to save the copy picture.

Ø **Filter Effects:** The [Filter Effects] option in the Retouch menu offers two choices that simulate the effects of a skylight or color correction (warm) filter. Select the image as described above and select the filter effect option before the thumbnail images are displayed.

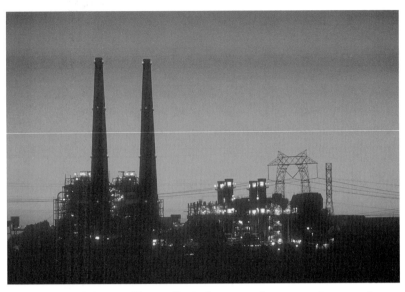

The Monochrome Picture Control can produce normal grayscale black-and-white images, as well as sepia or cyanotype black and white.

- **[Skylight]:** Nikon describes this option as emulating the effect of a Skylight filter. The effect is subtle, reducing the amount of blue in the image by a very modest amount.
- **[Warm filter]:** This effect increases the amount of red in the image and produces a result similar result to that of a Wratten 81-series color correction filter. Again the effect is subtle, and proper white balance control should eliminate the need to use it.
- **[Red intensifier]:** Intensifies red; use the multi selector button to select one of three levels: 1 (high), 2 (medium), or 3 (low).
- **[Green intensifier]:** Intensifies green; use the multi selector button to select one of three levels: 1 (high), 2 (medium), or 3 (low).
- **[Blue intensifier]:** Intensifies blue; use the multi selector button to select one of three levels: 1 (high), 2 (medium), or 3 (low).

- **[Cross screen]:** Adds a star-point effect to point light sources in the image.

  > [Number of points]: Select from 4, 6, or 8.
  >
  > [Filter amount]: Choose the brightness of the light sources affected.
  >
  > **[Filter angle]:** Select the angle of the star points.
  >
  > **[Length of points]:** Select the length of the star points.
  >
  > **[Confirm]:** Use to preview the effects of the filter. (To preview in full-frame press the ⊕ button.)
  >
  > **[Save]:** Create the retouch copy.

A preview image is displayed in all cases. After selecting the filter effect, press the Ⓞ button to apply it and create the copy image.

Color Balance: The [Color Balance] item is used to produce a copy image with a modified color balance from the original file. Select the image (as described above) and press the Ⓞ button to display to control options.

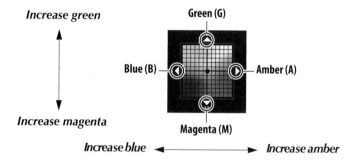

A thumbnail image of the selected picture is displayed alongside histograms for the composite red, green, and blue channels. Below the thumbnail is a two-dimensional CIE color space map with a vertical and horizontal axis aligned on its center. The central point of the color space map represents the color balance of the original file. Press the multi selector up to increase the level of green, and down to increase the level of magenta. Pressing the multi selector to the left increases the level of blue, and to the right increases the level of amber. The black square cursor will shift position accordingly, the histograms will reflect the altered color distribution, and the thumbnail image can be used to preview the effect.

To magnify a section of the preview image, press the ⊕ button; the histograms are updated to represent only the displayed portion of the image. When the preview image is enlarged, press the **?/⌦** button to switch back and forth between the magnifying function and the color-balance control. To move around the magnified image, use the ⬦ button.

Once you are satisfied with the adjustment, press the ⊛ button to apply the color shift and save a copy of the image.

⬛ **Small Picture:** The Small picture item offers options to reduce the resolution of the original image to create a copy that has a far smaller file size:

- **[640 x 480 pixels]:** suitable for playback on a television set.
- **[320 x 240 pixels]:** suitable for display on webpages.
- **[160 x 120 pixels]:** suitable for sending as an attachment to e-mail.

The selection of a picture for processing in this menu from single-image playback is as described above; however, when the [Small picture] item is selected from the Retouch menu, the method of selecting an image differs from the method described previously. It is necessary to select the image size as the first step, and then select the picture(s) to which the process will be applied.

Note: Copies created by Small picture cannot be modified further. Also, files created with the Small picture option have file names that begin with "SSC_" and end with the file extension ".JPG" (e.g., SSC_0001.JPG). Using the Retouch menu, proceed as follows:

1. Open the Retouch menu, highlight [Small picture] and press ⊕ to display two options: [Select picture] and [Choose size].

2. Use ⊕ to highlight [Choose size], and then press ⊕ to display the three size options (listed above), and highlight the required size.

3. Press the ⊗ button to confirm your choice and return to the previous page. Highlight [Select picture] and press ⊕ to display up to six thumbnail images. The currently selected image is shown framed by a yellow border.

4. Use the multi selector to highlight a desired image (the yellow border will shift accordingly), and then press ⊕▦ to select it (a small icon appears in the top-right corner of the thumbnail to indicate it has been selected). Press ⊕ to view an enlarged picture.

5. Repeat as required; once you have selected all the images you want to reduce in size, press the ⊗ button. A confirmation page will be displayed indicating how many images will be processed.

6. Select [Yes] to proceed with the process, or [No] to return to the previous page. If you select [Yes], press the ⊗ button to apply the effect and save the copy picture(s).

Note: Images saved using the Small picture item are identified with a gray border when displayed during full-frame playback, thumbnail playback, and when a picture selection dialog page is shown; it is not possible to use the ⊕ zoom function with these images.

🖭 **Image Overlay:** Image overlay is one of two methods available on the D90 that enable the combination of multiple images in one file. This method is limited to using a pair of NEF files and combining them to form a single, new image (the original image files are not affected by this process). The images do not have to be taken in consecutive order, but must have been recorded by a D90 and be stored on the same memory card.

Note: The new image is saved at the image quality and size currently set on the camera. Therefore, before using this feature, ensure the image quality and size are set to the values you desire. If you want to save the new image as an NEF file, set the image quality on the camera to NEF (RAW). To use Image Overlay:

1. Highlight the [Image Overlay] option in the Retouch menu and press the ⊙ button.
2. The Image overlay page will open with [Image 1] highlighted.
3. To select the first picture, press the ⊛ button; a thumbnail view of all NEF files stored on the memory card will be displayed. Scroll through the images using ⊕ to highlight the image you wish to select.
4. Press ⊛ and the selected image will appear in the [Image 1] box and the [Preview] box.
5. Adjust the gain value of [Image 1] by pressing ▲ and ▼ . The effect of the gain control can be observed in the preview box (the default value is 1.0x—0.5x cuts the gain in half, while selecting 2.0x doubles the gain).
6. Highlight the [Image 2] box and repeat steps 2 – 5 above.
7. Once you have adjusted the gain of both images to achieve the desired effect, highlight the [Preview] box by pressing ⊙ . Highlight [Overlay] using ⊛ and press ⊛ to display a preview of the combined images. If the result is satisfactory, press the ⊛ button to save the new image, otherwise press ⊟ to return to the previous step.
8. To save the image without displaying a preview, highlight [Save] at step 7 above instead of [Overlay], and press the ⊛ button. The new image will be displayed full-frame.

The image will be saved on the memory card using the quality and size settings currently selected on the camera. Image attributes such as white balance, sharpening, color mode, saturation, and hue will be copied from the image selected as [Image 1]. The shooting data is also copied from [Image 1]. Image Overlays saved as NEF files use the same compression and bit depth as the original files; JPEG overlays are saved using size-priority compression.

⊞ **NEF (RAW) Processing:** This item can be used to create JPEG copies of pictures saved and stored on the installed memory card at an image quality of NEF (RAW), or NEF (RAW) + JPEG. To use NEF (RAW) processing:

1. Highlight NEF (RAW) processing in the Retouch menu and press ⊛ .
2. Select the desired NEF picture from the displayed thumbnail pictures by pressing ⊕ . Note that only NEF pictures will be displayed. Press the ⊛ button to select the highlighted picture.
3. A preview image is now display next to a menu of options:
   • Image quality: Choose image quality from, JPEG Fine, JPEG Normal, or JPEG Basic.
   • Image size: Choose image size from, Large, Medium, or Small.
   • White balance: Choose white balance settings; specify fluorescent lighting type; and apply white balance fine-tuning, including photographs taken at a white balance of preset manual, but these can only be subjected to fine-tuning from the preset manual white balance option. The preset manual option is only available for pictures taken at this white balance setting.
   • Exposure compensation: Adjust the exposure level between ±3 Ev.
   • Set Picture Control: Choose a Picture Control option.
4. Highlight the desired option and press ⊛ . Select the required setting and press the ⊛ button to return to the preview image and menu display. Repeat the selection process for any other options to be used.
5. Once all settings have been adjusted, highlight EXE.
6. Press ⊛ to create and save a JPEG copy and return to the full-frame playback.
7. Press the **MENU** button to and return to the full-frame playback without creating a copy image.

Treat the Exposure compensation option with caution, as the ±3 Ev range is overly optimistic. The extended dynamic range of NEF files recorded by the D90 does permit some adjustment to the exposure level, but only across a far more limited range if image quality is to be preserved. I would suggest that ±2 Ev is the practical limit of adjustment using this option, and preferably lower. The original exposure should be as accurate as possible to maximize image quality.

Note: The exposure compensation option cannot be selected if the original picture was taken with Active D-Lighting. Also, the [White balance] option cannot be selected for a copy image created using the [Image overlay] feature. [Preset manual] white balance is only available if the original image was recorded using the [Preset manual] white balance. [White balance] and [Set Picture Control] options are not available for images recorded using the AUTO or Scene exposure modes.

Quick Retouch: This item can be used to make a rapid enhancement to color saturation and contrast; the D90 will apply D-Lighting accordingly to increase the brightness of strongly backlit subjects.

Select an image as described above and press ⓄⓀ to display the image alongside a preview image. Use ⓸ to select one of three values: [Low], [Normal], or [High]. Press and hold Ⓠ to view the preview image full-frame, and press ⓄⓀ to make the copy image. To return to the normal full-frame playback, press the (icon15) button.

Hint: This is about as "quick and dirty" as it gets as far as image adjustment goes; this item should only be considered when the need to expedite an image with adjusted color saturation and contrast is immediate and imperative!

Straighten: How often have you shot a picture with a hand-held camera with a horizon line or an area of water in the scene, only to notice afterwards that the camera was not perfectly horizontal! Nikon has introduced this remedy for the first time in the D90 to help correct sloping horizons.

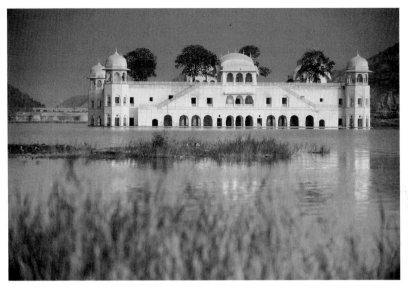

Use the Straighten option to fix lines that should be perfectly horizontal, but do not appear that way in the final image; or use the Distortion Control feature to fix any pincushion or barrel distortion that may occur in your pictures due to lens design.

Select an image as described above and press ⓄⓀ to display the image with a grid line pattern superimposed on it, and a scale (without units) shown along the bottom edge of the screen. Press ▶ to rotate the image clockwise by up to 5° in steps of 0.25°; pressing ◀ rotates the image in the opposite direction. Press ⓄⓀ to create the copy or ▶ to return to the playback display.

Note: To maintain a rectangular image, some degree of cropping will occur as the image is rotated; consequently, the geometry of elements in the image will also change.

⊙ **Distortion Control:** Many lenses, particularly zooms, exhibit optical aberrations that cause straight lines toward the periphery of the image to either bow outwards away from the center of the image (this is know as barrel distortion), or bend inwards toward the center of the image (this is known as pincushion distortion). This retouching item allows you to correct the effects of these types of distortion.

• **[Auto]:** Selecting this option activates automatic application of the distortion control, plus it is possible to apply a fine-tuning by pressing ▶ to reduce barrel distortion and pressing ◀ to reduce pincushion distortion.
• **[Manual]:** Apply distortion correction by pressing ▶ to reduce barrel distortion and pressing (icon123) to reduce pincushion distortion. No automatic correction is applied.

Select [Distortion control] and press ⊛ to display the two options; highlight [Auto] or [Manual] and press ⊙ to display thumbnail images. Select the desired image and press ⊛ . The image is displayed full frame with a scale set along the bottom edge of the screen. Press ◀ or ▶ , and the pointer on the scale will move accordingly. Press ⊛ to save the copy image. To cancel the process, press the ▶ button.

Note: The [Auto] option is intended for use with images recorded using D- and G-type Nikkor lenses (except PC, Fisheye, and the AF 35-70mm f/2.8D lenses).

▦ **Fisheye:** This rather interesting feature emulates the effects of using a non-rectilinear-type fisheye lens, which records straight lines as curved, with an increasing level of distortion the closer the line is to the periphery of the frame.

Select [Fisheye] and press ⊙ to display thumbnail images. Select the required image and press ⊛ . The image is displayed full frame with a scale set along the bottom edge of the screen. Press ◀ , and the pointer on the scale will move accordingly; the further the pointer shifts to

266

the right, the greater the fisheye distortion in the image becomes. Press ⊛ to save the copy image. To cancel the process, press the ▶ button.

Hint: There is a significant amount of cropping at the edges of the original image to fill the rectangular frame as the level of distortion is increased. Therefore, when shooting an image specifically to use this feature, do not frame it too tightly, rather leave plenty of space at the edges of the frame.

■→□ **Side-by-Side Comparison:** Use this item to compare a retouched copy with the original (source) file, as follows:

1. Select either a picture that has been retouched or a retouched copy (indicated by the ⬚ icon) for comparison to the original.
2. Press the ⊛ button to display the original source image to the left and the retouched copy on the right. The options used to create the copy are displayed above the two images.
3. Use ⊕ to switch between the two images; the selected version is shown with a yellow border. Press and hold ⊕ to view an enlarged view of the selected image.
4. If the image was created using the [Image Overlay] option, use ⊕ to view the second source image.
5. Press the **MENU** button to return to the Playback mode.
6. To return to Playback mode with the selected image displayed press ⊛ .

Note: There must be at least one retouched image or retouched copy file stored on the selected memory card for the [Side-by-side] item to be available in the Retouch menu.

📄 Recent Settings / 📋 My Menu

Recent Settings

In either [Recent settings] or [My menu], highlight [Choose tab], and press ⊙ to display two options: [My Menu] and [Recent settings]. Highlight the desired menu and press the 🆗 button.

Up to 20 of the most recently used menu items will be displayed in [Recent settings]. As different menu items are used, they will be added automatically to the top of the Recent Settings menu list in chronological order. To revert back to using the [My Menu] item, open the [Recent settings] item, highlight [Choose tab], and press ⊙ to again display [My Menu] and [Recent settings]. Highlight [My Menu] and press the 🆗 button.

My Menu

The [My Menu] allows you to create a customized menu from practically any combination of items in the Playback, Shooting, Custom Setting, Setup, or Retouch menus. Items can be added, deleted, and reordered at any time. Given the complexity and size of the menu system, this useful feature allows those frequently accessed menu items to be located in a single menu. Up to four items can be added to the [My menu] list of items before it becomes necessary to scroll to additional pages.

Add Menu Items: Follow these steps to add items to the My menu screen:

1. Open [My menu], highlight [Add items], and press ⊙ to display a list of the five primary menus.
2. Highlight the desired menu and press ⊙ .
3. Highlight the desired item within the menu and press the 🆗 button.
4. To position the selected menu item in the [My menu] list, use ▲ and ▼ . Once positioned, press the 🆗 button to add the new item.

Note: Any menu item previously selected and added to [My menu] will be displayed with a check mark when scrolling the various menus via the [Add items] option. Any item that is marked with a square that is scored through cannot be selected for [My menu]—[Format memory card] in the Setup menu, for example.

Delete Menu Items: Follow these steps to delete items from My menu:

1. Open [My menu], highlight [Remove items], and press ⊙ to display the list of items in [My menu].
2. Highlight the item to be removed and press ⊙ ; a check mark will be shown in the box to the right of the selected menu item.
3. To confirm the deletion of the selected item, highlight [Done] and press the ⊛ button. A confirmation dialog box is displayed with the message "Delete selected items?" Press the ⊛ button if you wish to proceed.

Re-order Menu Items: Follow these steps to change the order of items in My menu:

1. Open [My menu], highlight [Rank items], and press ⊙ to display the list of the menu items in [My menu].
2. Highlight the item to be relocated and press ⊛ .
3. Use ▲ and ▼ to position the item within the menu list; a solid yellow line indicates the location for the menu item.
4. Once positioned, press the ⊛ button and the menu item will be moved.

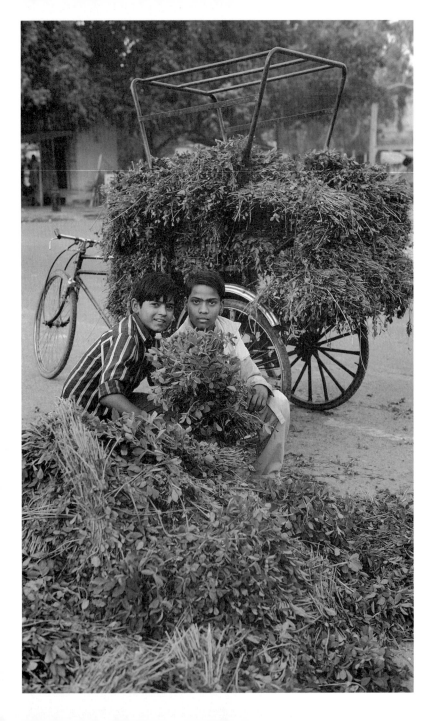

Image Resolution
and Processing

Secure Digital (SD) Memory Cards

These small, solid-state memory cards, which measure 1.3 x 0.9 x 0.08 inches (34 x 22 x 2 mm) offer a capacity of up to 2GB, and are structured rather like the hard drive disk of your computer in that they have a file directory, file allocation table, folders, and individual files. They are capable of retaining data even when they are not powered, and since they have no moving parts, they are reasonably robust, so a minor impact from the card being dropped eight to ten feet (2.7–3 m) or exposure to the natural elements should not cause any problems. Although total immersion in water should be avoided! Obviously, you should treat any memory card with the same care you would your camera equipment, and it is advisable to keep them in the small plastic case that is typically supplied with each card.

Generally, they have a temperature operating range of -4°F to 167°F (-20°C to 75°C), and no altitude limit. SD cards have a small, sliding write-protect switch on one edge that when set to the locked position prevents any data being written to or deleted from the card by either a camera or a computer (if you insert a locked SD card in to the D90, the camera will display $\mathbf{CHR}$ as a warning message). Finally, unlike photographic film, they are not affected by ionizing radiation from X-ray security equipment that is so widely used these days.

↶ *Although SDHC cards are available in capacities up to 32GB, I recommend using several smaller capacity cards, in order to mitigate the consequences of losing or damaging a card.*

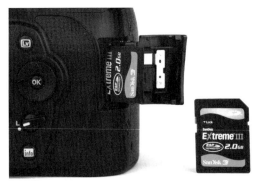

The D90 is compatible with both SD and SDHC memory cards.

Secure Digital High Capacity (SDHC) Memory Cards

To support the larger file sizes generated by contemporary digital cameras and other devices, there has been a growing requirement for SD cards with a capacity in excess of 2GB. To meet this demand, a new design of SD card has been introduced, although they retain the same physical dimensions and write-protect feature of standard SD cards. The new card type complies with the SD specification version 2.0, which supports a card capacity of 4GB and over, and is called Secure Digital High Capacity (SDHC). The SD Association has created and defined three speed classes for performance capabilities/minimum requirements of SDHC cards and products that support the SDHC format. Full details on the SD 2.0 specification can be viewed at: http://www.sdcard.org.

The D90 is fully compatible with memory cards that comply with the SDHC standard and at the time of writing, most manufacturers already offer card capacities up to 16GB, with some producing 32GB cards. While such capacious storage may sound tempting, I believe it is important to consider the potential risks of placing all your proverbial "eggs in one basket," and suggest it would be prudent to spread out the risk of loss or corruption of image data by using a number of cards with smaller capacities.

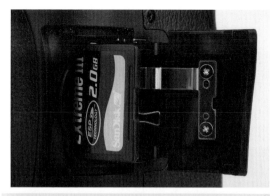

An SD memory card is shown here, partially inserted in the D90.

Note: The D90 supports standard SD cards and SDHC cards; if you use any other device, such as a card reader, it is important to remember that while an SDHC-compliant device supports both SD and SDHC cards, a device that is only compliant with SD cards cannot support SDHC cards.

Insert/Remove Memory Card

Before inserting a memory card in the D90, switch the power off. Open the card port door by sliding it toward the back of the camera; the door will spring open and swing back to reveal the memory card port. Insert the card with its contact terminals pointing toward the front of the camera and the main (top) label of the card facing toward the back of the camera (i.e., toward yourself, assuming the camera is being held normally). The card will slide in so far and then you will feel a slight resistance. Keep pushing the card until it locks in to place (the green memory card access lamp illuminates briefly as a confirmation that the card is installed properly). If **Far** is displayed in the control panel, the memory card requires formatting (see pages 277-278).

To remove the card, switch the camera off, open the card port door, and press the exposed edge of the card toward the camera, and then release it. The card will pop out of its port so far; then just slide it free from the camera. Memory cards can become warm during use; this is normal and not an indication of a problem.

If no memory card is inserted when a charged battery is installed in the camera or it is connected to an AC power supply, and the camera is powered on, (**-E-**) appears within the exposure counter brackets in both the viewfinder and control panel displays. If the camera is turned off while a charged battery is installed and there is no memory card, then (**-E-**) is only displayed in the control panel.

The SD and SDHC cards used by the D90 have a write-protect switch that can be used to prevent inadvertent loss of data; when this switch is in the locked position, data cannot be written to or deleted from the memory card, and the card cannot be formatted. To use the card, slide the switch out of the locked position.

Approved Memory Cards
There are a plethora of memory cards on the market, but Nikon has only tested and approved those listed in the table below for use with the D90.

SD and SDHC card technology is well established, so although Nikon will not guarantee operation with other makes of cards, you should not experience any problems or have any concerns if you use an alternative brand. If you have any doubt, test your memory card before using it to record any important pictures.

Nikon Approved Memory Cards for the D90
All cards of make and capacity listed here can be used, regardless of their read/write speed.

Manufacturer	Card Capacity
Lexar Media	512MB, 1GB, 2GB, and 4GB Platinum II: 512MB, 1GB, 2GB, and 4GB Professional: 1GB, 2GB, and 4GB
Panasonic	512MB, 1GB, 2GB, 4GB, 8GB, 16GB, and 32GB
SanDisk	512MB, 1GB, 2GB, 4GB, and 8GB
Toshiba	512MB, 1GB, 2GB, 4GB, 8GB, 16GB, and 32GB

Nikon states that other brands and capacities of cards have not been tested with the D90; therefore, operation cannot be guaranteed. Although problems are unlikely to occur, always test a new memory card a few times before using it for any important photography. Should you experience any problems related to the memory card, use one of the approved cards for the purpose of troubleshooting.

Memory Card Capacity

When considering the capacity of the memory cards you will use, bear in mind that the 12.3MP resolution of the D90 will result in larger file sizes compared with those of lower resolution cameras, such as the D200 or the D80 models. So, if you regularly use 1GB or 2GB memory cards with your 6 to 10MP digital SLR, you may want to think about stepping up to 4GB. On average, I find when shooting NEF (RAW) files I can expect to record about 250 to 270 images on a 4GB card. This provides plenty of scope, especially if you shoot for techniques such as high dynamic range (HDR) or panoramic, which require stitching multiple images together. I find that a 4GB card offers a good compromise between storage capacity and the risks (card failure or loss) inherent with saving all your shots to a single, higher capacity 8GB or 16GB card. Furthermore, if you expect to make regular use of the video recording capability of the D90, you will want to use at least a 4GB card and probably even an 8GB one, as the video recording consumes storage at a rate of about 100MB/minute, or about 2GB for two five-minute clips.

The table on the next page provides information on the approximate number of images that can be stored on a typical 2GB SD memory card at the various image quality and size settings available on the D90. All memory cards use a small proportion of their memory capacity to store data required for the card to operate. Therefore, the amount of memory available for storing image files will be slightly less than the quoted maximum capacity of the card. Likewise, capacities may vary slightly if you use a different brand of memory card.

Quality	Image Size	File Size (MB)[1]	No. Images[1]	Buffer Capacity[2]
NEF (RAW)	–	10.8	133	9
NEF (RAW) +	L	16.9	89	7
JPEG Fine [3]	M	14.4	104	7
	S	12.4	118	7
NEF (RAW) +	L	13.9	106	7
JPEG Normal [3]	M	12.6	116	7
	S	11.6	124	7
NEF (RAW) +	L	12.3	118	7
JPEG Basic [3]	M	11.7	123	7
	S	11.2	128	7
JPEG Fine	L	6.0	271	25
	M	3.4	480	100
	S	1.6	1000	100
JPEG Normal	L	3.0	539	100
	M	1.7	931	100
	S	0.8	2000	100
JPEG Basic	L	1.5	1000	100
	M	0.9	1800	100
	S	0.4	3800	100

1. File size will vary according to the scene photographed and the make of memory card used. Therefore, all figures are approximate.
2. This is the maximum number of image files that can be stored in the buffer memory. Capacity of the buffer will be reduced by the following: ISO sensitivity is set to Hi 0.3 or higher, [High ISO NR] is [On] while ISO is set to 800 or higher, long exposure noise reduction is on, or Active D-lighting is on.
3. File size is the combined total for the NEF (RAW) and JPEG files. The size of an NEF (RAW) file cannot be altered, so the image size applies to JPEG files only.

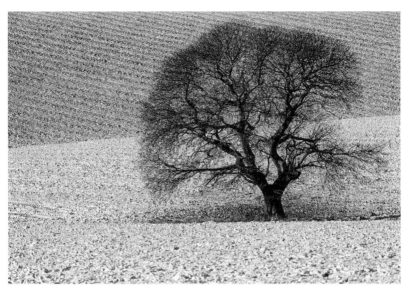

Although Nikon states that formatting a memory card will delete all the images on it, this is only partly true. If you have accidentally formatted a card, there is a good chance that using an image-recovery software, you can rescue the deleted photos, particularly if you have yet to record any new images on the card since it was formatted.

Formatting a Memory Card

As mentioned earlier in this chapter, the memory of a Secure Digital card is similar a hard disk drive. As data is written to and deleted from the card, small areas of its memory can become corrupted and files can become fragmented. This is particularly true if you delete individual image files. Formatting the card in the camera will clean up the majority of the worst effects of fragmentation.

In the D90 instruction book, Nikon states that formatting memory cards will "permanently delete any data they may contain." While this is a salutary warning, it is somewhat misleading. The formatting process actually causes the existing file directory information to be overwritten, so that the indicators that direct any reading device, including the camera itself, to the image data held on the card are removed; it does not actually delete/erase all the data, as Nikon claims.

This makes it extremely difficult, although not impossible, to recover previously written data from a card once it is formatted. If you inadvertently format a card, it is often possible to recover the image files by using appropriate recovery software, provided no further data is written to the card. Since prevention is better than a cure, always save your images to a computer or other storage device before formatting a card. Also, make sure to create back-up copies of these files.

To format a card using the D90, insert a memory card and turn the camera on. Press and hold the FORMAT buttons (☷ & 🗑) for approximately two seconds until **Fo⌐** flashes in the control panel, together with a flashing frame count display. To proceed with the formatting process, you must release the FORMAT buttons momentarily and then press them again. Alternatively, you can use the [Format] option in the Setup menu.

During formatting, **Fo⌐** appears continuously in place of the shutter speed display of the control panel and viewfinder. Once complete, the remaining exposure display shows the approximate number of photographs that can be recorded on the installed memory card at the current size and quality settings. The displayed figure is only an approximation because file size will vary due to file compression; it is often possible for the camera to record and store more images than the remaining exposure count display suggests initially after formatting.

Hint: After ensuring its contents have been saved and backed up, the memory card should be formatted each time you insert it into the camera. This is especially important if it has been used in a different camera model or formatted by a computer or other device. Failure to follow this procedure may lead to image files being rendered unreadable or becoming corrupted.

Note: If you press any other button after **Fo⌐** begins to flash, the format function is cancelled, and the camera returns to its previous state.

Note: You should never switch the camera off or otherwise inter-rupt the power supply to the camera during the formatting process, as this can result in corruption of the memory card.

Image Quality and File Formats

The D90 saves still picture images to the memory card in two file formats, Joint Photographic Experts Group (JPEG) and Nikon Electronic File (NEF) RAW format, which are dis-cussed at length in the following sections.

When it records video, the D90 uses the Open DML JPEG video format, which is known more commonly as Motion JPEG (M-JPEG). These files are saved as Audio Video Inter-leave (AVI) files (see page 124 for full details).

Expeed Image Processing

Expeed is the generic name given by Nikon to its latest in-camera image-processing regime; in combination with the Picture Control System (see pages 77-79 for more informa-tion), its purpose is to ensure consistency in the appearance of images in terms of color and contrast, although compo-nent parts of the system—both hardware and software—may differ from camera model to camera model. If you have the experience of shooting film, it might help to understand the concept by thinking about the way a specific film can be matched with particular developer to produce consistent, repeatable results, regardless of which camera was used.

The Expeed processing concept is applied to the D90, and is the same as that used by the D300, D700, and D3 models. When the camera is set to record images in the JPEG file format, it uses the integrated ADC (analog to digital converter) on the sensor to convert the electrical signals generated by the photodiodes at a 12-bit depth to produce 12-bit raw data before the value for each pixel is rendered via a de-mosaicing (conversion) process to 12-bit RGB data. Remember, each photodiode only records a value for red, green, or blue, so the de-mosaicing process is necessary to render an RGB value for each pixel.

Next, the 12-bit RGB data is passed to the Expeed processing engine where all further processing, such as color manipulation, contrast control, and sharpening (plus an automated reduction of the effects of lateral chromatic aberration to reduce color fringing at distinct edges in image detail) is performed in a 16-bit depth space to ensure that there is no compromise of the data. The final stage of the image processing is the encoding of the data to create the JPEG file; it is only at this point that the 12-bit data is reduced to 8-bit. The result is a noticeable improvement in image quality compared with JPEG files generated by earlier Nikon D-SLR camera models, particularly in the lower shadow tones. This is of particular benefit if the finished 8-bit JPEG files are to be subjected to post-processing in a computer, which would otherwise compound errors generated during in-camera processing had this been performed on 8-bit data rather than the 12-bit data handled by the D90.

When the D90 is set to record an image in the Nikon Electronic File (NEF) format, the data saved is essentially the "raw" data generated by the ADC with no interpolation or other adjustment of the information from the sensor. The settings for the Picture Control System are not applied in-camera, but recorded and appended to the RAW file as a set of instructions to be read by the file converter used to open the NEF (RAW) file subsequently. The lack of processing is the reason such files are referred to as "RAW" files, and the ability to modify the instruction set to each RAW file at any subsequent point after the original image is recorded in a camera is the key to the tremendous flexibility offered by this particular format.

However, unlike other more highly specified Nikon camera models, which offer a choice of bit depth, the D90 can only record NEF files at a 12-bit depth and it always applies compression to the image data. So, the ADC performs the conversion of the information from the sensor at 12-bits. The data is maintained in the selected bit depth while it is built and output, which means that at a 12-bit depth, each pixel can have one of 4,096 distinct values. Essentially, an NEF file uses the same structure as a TIFF file; it starts with tags that point to the EXIF (camera settings) and white balance value information, then saves a small thumbnail image as a JPEG file, followed by the raw pixel data. However, since the D90 can only save NEF files in a compressed form, some of the original information captured by the sensor is discarded in a process that Nikon describes as being "visually lossless" (see pages 286-288 for the explanation of what actually occurs).

To summarize, when comparing between the JPEG and NEF formats, the principal differences lie in how the camera deals with the data from the sensor that forms the image. Using the JPEG format, the camera produces a finished image, based on the sensor data and camera settings at the time of the exposure, selected by either you or the camera. Although it is possible to use these finished files directly from the camera to produce a print or post to a web site, these files can still be post-processed after they have been imported to a computer if required. However, using the NEF format requires the work necessary to produce a finished image to be done by the photographer, after the fact, using a computer with NEF compatible software.

If you are beginning to form the impression that to eek out every last ounce of quality the D90 has to offer you should shoot in the NEF format, you are not too far off the mark! However, while many photographers refer to the NEF format as being better than JPEG or TIFF, I prefer to consider this issue in terms of the flexibility the formats offer and recommend that you use the one that is best suited to your specific requirements.

JPEG

Probably the greatest benefit of the JPEG format it that it can be read by most software and it supported by HTML, the computer language used to build web pages. Such ubiquitous acceptance of the JPEG format enables these files to be shared widely, regardless of the type of computer or software that may be used.

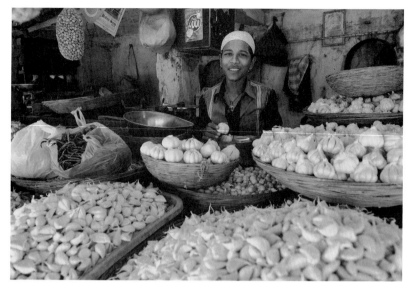

Although JPEG image files degrade each time they are altered and resaved, they offer the benefit of being small and manageable file types. If you plan to print directly from the camera or memory card, without performing any post-processing, I recommend shooting JPEGs.

Note: Strictly speaking, JPEG is a data compression regime and not a file format, but since a file saved using this regime is usually assigned an extension of .jpg or .jpeg, common convention refers to JPEG as a file format.

The process of saving a file as a JPEG involves taking 8 x 8 blocks of pixels and subjecting each block to a series of calculations that determines the compression of the file. Essentially, the numerical values of the pixels are converted into an equation that represents an average value of the pixels in that block. The compressed result for each block is then brought together as a single sequence of binary values, which is encoded using a further lossless form of compression. While the compression process varies, depending on the range of pixel values in each block, it will ultimately result in the permanent loss of some data. As a rule of thumb, using a JPEG compression ratio of 1:4 or less will produce an image in which the effects of the compression process are all but imperceptible. However, the JPEG format has three properties that can potentially influence image quality in an adverse manner:

1. The in-camera processing reduces the 12-bit data from the sensor to 8-bit values when it creates a JPEG file. The D90 does offer the advantage that it makes all in-camera adjustments to image attributes (i.e., sharpening, contrast, and saturation) at a 12-bit level before the data is reduced to an 8-bit level. Therefore, if you have no intention of doing any post processing work on your images, the reduction to 8-bits is of no real consequence. However, if you make significant changes to an image using software in post processing, the 8-bit data of a JPEG file can impose limits on the degree of manipulation that can be applied. This is particularly true with the level of color, sharpening, and contrast adjustments that can be made. In respect of the two latter attributes, it appears that Nikon has changed course somewhat with the D90, insomuch as the default settings for both are appreciably lower compared with their other recent D-SLR camera models; as a consequence, JPEG files straight from the D90 look noticeably softer and have a flatter contrast.

2. When the camera saves an image using the JPEG format, it encodes most of the camera settings for attributes such as white balance, sharpening, contrast, saturation, and hue into the image data. If you make an error and inadvertently select the wrong setting, you will need to try to fix your mistake in post-processing. Inevitably, this is time-consuming and there is no guarantee it will be successful, particularly if you're trying to reduce the effects of over-sharpening, reduce contrast, or correct color because the wrong white balance setting was used for the original image.

3. The technology of digital imaging is fast-paced and the electronics used in any particular camera are only as good as the day the manufacturer decided on the specifications and finalized the design of the camera. Granted, most modern cameras can have their firmware (installed software) upgraded by the user. This helps to offset obsolescence, but it is only effective for so long. By processing images in software on a computer, you can often take advantage of the very latest advances in image processing, which are unavailable in the camera.

JPEG Image Quality: The D90 allows you to save JPEG files at one of three different levels of quality.

- **FINE:** Uses a low compression ratio of approximately 1:4
- **NORMAL (default):** Uses a moderate compression ratio of approximately 1:8
- **BASIC:** Uses a high compression ratio of approximately 1:16

As the processing involved in the creation of JPEG files uses compression that discards data, to maintain the highest image quality you should select the lowest level of compression. A file saved at the FINE setting will be visually superior to a file saved at the BASIC setting.

JPEG Image Size: Each JPEG can be saved by the D90 at one of three different sizes:

- **L:** Large (4,288 x 2,848 pixels)
- **M:** Medium (3,216 x 2,136 pixels)
- **S:** Small (2,144 x 1,424 pixels)

Note: JPEG compression can generate visual "artifacts." The higher the compression ratio and smaller the image size, the more apparent these become. If you are shooting for web publication, this is unlikely to be an issue, but if you intend to make prints from your JPEG file pictures, you will probably want to use the Large FINE settings.

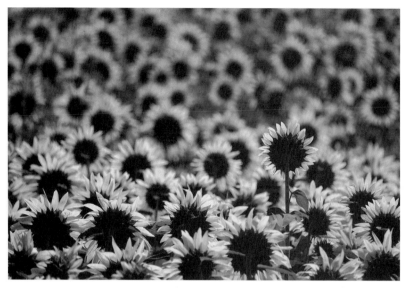

RAW image files are ideal for getting the best possible image quality and flexibility out of your pictures. Although they require some post-processing, the ability to change exposure and white balance settings, among other things, makes the additional work worthwhile.

Note: Image size is not applicable to NEF files, which always have the dimensions of an image saved at the [Large] size option when opened in appropriate software, such as Nikon View NX or Nikon Capture NX2.

NEF (RAW)

Using the NEF format has only two real disadvantages in my mind—the extra time you will need to invest in post-processing each image to produce a finished picture is one. The larger file size of the NEF format can present an issue in terms of the amount of available storage in your memory card or external storage device. But modern data storage devices are relatively cheap, so this shouldn't be too much of a concern. Equally, there can be limitations and variability with a third party software's ability to read and interpret Nikon NEF files.

The benefits of NEF format include:

- More consistent and smoother tonal gradations
- Color that is more subtle and accurate to the original subject or scene
- A slight increase in the level of detail that is resolved compared with JPEG
- The ability (within certain parameters) to adjust exposure in post-processing to correct for slight exposure errors, or to help extend the dynamic range of an image; for example, it is often possible to gain an extra stop (1EV) in the highlights of an image to reveal more detail and tonal gradation
- The increased post-processing ability to correct and/or change image color by resetting attributes such as the white balance value, saturation, and hue; plus, control over image contrast and brightness is also improved

Note: NEF (RAW) files taken with the D90 using the [Monochrome] option in the Set Picture Control menu are only slightly smaller than color files because the NEF file retains all of the original data, including the color information. Consequently, using the appropriate options in a RAW file converter, an NEF file saved as a black-and-white image can be converted to produce a color image.

Note: Black-and-white NEF (RAW) files from the D90 are slightly smaller than color NEF (RAW) files only due to the thumbnail image embedded in the NEF file being a smaller grayscale file with no color information.

Compressed NEF (RAW): Since you have no option but to record compressed NEF (RAW) files with the D90, the question is what, if any, effect does this have on image quality, because when the camera records a compressed NEF file, some of the image data is discarded.

Nikon has described the compression applied to NEF files as "visually lossless," by which they mean it is almost impossible to visually differentiate between an image produced from an uncompressed file and one produced from a compressed file.

The compression process used by Nikon is selective; it only works on certain image data while leaving other data unaffected. Nikon's use of the word "compression" in this context is rather misleading, as the process involves two distinct phases. The first phase sees certain tonal values grouped and then rounded, and the second phase is the point at which a conventional, lossless compression is applied. Once the analog signal from the sensor has been converted to digital data, the first phase of the compression process separates the values that represent the very darkest tones from the rest of the data. Then, the data with values that represent the remaining lighter tones are divided into groups, but this process is not linear. As the tones become lighter, the size of the group increases, so the group with the lightest tones is larger than a group containing midtone values. A lossless compression is then applied to each individual dark tone value and the rounded value of each group in the midtones and light tones.

When an application such as Nikon Capture NX2 opens an NEF (RAW) file recorded by the D90, it reverses the lossless compression process. The individual dark tone values are unaffected (remember, the compression applied here is lossless) but, and here is the twist, each of the grouped values for the midtones and light tones must be expanded to fit its original range. Since the rounding error in each group becomes progressively larger as the tonal values it represents become lighter and lighter, the gaps in the data caused by the rounding process also become progressively larger at lighter tonal values.

It is important to put these data gaps into perspective. A single compression/decompression cycle performed on an NEF file produces an image that is for most intents and purposes indistinguishable from one produced from an uncompressed NEF file. The human eye does not respond in a linear way to increased levels of brightness; therefore it is incapable of resolving the very minor changes that have taken place, even in the lightest tones where the rounding error is greatest and therefore the data gap is largest (remember Nikon's phrase, "visually lossless").

Furthermore, our eyes are generally only capable of detecting tonal variations equivalent to those produced by 8-bit data. Since even a compressed NEF file has the equivalent to more than 8-bit data, the data gaps caused by Nikon's compression process are of no consequence. Similarly, many photographers will ultimately reduce their 12-bit NEF file to an 8-bit RGB TIFF or JPEG file prior to printing, which can mask any loss of tonal gradation caused by compressing the original NEF file.

In spite of our eyes' inability to recognize these changes, it is important to understand that the data loss caused by compression of an NEF (RAW) file can affect final image quality. Thankfully, this unwanted effect is rare and is likely to only to manifest in the highlight area(s) of an image that has been subjected to a significant level of color and/or contrast adjustment during post-processing, or where excessive sharpening is applied; the result can be posterization, which creates course shifts in color and tone where there should be gentle, smooth transitions.

Which Format?

In considering the attributes of the JPEG and NEF formats, many photographers make an analogy with film photography; they consider the NEF file as though they have the original film negative to work from, and the JPEG file as being akin to a machine-processed print. I do not disagree, but this is where my point about the flexibility of the two formats comes back to be relevant; not every photographer has the desire, ability, or time to spend post-processing NEF files. The good news is that we have a choice, so consider the points made in this section and make your decision based on which format is best suited to your purposes. If you have sufficient storage capacity on your memory card(s), you could always select one of the NEF + JPEG combinations from the [Image Quality] options, as the D90 can record a picture in both formats simultaneously.

Setting Image Quality and Size

To set image quality on the D90, open the Shooting menu and use (⊕) to highlight the [Image Quality] option, press (⊕) to open the list of options and use (⊕) to highlight the required setting, then press the (OK) button to confirm the selection. Alternatively, and in my opinion by far the more convenient and quicker way to select image quality, is to use the button and dial method. Press and hold the **QUAL** button and rotate the main command dial; the selected value is displayed in the control panel. There are seven options available: NEF (RAW), JPEG Fine, JPEG Normal, JPEG Basic, NEF + JPEG Fine, NEF + JPEG Normal, and NEF + JPEG Basic.

To set image size for the JPEG format on the D90, open the Shooting menu and use (⊕) to highlight the [Image Size] option (note if you only have NEF selected for [Image Quality], this option is grayed out); press (⊕) to open the list of options and use (⊕) to highlight the required setting. Again, in my opinion, using the alternative button and dial method is the more convenient and quicker way. Press and hold the **QUAL** button, then rotate the sub-command dial; the selected value is displayed in the control panel as L (large), M (medium), or S (small).

Note: At the NEF + JPEG Fine, NEF + JPEG Normal, and NEF + JPEG Basic settings, two images are recorded—one NEF and a JPEG at the relevant image quality, but always at an image size of [Large]. When reviewing a picture recorded using one of the dual-format options, only the JPEG image is displayed; however, when pictures recorded at these settings are deleted, both image files are deleted.

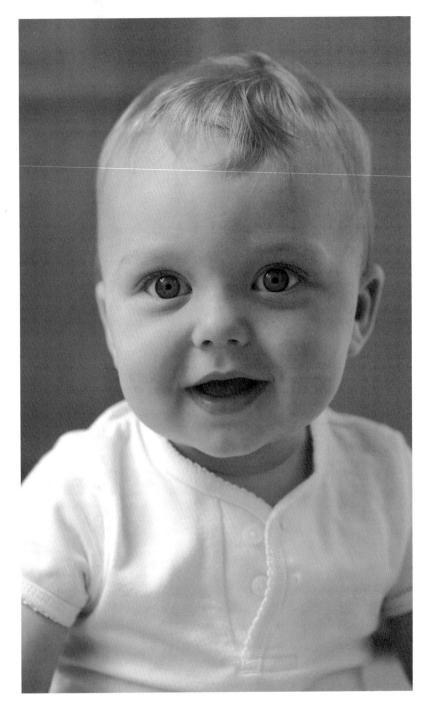

Nikon Flash Photography

Before we take a look at the flash capabilities of the D90, it is important to understand a little bit about the physics of light and flash exposure. Light from a flash unit falls off, as it does from any light source, by what is known as the Inverse Square Law; put simply, if you double the distance from a light source, its intensity drops by a factor of four. This is because as light travels it spreads out and subsequently illuminates a wider area. Since a flash unit emits a precise level of light, it will only light the subject correctly at a specific distance, depending on the intensity of the light, the lens aperture, and the ISO sensitivity. If the flash correctly exposes the subject, anything closer to the flash will be overexposed and anything farther away will be increasingly underexposed. So, to produce a balanced exposure between the subject and its surroundings, particularly the background, it is often necessary to balance the light from the flash with the ambient light.

The output of an electronic flash unit is quantified by its guide number (GN). The higher the guide number, the more powerful the flash unit. Guide numbers are stated at a given ISO and are expressed in either feet or meters, so make sure when comparing guide numbers that you are working with the same system of measurement and ISO value. The formula for guide number is GN = distance x aperture. Zoom head position also affects guide number.

◁ *Flash may be one of the most challenging aspects of photography, but this chapter will give you the tools to use it confidently and effectively.*

The SB-600 is one of several flash units that are totally compatible with Nikon's new Creative Lighting System.

The Creative Lighting System (CLS)

Nikon's most sophisticated flash control system to date, the CLS encompasses a range of features and functions that is as much a part of the cameras as it is of the Speedlight flash units themselves. These features include: i-TTL, Advanced Wireless Lighting that provides wireless control of multiple Speedlights using i-TTL flash exposure control, Flash Value (FV) Lock, Flash Color Information Communication, Auto FP High-Speed Sync, and Wide-Area AF-Assist Illuminator. The CLS has expanded and, at present, camera compatibility extends to the D3, D2-series, D700, D300, D200, D90,

D80, D70-series, D60, D50, D40-series, and F6 cameras, although the D70-series, D60, D50, and D40-series camera models do not support all the features of the CLS.

TTL Flash Modes

The D90 supports two methods for TTL control flash exposure, either with its built-in flash unit or with a compatible external Speedlight, when used in combination with a CPU-type lens.

i-TTL Balanced Fill-flash
This is Nikon's third generation of TTL flash exposure control—the most sophisticated to date. When the D90 is set to Matrix metering, a D- or G-type Nikkor lens is mounted, and the built-in Speedlight (or an external Speedlight such as the SB-600, SB-800, or SB-900) is activated, i-TTL Balanced Fill-flash will attempt to balance the ambient light to the flash output.

It is important to note that whenever you see the term i-TTL Balanced Fill-flash, existing ambient light and flash are being mixed in a fully automated process to produce the final exposure; how the two light sources are mixed and in what proportion will depend on a wide variety of factors, including ISO sensitivity, lens aperture, exposure mode, exposure compensation value, brightness of both the ambient and flash illumination, and nature of the scene being photographed.

If you want to achieve consistent, repeatable results when using a true fill-flash technique—where the flash is the supplementary light—I recommend you use standard i-TTL flash, as any flash output compensation, or exposure compensation you set will be applied without influence from the camera. Likewise, in any situation where you wish to use flash as the main source of illumination and have control over the flash output level as well as the exposure of ambient light, I suggest you select standard i-TTL flash.

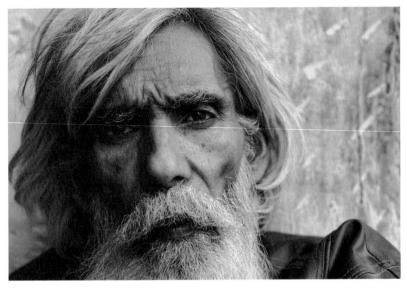

When using fill-flash, or when the exposure of the background is relatively unimportant, Standard i-TTL flash may be the better option.

Standard i-TTL Flash

This differs from the i-TTL Balanced Fill-flash method just described in that the 420-pixel RGB metering sensor and the metering system of the D90 only determines the output of the flash. The measurement of ambient light in the scene remains wholly independent, and is not integrated in any way with the flash exposure calculations. For reasons explained above, Standard i-TTL flash exposure control is often the best option when the flash exposure of the main subject is the priority, or when flash output compensation is used, for example with fill-flash.

Note: Selecting spot metering on the D90 will cause the flash exposure control of the built-in Speedlight and the SB-400, SB-600, SB-800 and SB-900 to default to standard i-TTL flash.

Using i-TTL Flash Exposure Control

i-TTL offers an enhanced and refined method of flash exposure control. Currently, the SB-900, SB-800, SB-600, SB-400, and SB-R200 are the only external Speedlights that support i-TTL and the CLS, while the SU-800 Wireless Speedlight Commander can be used to control any of these units with the exception of the SB-400. If any other external Nikon Speedlight is attached to the D90, TTL flash exposure control is not supported; this applies to all earlier Speedlights, even DX-type Speedlights like the SB-80DX, designed for earlier digital SLR cameras.

The following are technical details on how i-TTL works with the D90:

- i-TTL uses fewer monitor pre-flashes than other systems, but they have a higher intensity. This greater intensity improves the efficiency of obtaining a measurement from the TTL flash sensor, and by using fewer pulses, the amount of time taken to perform the assessment is reduced. This enables the camera to perform flash output assessment before the mirror lifts.
- The D90 uses its 420-pixel RGB metering sensor located in the prism head to control flash exposure, regardless of whether a single Speedlight or multiple Speedlights is/are used as part of a wireless TTL configuration. In both configurations, monitor pre-flashes are always emitted before the reflex mirror is raised.
- The i-TTL system is designed to work with ISO sensitivities between 200 and 6400; Nikon states that outside of this range, flash exposure control may be less accurate.

The following is a summary of the sequence of events used to calculate flash exposure in the D90, when it is used with a single or multiple compatible Speedlights (i.e., SB-900, SB-800, SB-600, SB-400, or SB-R200) and a D- or G-type Nikkor lens:

1. Once the shutter release is pressed, the camera reads the focus distance from the D- or G-type lens.

2. The camera sends a signal to the Speedlight to initiate the pre-flash system, which then emits the monitor pre-flashes (pulses of light) from the Speedlight(s).

3. The light from these pre-flashes is bounced back from the scene, through the lens, and onto the 420-pixel RGB metering sensor via the reflex mirror.

4. The information from the pre-flashes gathered by the 420-pixel RGB metering sensor is analyzed along with measurements of the ambient light in the scene and information supplied by the focusing system. The camera then determines the amount of light required from the Speedlight(s) and sets the duration of the flash discharge accordingly.

5. The reflex mirror lifts up out of the light path to the shutter, and the shutter opens.

6. The camera sends a signal to the Speedlight(s) to initiate the main flash discharge, which is quenched the instant the amount of light pre-determined in Step 4 has been emitted.

7. The shutter closes at the end of the predetermined shutter speed duration, and the reflex mirror is lowered to its normal position.

Note: In the D90, the emission of the monitor pre-flashes occurs before the reflex mirror is raised. Thus, there is a slight chance that, during the short delay between the mirror being raised and the shutter opening, the light from the pre-flash may cause the subject to blink.

Note: Due to its design, the SB-R200 cannot be mounted on the accessory shoe of a camera; it can only be used as a wireless remote flash controlled by either the SU-800 Commander unit, an SB-800 Speedlight, or the SB-900 Speedlight.

Flash Output Assessment

The crucial phase in the sequence described above is step 4, which is the point when the required output from the flash is calculated. As stated previously, this is accomplished using the D90's 420-pixel RGB metering sensor that is positioned in the viewfinder head. The ability of this sensor is enhanced by the

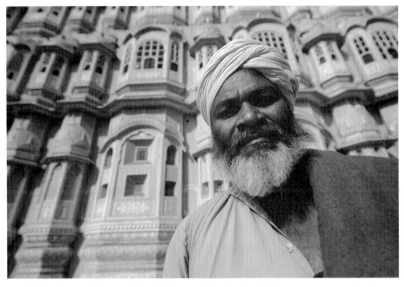

The Scene Recognition System detects typical image components like faces, buildings, landscapes, and backgrounds to determine how to expose each photo, and it is particularly sensitive to skin-tones. The D90's i-TTL flash works with the SRS to help achieve evenly exposed flash pictures.

recently developed Scene Recognition System (SRS), which made its debut in the D300 in mid-2007. It separates light into its component colors using a diffraction grating, enabling the 420-pixel sensor to recognize shapes and objects by the distribution of color and contrast, so it can work more effectively and efficiently. It is particularly sensitive to skin tones. This Scene Recognition System operates only with Matrix metering; if center-weighted or spot metering is selected, the D90 uses a simple grayscale metering system (i.e., it is not sensitive to color).

This evaluation of the shape and color of elements in the scene is performed together with conventional assessments of overall levels of brightness and contrast. These are combined with information from the autofocus (AF) system, which determines the approximate distance of the subject from the flash and its location within the frame (the camera assumes the subject is at the point of focus).

The camera compares the relative brightness of each Matrix metering segment using its 420-pixel RGB meter. For example, if a majority of the segments in the outer parts of the frame exhibit a high level of brightness and those close to the center of the frame have a much lower level of brightness, the system is likely to conclude that there is strongly backlit subject near the center of the frame.

Once the camera has collected all the information pertaining to the shapes, colors, brightness, and range of contrast in the scene, it compares these values against information from actual photographs held in a database of over 30,000 sample exposures, covering an enormous range of lighting conditions. If the first comparison generates conflicting assessments, the segment pattern may be re-configured and further analysis performed. For example, if any segment (or group of segments) reports an abnormally high level of brightness in comparison to the others, the metering system will usually ignore this information in its flash exposure calculations. This might occur if there is a highly reflective surface such as glass or a mirror in a part of the scene.

Focus Information

Focus information is provided in two forms: camera-to-subject distance, and the level of focus/defocus at each focus point. Generally, the focus distance information will influence which segment(s) of the 420-pixel RGB metering sensor affect overall exposure calculations. For example, assuming the subject is positioned in the center of the frame and the lens is focused at a short range, the camera will generally place more emphasis on those segments that cover the outer part of the frame area and less on the central ones. An exception to this occurs if the camera detects a very high level of contrast between the central and outer areas of the frame; it may, and often does, reverse the emphasis and weights the exposure according to the information received from central segments of the 420-pixel RGB metering sensor. Conversely, if the subject is positioned in the center of the frame and the lens is focused at a mid-to long range, the camera will place more emphasis on the segments at the center of the frame and less on those in the outer areas. Essentially, what the camera is trying to do in both cases is prevent overexposure of the subject, which it assumes is in the center of the frame.

Note: There must be a D- or G-type lens mounted on the camera for the focus distance information to be accurately assessed.

Individual focus point information is integrated with focus distance information, as each AF point is checked for its degree of focus. This provides the camera with information about the probable location of the subject within the area of the scene. Using the examples given in the previous paragraph, the camera notes that the central AF point has acquired focus while the other AF points each report varying levels of defocus. Therefore, exposure is calculated on the assumption that the subject is in the center of the frame and the camera biases its computations according to the focus distance information it receives from the lens as described.

However, it is important to understand that other twists occur in this story of interaction between exposure calculation and focus information. For example, when you acquire and lock focus on a subject using the center AF point and then recompose the shot so that the subject is located elsewhere in the frame (the central AF point consequently no longer detects focus), the camera will generally use the exposure value it calculated when it first acquired focus. However, if it detects that the level of brightness detected by the metering segments at the center of the frame has changed significantly from the level when focus was first acquired with the subject at that position, the camera can, and often does adjust its exposure calculations—sometimes not necessarily for the better. To help improve flash exposure accuracy in such situations, use the flash value (FV) lock feature (see pages 319-320).

The Built-in Speedlight

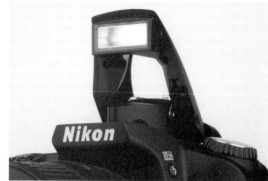

The built-in Speedlight of the D90 has a Guide Number of 56 feet at ISO 200 in its automatic mode.

The D90 has a built-in Speedlight with an automatic flash Guide Number of 56 feet (17 m) at ISO 200, 68°F (20°C), and 59 feet (18 m), ISO 200, 68°F (20°C) for manual flash. The camera has a standard flash synchronization speed of 1/200 second, although this can be increased when using an external Speedlight that supports the Auto FP high-speed flash sync feature of the CLS. There is a minimum range of 2 feet (0.6 m) below which the camera will not necessarily calculate a correct flash exposure. Operation of the built-in Speedlight must be selected manually in P, S, A, and M modes by pressing the ⚡ flash release button that is

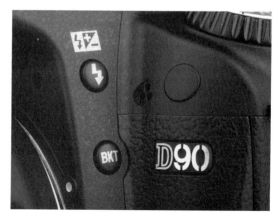

The release button for the built-in flash can be seen in the top left of this picture.

located immediately below the ⚡️ flash exposure compensation icon on the lower left side of the viewfinder head, which will cause the flash head to lift. If the camera is set to one of the automatic Scene modes and the meter determines that flash is needed, it will pop up automatically.

The built-in Speedlight draws its power from the camera's main battery, so extended use of the flash will have a direct effect on battery life. As soon as the flash unit pops up, it begins to charge. The flash-ready symbol ⚡ appears in the viewfinder to indicate charging is complete and the flash is ready to fire. If the flash fires at its maximum output, the same flash-ready symbol will blink for approximately three seconds after the exposure has been made, as a warning of potential underexposure (see page 318 for details on how to apply flash output compensation to the built-in Speedlight). The flash-ready symbol operates in exactly the same way when an external Speedlight is attached and switched on as it does with the built-in Speedlight.

Range, Aperture, and ISO Sensitivity
The built-in flash unit's shooting range will vary depending on the values set for the lens aperture and ISO sensitivity:

Lens aperture at ISO (sensitivity)					Range	
200	400	800	1600	3200	Meters	Feet
1.4	2	2.8	4	5.6	1.0 - 8.5	3' 3" – 27' 11"
2	2.8	4	5.6	8	0.7 - 6.1	2' 4" – 20'
2.8	4	5.6	8	11	0.6 - 4.2	2' – 13' 9"
4	5.6	8	11	16	0.6 - 3.0	2' – 9' 10"
5.6	8	11	16	22	0.6 - 2.1	2' – 6' 11"
8	11	16	22	32	0.6 - 1.5	2' – 4' 11"
11	16	22	32	-	0.6 - 1.1	2' – 3' 7"
16	22	32	-	-	0.6 - 0.8	2' – 2' 7"

Limitations of the Built-in Speedlight
While the built-in Speedlight of the D90 is not as powerful as an external Speedlight, it can still provide a useful level of illumination at short ranges; especially for the purpose of

fill-flash, since it supports flash output level compensation. However, if you want to use this built-in Speedlight as the main light source, you should be aware of the following:

- The Guide Number (GN) is limited, thus flash shooting ranges are relatively short (see table above).
- The proximity of the flash head of the built-in Speedlights is much closer to the central lens axis compared with an external flash; hence, the likelihood of red-eye occurring is increased significantly.
- This close proximity of the built-in Speedlight to the central lens axis often means that the lens obscures the output of the flash, especially if it has a lens hood fitted. For example, if the camera is held in a horizontal orientation, the obstruction of the light from the flash will cause a shadow to appear on the bottom edge of the picture.
- The angle of coverage achieved by the built-in Speedlight is limited, and only extends to cover the field-of-view of a lens with a focal length of 18mm or more. If used with a shorter focal length lens, the flash will not be able to illuminate the periphery of the frame and these areas will appear underexposed. Even at the widest limit of coverage, it is not uncommon to see a noticeable falloff of illumination (vignetting) in the corners of the frame.
- The built-in Speedlight draws its power from the camera's battery, so extended use will exhaust it quite quickly.

Lens Compatibility with the Built-in Speedlight

The built-in flash can be used with CPU lenses (i.e., all AF and Ai-P types) with focal lengths between 18mm and 300mm, but always remove the lens hood to prevent light from the flash from being obscured. Regardless, the built-in flash has a minimum range of 2 feet (0.6 m); therefore it cannot be used at the close focus distances of macro zoom lenses. Furthermore, it is not possible to use the built-in Speedlight with the AF-S 14–24mm f/2.8G ED, as light is always obscured regardless of focal length. The built-in flash may be unable to illuminate the entire frame area evenly when using the following lenses at a focus distance less than those given in the following table:

Zoom Lens Focal length / Minimum Shooting Range:

Lens	Focal length	Minimum distance
AF-S DX 12–24mm f/4G ED	20mm	6 ft, 7 in / 2 m
	24mm	3 ft, 3 in / 1 m
AF-S DX 16-85mm f/3.5-5.6G ED VR	18mm	6 ft, 7 in / 2 m
	20mm	3 ft, 3 in / 1 m
AF-S 17–35mm f/2.8D ED	24mm	6 ft, 7 in / 2 m
	28mm, 35mm	3 ft, 3 in / 1 m
AF-S 17–55mm f/2.8G ED	28mm	4 ft, 11 in / 1.5 m
	35mm	3 ft, 3 in / 1 m
AF 18–35mm f/3.5–4.5D ED	24mm	3 ft, 3 in / 1 m
AF 18–70mm f/3.5–4.5D ED	18mm	3 ft, 3 in / 1 m
AF-S DX 18-105mm f/3.5-5.6G ED VR	20mm	8 ft, 2 in / 2.5 m
	24mm	3 ft, 3 in / 1 m
AF-S DX 18-135mm f/3.5-5.6G ED	18mm	4 ft, 11 in / 1.5 m
AF-S DX 18-200mm f/3.5-5.6G ED	24mm, 35mm	3 ft, 3 in / 1 m
AF 20–35mm f/2.8D	20mm	4 ft, 11 in / 1.5 m
	24mm	3 ft, 3 in / 1 m
PC-E 24mm f/3.5D ED	24 mm	4 ft, 11 in / 1.5 m
AF-S 24–70mm f/2.8G ED	35mm	4 ft, 11 in / 1.5 m
AF-S VR 24-120mm f/3.5-5.6G ED	24mm	3 ft, 3 in / 1 m
PC-E 24mm f/3.5D	24mm	6 ft, 7 in / 2 m
AF-S 28–70mm f/2.8D ED	35mm	4 ft, 11 in / 1.5 m
	50mm	3 ft, 3 in / 1 m
AF-S VR 200-400mm f/4G	200mm	9 ft, 10 in / 3 m
	250mm, 300mm	8 ft, 2 in / 2.5m

Using External Nikon Speedlights

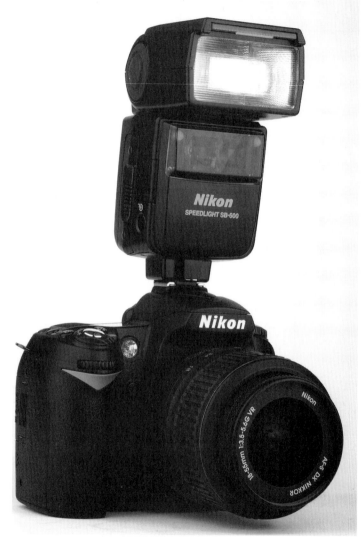

The D900 is pictured here with the SB-600 Speedlight.

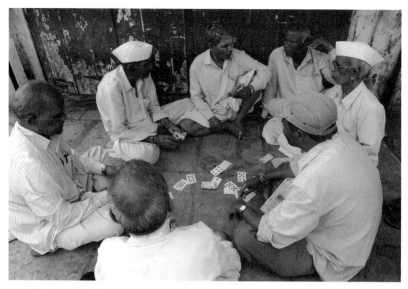

The capabilities and range of the built-in Speedlight on the D90 are limited. For more flexibility and power, consider adding an external Speedlight to your system.

The D90 offers full i-TTL flash exposure control with four external Nikon Speedlights (flash units) that are compatible with the CLS:

- SB-400 with a GN of 98 feet (30 m) at ISO 200
- SB-600 with a GN of 138 feet (42 m) at ISO 200 with the flash head set to 35mm
- SB-800 with a GN of 175 feet (53 m) at ISO 200 with the flash head set to 35mm
- SB-900 with a GN of 157 feet (48 m) at ISO 200 with the flash head set to 35mm (and with Normal light distribution selected)

All models can either be attached to the camera directly or via the dedicated Nikon TTL remote flash cords: SC-28, SC-29, or the now discontinued SC-17. The SB-R200, which has a GN of 49 feet (14 m) at ISO 200, can only be controlled as part of the Nikon Advanced Wireless Control

(AWL) flash system via either the SU-800 commander unit, or the SB-800 and SB-900 Speedlights when used as a master flash unit.

These four Speedlights offer further versatility since their flash heads can be tilted and – in the case of the SB-600, SB-800, and SB-900 – swiveled for bounce flash. Unlike earlier Nikon Speedlights, which cancelled monitor pre-flashes if the flash head was tilted or swiveled for bounce flash, the SB-400, SB-600, SB-800, and SB-900 emit pre-flashes regardless of the flash head orientation. The three latter units also have an adjustable auto zoom-head (SB-600: 24-85mm, SB-800: 24-105mm, SB-900: 12-200mm) that controls the angle of coverage, and a wide-angle diffuser to allow them to illuminate an even wider field of view. With the diffuser, the SB-600 and SB-800 can cover down to 14mm, while the SB-900 can cover down to 12mm.

Hint: The coverage of the SB-600 and SB-800 is set to correspond to the field of view of a lens with one of the focal lengths within the range of its zoom head. However, this is based on the assumption that the Speedlight is attached to a camera with an FX-format (35mm, or full frame) sensor (when used with the D90, the SB-900 automatically adjusts its coverage to match the DX format). The DX-format of the D90 corresponds to a reduction in the angle of view for the same focal length when used on the FX-format, so the flash will illuminate a greater area with the D90 than is necessary. Consequently, this will restrict the potential shooting range and squander flash power. In this situation, use the following table to adjust the zoom head position and thus maximize the performance of the flash unit:

Focal length of lens (mm)	Zoom head position (mm)	Focal length of lens (mm)	Zoom head position (mm)
14	20	35	50
18	24	50	70
20	28	70	85
24	35	85	105 [1]
28	50		

1 - Available on SB-800 only.

Automatic (Non-TTL) Flash with the SB-800 and SB-900 Speedlights

When using the SB-800 and SB-900 external Speedlights with the D90, there are two additional non-TTL flash modes available; these are selected on the Speedlight:

Auto Aperture (AA): In this mode, the SB-900 and SB-800 read the ISO sensitivity setting, lens aperture, and the command to fire the flash from the camera automatically. The AA flash mode can be used in Aperture-priority or Manual exposure mode. Thereafter, the flash output level is determined using a sensor on the front panel of the Speedlight to monitor the flash exposure and as soon as this sensor detects that the flash output has been sufficient, the flash pulse is quenched. If, between exposures, you decide to alter the focal length or change the lens aperture, the Speedlight will adjust its output accordingly to maintain a correct flash exposure. The problem with this option is that the sensor does not necessarily "see" the same scene as the lens does, which can lead to inaccuracies in flash exposure.

Automatic (A): This is the only automatic, non-TTL flash mode available with the SB-800 and SB-900 Speedlights. It can be used in Aperture-priority or Manual exposure mode. Similar to in the AA mode, a sensor on the front of the SB-800, SB-900, or DX-type Speedlight monitors flash levels and shuts off the flash when the Speedlight calculates that sufficient light has been emitted. However, the lens aperture and ISO sensitivity values must be set manually on the Speedlight to ensure that the subject is within the flash shooting range. As with the AA mode, the sensor does not necessarily "see" the same scene as the lens does, which can lead to inaccuracies in flash exposure.

Manual Flash Exposure Control

In Manual flash mode, you set the output of the Speedlight (built-in or external) to a fixed level. It is necessary to calculate the correct lens aperture as determined by the flash-to-subject distance and the Guide Number (GN) of the Speedlight.

For example, at its base sensitivity of ISO 200, the built-in Speedlight of the D90 has a guide number (GN) of 59 ft (18 m). The output level of the built-in Speedlight is determined by CS-e2, where a value between 1/1 (full output) to 1/128 can be selected. Since there is only one specific exposure value for any given level of sensitivity (ISO) at a particular flash-to-subject distance, it is necessary to calculate the lens aperture required to record a proper exposure.

Use the following equation:

• Aperture = GN / Distance

Therefore, with the built-in Speedlight of the D90 set to 1/1 (full output) at a flash-to-subject distance of exactly 10.5 feet (3.2 m), the lens aperture required to obtain a correct exposure of the subject will be f/5.6. (5.6 = 59/10.5). Similar calculations will have to be performed when using an external Speedlight in Manual flash mode. Check the Guide Number (GN) for the particular Speedlight model and ensure that you conduct the calculations using the same unit of distance throughout.

Repeating Flash

The purpose of the repeating flash function, which is supported both by the built-in and external Speedlight flash units, is to enable you to take a picture with a stroboscopic lighting effect. The very brief, high-frequency pulses of light output from the flash can reveal the motion of a subject that is moving very rapidly by essentially breaking the exposure down in to a series of separate exposures, each lit by the successive pulses of light. The technique works best when the flash is the only light source so that the ambient light will not have any effect. For example, you could photograph a bouncing tennis ball using a single one-second exposure, where the flash fired at a frequency of 10Hz (i.e., ten times during the total exposure duration), to capture ten successive exposures of the ball all within the same image, each lit by one pulse of light from the flash, showing it as it fell and then struck the floor and finally rebounded.

To configure repeating flash with the built-in Speedlight, use the relevant option at CS-e2 [Flash Cntrl for Built-in Flash]. Highlight [Flash Cntrl for Built-in Flash] and press ⊕ , highlight [Repeating flash] and press ⊕ again. Use ◄ or ► to select one of the three options that must be set; then use ▲ or ▼ to select the required value. Press ⊛ to return to the Custom Setting menu once each value has been set.

Option	Description
Output	Select the required flash output (it is expressed as a fraction of the maximum output between 1/4 and 1/128).
Times	Select the number of times the flash will fire at the selected output level. Depending on the shutter speed used and the frequency selected, the number of frames may be less than selected.
Frequency	Select how often the flash fires per second (1Hz = 1 per second).

The values available for Times is dependent on the output level of the flash.

Output	Times (Number of times the flash will fire)
1/4	2
1/8	2-5
1/16	2-10
1/32	2-10, 15
1/64	2-10, 15, 20, 25
1/128	2-10, 15, 20, 25, 30, 35

Flash Mode Display

The flash mode is displayed in the shooting information display for both the built-in and external Speedlights as follows:

	i-TTL		Auto aperture [1] (AA)		Manual	
	Built-in	**External**	**Built-in**	**External**	**Built-in**	**External**
TTL [2]	⚡ TTL	⚡ ⇄ TTL	----	⚡ ⇄	⚡	⚡ ⇄
Auto FP	----	⚡ ⇄ TTL FP	----	⚡ ⇄ FP	----	⚡ ⇄ FP
Repeating flash [2]	----	----	----	----	⚡ RPT	⚡ ⇄ RPT
Commander mode [2]	⚡ TTL CMD	⚡ ⇄ TTL CMD	----	⚡ ⇄ CMD	⚡ CMD	⚡ TTL

1. *Only available with the SB-900 and SB-800 Speedlights*
2. *The flash mode for the built-in Speedlight is set using CS-e2 [Flash Cntrl for Built-in Flash]*

Flash Synchronization

The maximum flash synchronization (sync) speed is the briefest shutter speed that can be set while maintaining full illumination of the frame area by a flash unit and have the flash produce its maximum output if required. On the D90 the maximum flash sync speed is normally 1/200 second.

Using the Auto FP (Focal Plane) high-speed flash sync feature, it is possible to synchronize external Speedlights compatible with the Creative Lighting System (CLS) at shutter speeds between 1/200 and 1/4000 second (this feature is only available in the P, S, A, and M exposure modes); select [On] under CS-e5 (see below for a full description).

Flash (Sync) Modes

Not to be confused with the flash exposure control modes available on the D90 (e.g., i-TTL Balanced Fill-flash, or Standard i-TTL flash) described earlier, the flash synchronization (flash sync) modes determine when the flash is fired in relation to the opening and closing of the shutter. The availability of a particular flash sync mode will depend on the exposure mode selected via the mode dial. In turn, the choice of flash sync mode will influence the range of shutter speeds that is available (see chart below, under Shutter Speed Restrictions).

To set a flash sync mode on the D90 when used with a compatible Nikon Speedlight, press and hold the $\sharp$ button, and rotate the main command dial to scroll through the various options until the icon for the desired mode appears in the control panel. The options available are as follows:

Using **ISO** , $\mathbf{\Sigma}$, $\clubsuit$, and $\boxed{\mathbf{\Xi}}$ Scene modes:

$\boxed{\text{\tiny AUTO}}$ **Auto flash:** The built-in flash will pop up automatically if the camera determines that the ambient light level is low or the subject is backlit strongly. In **ISO** and $\mathbf{\Sigma}$ Scene modes, the shutter speed is restricted to 1/200 – 1/60 second; while using $\clubsuit$, shutter speeds of 1/200 – 1/125 second are available.

$\boxed{\text{\tiny AUTO}}$ **Auto flash with slow sync:** Only available in the $\boxed{\mathbf{\Xi}}$ Scene mode, the built-in flash pops up automatically when the camera detects low-level ambient light, but this option offers an extended range of shutter speeds between 1/200 and 1 second to enable the camera to record the ambient light.

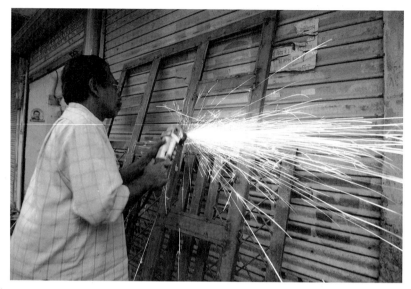

Use slow sync flash to illuminate the subject without cancelling out ambient light.

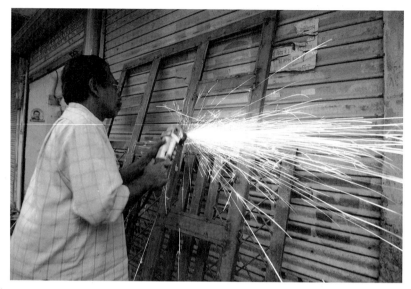 **Auto flash with red-eye reduction:** This operates in the same way as Auto flash, except the red-eye reduction lamp will illuminate briefly before the flash fires.

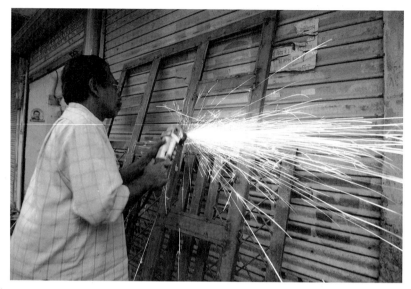 **Auto flash with slow sync and red-eye reduction:** This operates in the same way as Auto flash with slow sync, except the red-eye reduction lamp will illuminate briefly before the flash fires.

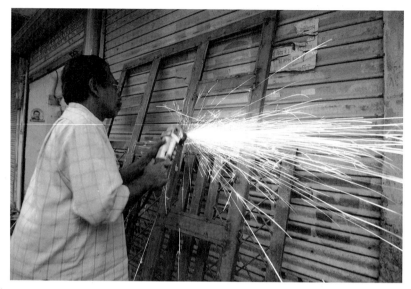 **Flash off:** Operation of the flash unit is cancelled regardless of the prevailing light conditions.

Using P, S, A, and M Exposure Modes:

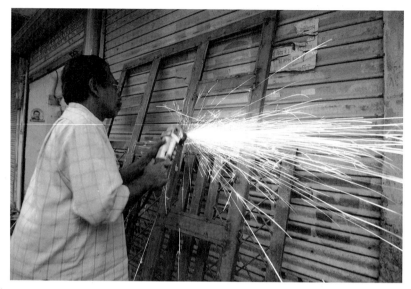 **Front-curtain sync:** The flash fires as soon as the shutter has fully opened. In P and A exposure modes, the shutter speed range is restricted to between 1/60 and 1/200 second, unless a lower speed between 1/60 second and 30 seconds has been selected via CS-e1 [Flash Shutter Speed]. In S and

M exposure modes, the Speedlight synchronizes at shutter speeds between 30 seconds and 1/200 second.

⬚ **Slow-sync:** Only available in P and A exposure modes, the flash fires as soon as the shutter has fully opened and at all shutter speeds between 30 seconds and 1/250 second. It is useful for recording low-level ambient light as well as those areas of the scene or subject illuminated by flash (see below for a full description).

⬚ **Rear-curtain:** In S and M exposure modes, the flash fires just before the shutter closes at all shutter speeds between 30 seconds and 1/200 second. Therefore, any image of a moving subject recorded by the ambient light exposure will appear to follow the image of the subject illuminated by the flash output (see below for a full description). In P and A exposure modes ⬚ , slow rear-curtain sync is set when the ↯ button is released.

⬚ **Red-eye reduction:** This mode is only available with the built-in Speedlight or the SB-400, SB-600, SB-800, and SB-900 external Speedlights; it operates in one of two ways depending on the type of Speedlight used. With the built-in unit, the red-eye reduction lamp lights for approximately one second before the main flash output, while with an external Speedlight a short series of low-intensity light pulses are emitted before the main output. The purpose is to try to induce the pupils in the subject's eye to constrict, thus reducing the risk of red-eye. Shutter speed synchronization is the same as for front-curtain sync.

Hint: This mode not only alerts your subject that you are about to take a picture, but it also causes an inordinate delay in the shutter's operation, by which time the critical moment has generally passed and you have missed the shot! Personally, I never bother with this feature. Red-eye can easily be edited out later.

⬚ **Red-eye reduction with slow sync:** This is only available in P and A exposure modes. The flash fires as soon as the shutter has fully opened at all shutter speeds between 30 seconds and 1/200 second. It is useful for recording low-level ambient light as well as those areas of the scene or subject illuminated by flash (see full description below).

Hint: The same advice applies here as with regular red-eye reduction; it may be better to use the non-red-eye flash modes and edit later if necessary.

Shutter Speed Restrictions

When Vibration Reduction is switched off and either the built-in Speedlight or an external Speedlight (SB-900, SB-800, SB-600, or SB-400) is used with the D90 the range of available shutter speeds varies according to the selected exposure mode as follows:

Mode	Shutter speed range
AUTO 🖼 🏃 P * A *	1/200 – 1/60 second
🌷	1/200 – 1/125 second
🖼	1/200 – 1 second
S, M	1/200 – 30 seconds

* If ⚡SLOW slow flash sync is selected, the shutter speed range is extended to 1/200 – 30 seconds. Alternatively, the lower shutter speed value in the range can be set via CS-e1 [Flash shutter speed] with values between 1/60 and 30 seconds available.

Aperture Restrictions

When the built-in Speedlight is used in combination with the Programmed-auto (P) exposure mode and a number of the Scene modes, the maximum aperture (lowest f/number) available on any lens is limited according to the ISO sensitivity set, as follows:

Mode	Maximum aperture at ISO sensitivity setting				
	200	**400**	**800**	**1600**	**3200**
P ISO 🏃 🖼	2.8	3.3	4	4.8	5.6
🌷	5.6	6.7	8	9.5	11

The following table summarizes how the shutter speed and lens aperture values are influenced by which exposure mode is active when an external Speedlight is used:

Exposure mode	Shutter speed	Lens aperture
Programmed-auto (P)	Set automatically by camera (1/200 – 1/60 second) [1, 2]	Set automatically by the camera
Shutter-priority (S)	Value selected by user (1/200 – 30 seconds) [2]	
Aperture-priority (A)	Set automatically by camera (1/200 – 1/60 second) [1, 2]	Value selected by the user[3]
Manual (M)	Value selected by user	

1. Shutter speed may be set as slow as 30s in slow sync, slow rear-curtain sync, and slow sync with red-eye reduction flash modes.

2. Speeds as fast as 1/4000 s are available with optional SB-900, SB-800, SB-600, and SB-R200 flash units when [On] is selected for CS-e5 [Auto FP].

Slow Synchronization Flash
As described above, the camera will set a shutter speed that is within a restricted range when you're using the built-in flash or a compatible Speedlight mounted directly in the accessory shoe (or connected via a dedicated TTL flash cord such as the SC-28 or SC-29) and the camera is in Program (P), Aperture-priority (A), **ISO** , 🏃 , 🌷 , or 🗻 mode. The actual speed that is used within this narrow range depends on the level of ambient light (the brighter the conditions the shorter the shutter speed).

This restriction can have a significant effect on the overall exposure. For example, in situations when you photograph a subject outside at night or in a dark interior, any area of the scene illuminated by ambient light alone will be lit dimly compared with those areas that will be illuminated by the flash. It is more than likely that the level of ambient light will not be sufficient for a proper exposure within this restricted range of shutter speeds; consequently these areas of the scene will be underexposed. A typical photograph taken under these conditions has a well-exposed subject set against a dark, featureless background.

To prevent this, select the appropriate slow-sync mode. This enables the camera to use a wider range of slower shutter speeds. The camera will be able to select a more appropriate shutter speed for the low level of ambient light, so the correct exposure can be achieved for the background (remember the flash output will have little if any effect in this region because the intensity of light from the flash will diminish according to the Inverse Square Law). However, the flash output will be controlled for a proper exposure of the subject and its surroundings.

Hint: Since the shutter speed may be quite slow when using slow sync flash mode, consider using a tripod or other camera support to avoid the effects of camera shake.

Rear-Curtain Synchronization

If a subject you want to photograph is moving, it is possible to achieve some interesting effects by using slow sync flash mode in combination with a slow shutter speed, as the flash will illuminate the subject briefly to record it as sharp, while the slow shutter speed records the subject's motion as a blur. This technique can be particularly effective when used with ⌐ rear-curtain sync flash mode in either Shutter-priority (S) or Manual (M) exposure mode. Alternatively, in Programmed-auto (P) or Aperture-priority (A) exposure modes, use ⌐ slow rear-curtain sync flash mode. In each case, it will cause the blur due to subject movement to follow the sharp image of the subject formed by the flash illumination, to produce a more natural appearance of subject movement.

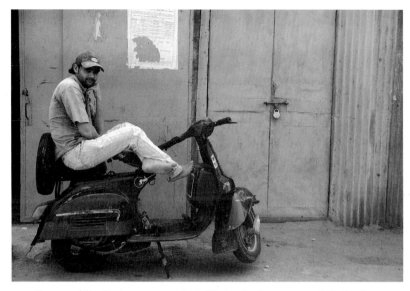

For a subtle flash exposure that fills in shadows, especially in daylight, use high-speed sync.

Auto FP (Focal Plane) High-speed Sync

Available with the SB-900, SB-800, and SB-600 Speedlights, or the SB-R200 when it is used as part of a wireless flash control system, this feature is set on the D90 via CS-e5 [Auto FP].

One of the limitations of using daylight fill-flash is the maximum flash sync speed of the D90, which is 1/200 second. When working in bright lighting conditions it is often not possible to open the lens aperture very far, due to this restriction of the maximum (briefest) shutter speed imposed by the use of flash. The Auto FP high-speed sync feature allows compatible external Speedlights to sync at any shutter speed beyond a 1/200 second to the shortest shutter speed available on camera, 1/4000 second. The flash output is adjusted automatically, which makes using fill-flash far more flexible. To achieve this, the flash emits its output as a very rapid series of pulses instead of a single continuous pulse. However, this has the effect of reducing the intensity of the light, so as the flash is synchronized with increasingly faster shutter speeds, its output is progressively reduced, which in turn reduces its effective shooting range.

Flash Output Compensation

Flash compensation is used to modify the level of flash output; it can be applied to the built-in Speedlight of the D90 by pressing and holding the ⚡ button while turning the sub-command dial. Compensation can be set in increments of either 0.3 Ev or 0.5 Ev (subject to setting in CS-b1 [EV steps for exposure cntrl]) over a range of +1 Ev to –3 Ev; ⚡± is displayed in the control panel, viewfinder, and shooting information display. To check the flash output compensation value, press the ⚡ button.

Flash output compensation can also be applied directly on compatible external Speedlights: SB-900, SB-800, and SB-600. If flash output compensation is applied on the D90 and on an external Speedlight at the same time, the effect is cumulative. For example, applying a value of +1 Ev to both the camera and external Speedlight results in a flash output compensation of +2 Ev.

As discussed earlier in this chapter, the default i-TTL Balanced Fill-flash mode will automatically set a flash compensation based on scene brightness, contrast, focus distance, and a variety of other factors. The level of automatic adjustment applied to flash output by the D90 will often cancel out any compensation value entered manually. Since there is no way of telling what the camera is doing, you will never have control of the flash exposure. To regain control, set the flash mode to standard i-TTL by either selecting spot metering on the camera (this is the only option for the built-in Speedlight), or set the flash control mode on an external Speedlight accordingly, ensuring that only TTL is displayed in its control panel and not TTL-BL.

Flash Value (FV) Lock

Flash Value (FV) Lock allows you to use the camera and Speedlight to estimate the required flash output for a subject and then
retain this value temporarily, before making the main flash illuminated exposure. This is a very useful feature if your want to
compose a picture with the main subject located toward the
edge of the frame area, particularly if the background is very
bright or very dark. Under these circumstances, using the normal i-TTL flash exposure control, there is a risk that the camera
may calculate an incorrect level of flash output and cause the
main subject to be either under- or overexposed.

On the D90, the FV Lock feature can be activated via two
different routes. The following describes how to assign its
operation to the Function button (the FV Lock function can
also be assigned to the AE-L/AF-L button via CS-f4). Navigate
to CS-f3 [Assign FUNC button] and press ⊚ ; highlight
[FV Lock] and press ⓄⓀ .

Use either the built-in Speedlight or attach a compatible
Speedlight to the D90 (FV Lock is supported by the following external Speedlights: SB-900, SB-800, SB-600, and SB-
400). Whichever Speedlight is used must be set to perform
TTL flash control; additionally, the SB-900 and SB-800 can
also be used in Auto Aperture (AA) flash exposure control
mode (the FV Lock feature is also supported by the SU-800
controlling CLS compatible Speedlights in a wireless remote
lighting setup). Check that the flash ready light **⚡** is lit,
then compose the picture with the main subject in the center of the frame area; acquire focus by half-depressing the
shutter release before pressing the Fn button. The Speedlight
will emit a pre-flash, which is used to assess the required
amount of flash output. The calculated value for flash output
is stored by the camera and **⚡L** is shown in the
viewfinder to indicate that the FV Lock function is active.
Now you can recompose the picture placing the subject
toward the edge of the frame area. Finally, make the exposure by fully depressing the shutter release button. The flash
will fire at the predetermined level.

If you alter the focal length of a zoom lens or adjust the lens aperture, the FV Lock function will compensate the flash output automatically. However, the camera-to-subject distance must remain unaltered during the use of the FV Lock function; otherwise, the flash exposure may be inaccurate. To release the FV Lock, press the Function button and ensure that **EL** is no longer displayed in the viewfinder.

The area of the frame from which the camera takes a meter reading when the FV Lock function is active varies according to the number of Speedlights and the flash control mode in use.

Metering Area with FV Lock

When using an external Speedlight or multiple Speedlights, the area metered by the D90 for the purposes of assessing the flash exposure will vary according to the flash mode and the number of Speedlights in use, as follows:

Speedlight	Flash Mode	Metered Area
Single Speedlight connected to the camera	i-TTL	4 mm circle at center of frame
	AA (SB-900 and SB-800 only)	Area metered by built-in sensor on Speedlight
Speedlight used with others as part of wireless flash control system	i-TTL	Entire frame
	AA (SB-900 and SB-800 only)	Area metered by built-in sensor on Speedlight
	A (master flash only)	

Flash Color Information

When automatic white balance is selected on the D90 and it is used with the SB-900, SB-800, SB-600, or SB-400 Speedlights, the external flash automatically transmits information to the camera about the color temperature of the light it emits. The camera will then use this information to adjust its final white balance setting in an attempt to match the color

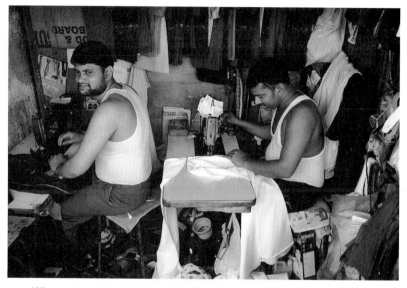

When automatic white balance on the D90 is activated, the camera will try to match its white balance setting to a combination of the ambient value and that of the flash.

temperature of the light from the flash and the color temperature of the prevailing ambient light.

Wide-Area AF-Assist Illuminator (External Units Only)

The purpose of the wide-area AF-assist illuminator built into the SB-900, SB-800, and SB-600 Speedlights and the SU-800 wireless commander unit is to facilitate autofocus in low-light situations. The AF-assist illuminator of these Speedlight units lights a much wider area than the AF-assist illuminator of previous Speedlights, in order to match the broader coverage of the multiple AF points in many CLS-compatible cameras. These external lamps are also much more powerful than the built-in AF-assist illuminator of the D90, which has the further disadvantage of being obstructed by many Nikkor lenses due to its proximity to the lens mount (see pages 189-191 for further details of the built-in and external AF-assist illuminators).

When a compatible external Speedlight with an AF-assist illuminator is used off the camera (see below), the light emitted by the lamp may not be reflected with sufficient strength to be effective if it strikes the subject at an oblique angle. In this situation, consider using the Nikon SC-29 TTL flash cord, which has a built-in AF-assist illuminator in its terminal block that attaches to the camera accessory shoe. This places the AF-assist illuminator immediately above the central axis of the lens to help improve the accuracy of autofocus.

Off-Camera Flash

Using a TTL Cord

When you work with a single external Speedlight, it is often desirable to take the flash off the camera. There are several different dedicated Nikon cords for this purpose: the SC-17 (discontinued), SC-28, and SC-29. All three cords are 4.9 feet (1.5 m) long: up to three SC-17 or SC-28 cords can be connected together to extend the operating range away from the camera. Whenever you take a Speedlight off the camera and use any TTL flash mode that will incorporate focus distance information in the flash output computations, take care as to where you position the flash. If the Speedlight is moved closer or further away by a significant amount compared with the camera-to-subject distance, the accuracy of the flash output may be compromised, as the TTL flash control system works on the assumption that the flash is located at the same distance from the subject as the camera. Likewise, when using Manual flash exposure control, remember to calculate the lens aperture based on the flash-to-subject distance, not camera-to-subject distance.

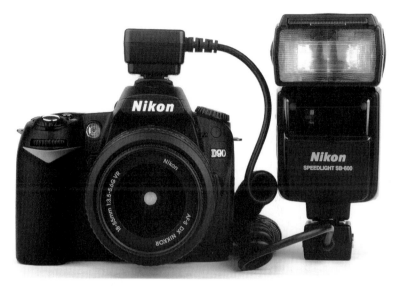

The SC-28 TTL cord is one of three cords that can be used to connect external Speedlights to the D90. It is pictured here with the D90 and an SB-600 Speedlight.

The benefits of taking a Speedlight off the camera include:

- Increasing the angular separation between the central axis of the lens and the flash head will significantly reduce the risk of the red-eye effect with humans or eye-shine with other animals.
- In situations when it is not practicable to use bounce flash, moving the flash off-camera will usually improve the quality of the lighting, especially the degree of modeling it provides, compared with the typical flat, frontal lighting produced by a flash mounted on the camera.
- By taking the flash off-camera, and directing the light from the Speedlight accordingly, it is often possible to control the position of shadows so that they become less noticeable.
- When using fill-flash, it is often desirable to direct light to a specific part of the scene to help reduce the level of contrast locally.

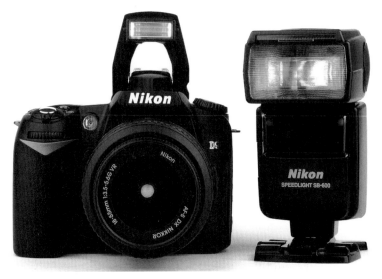

The built-in Speedlight of the D90 can control compatible remote Speedlights wirelessly, such as the SB-600 shown here.

- A Speedlight connected to the camera via one of Nikon's dedicated TTL cords can be used as the master flash to control multiple Speedlights off-camera using the Advanced Wireless Lighting system (see below).

Using the Built-in Speedlight in Commander Mode

In addition to being used for conventional flash photography, the built-in Speedlight of the D90 camera can be set to control one or more remote Speedlight(s) wirelessly in P, A, S, and M exposure modes. This feature is compatible with the SB-900, SB-800, SB-600, and SB-R200. The remote Speedlights can be controlled in a variety of flash modes: TTL, Auto Aperture (for use with remote SB-900/SB-800 Speedlights only), or Manual. Control is limited to a maximum of two independent groups, named A and B, using any one of four communication channels (1 to 4).

To use the Commander mode, which sets the built-in Speedlight of the Nikon D90 camera to act as either the master flash where it will contribute to the flash exposure as well as emitting the control signals for the remote Speedlights, or as the commander unit (use the [—] option), where it will only emit the control signals for the remote Speedlights and not contribute light to the flash exposure:

1. Open the Custom Setting menu and navigate to CS-e2 [Flash cntrl for built-in flash], and then press ⊙ .

2. Highlight the [Commander mode] option and press ⊙ to open a sub-menu of flash mode and flash output level compensation, together with flash group and control channel options.

3. Highlight Built-in flash / Mode to set the required flash mode and use ▲ or ▼ to select [TTL], [M], or [- -] (flash cancelled). If [TTL] or [M] is selected, press ▶ to highlight [Comp] (flash output level compensation) and use ▲ or ▼ to select the required value. In TTL mode, the flash output compensation can be set over a range of ±3 Ev in steps of 1/3 Ev; in Manual flash mode, the output can be set to between full output and 1/128 of full output. Finally, press ▶ to set and confirm the value, and highlight Group A / Mode.

4. Set the required flash mode for group A by using ▲ or ▼ to select [TTL], [AA] (SB-900/SB-800 only), [M], or [- -] (flash cancelled). If [TTL], [AA], or [M] is selected, and you want to set a flash output compensation level, repeat the procedure from Step 3; otherwise, press the multi-selector switch to the right to highlight Group B / Mode. Repeat Steps 3 and 4 to set the flash mode and flash exposure compensation for Group B.

5. Highlight Channel and use ▲ or ▼ on the multi-selector switch to select the required channel number.

6. Finally, press the ⊛ button on the back of the camera to confirm and lock the settings made in Steps 3 – 5 above.

7. Check that each remote Speedlight is set to operate as a remote flash unit, and that each unit is also set to the same channel as selected on the D90 at step 5 above.

The D90 with SU-800 Commander unit, which enables the independent control via wireless communication of up to three separate groups of compatible Nikon Speedlights; each group can comprise one or more Speedlight(s).

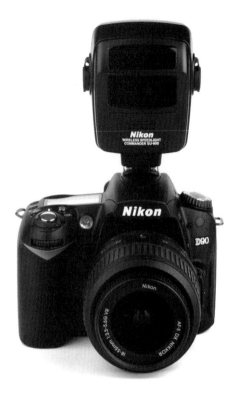

8. Press the flash pop-up button to raise the built-in Speedlight of the camera and ensure the ready light of each flash unit is lit. The system is now ready to be used.

Note: If the SB-400 is attached to the D90 and turned on, CS-e2 changes to [Optional flash], which allows the flash control mode of the SB-400 to be chosen from either TTL or Manual; the Repeating flash and Commander flash options are not available.

Commander Flash: Effective Ranges: When the following units are used as the master flash or commander unit for wireless control of compatible remote Speedlights (SB-900, SB-800, SB-600, and SB-R200) the effective range of operation is:

- **D90 built-in Speedlight / SB-900 / SB-800:** when either the D90 built-in Speedlight, SB-900, or SB-800 is used as a master flash, the maximum effective operating range between it and the remote Speedlights is 33 feet (10 m) within 30° of the central axis of the lens, and 16 feet (5 m) within 30 to 60° of the central axis of the lens.
- **SU-800:** the SU-800 is a dedicated IR transmitter (i.e., unlike flash units that emit control signals as part of a full spectrum emission, the SU-800 only emits IR light). It is a more powerful unit compared with the Speedlights that can perform the master flash role, and is capable of controlling remote SB-900, SB-800, and SB-600 Speedlights from up to 66 feet (20 m).
- **SU-800 / SB-R200:** Nikon states that when the SU-800 is used as the commander unit, the maximum effective operating range between it and remote SB-R200 Speedlights is 13 feet (4 m) along the central axis of the lens, and 9.8 feet (3 m) within 30° of the central axis of the lens.

I have found the quoted maximum operating ranges for the components of the Advanced Wireless Lighting system to be very conservative. For example, I have used SB-800 Speedlights as master and remote units at ranges outdoors of 100 feet (30 m) or more, even in situations where there have been reflective surfaces like walls and foliage close by, which is three times greater than the suggested maximum range. However, in bright sunlight, which contains a high level of naturally occurring IR light, you may find the practical limit of the operating range is reduced. I have used remote flash units very successfully without line-of-sight between the master flash and the sensor on the remote Speedlight(s). However, every shooting situation is different, so my advice is to set up the lighting system to your requirements, and always take test shots to ensure that it works as intended.

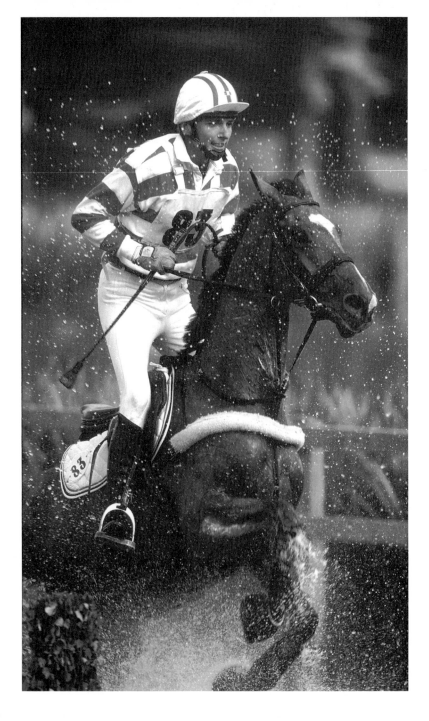

Using Nikon Lenses

Nikon currently makes a wide variety of lenses, known by their proprietary name, Nikkor, for their D-SLR and film camera models. The "F" mount used on these lenses is legendary; it has been used on all Nikon 35mm film and digital SLR cameras, virtually unchanged, since the original Nikon F SLR in 1959. As such, a great many of the lenses Nikon has produced in the past five decades can be mounted on the D90, including most manual focus lenses that conform to the Ai lens mount standard. The fullest level of compatibility is offered by modern autofocus Nikkor lenses (D- and G-types), but the D90 can be used with many earlier manual focus lenses (although lacking support for TTL metering and restricted to just manual exposure mode).

Mounting/Removing a Lens

Whenever you attach or detach a lens from the D90, make sure the camera is turned off. Identify the mounting index-mark (white dot) on the lens, and align it with the mounting index-mark (white dot) next to the bayonet ring of the camera's lens mount. Enter the lens bayonet into the camera and rotate the lens counter-clockwise until it locks into place with an audible click. To remove a lens from the camera, press and hold the lens-release button (located on the front of the camera to the left of the lens mount), and then rotate the lens until the two index-marks are aligned before lifting the lens clear of the camera body. If you do not intend to immediately mount another lens, make sure you place the BF-1A body cap back onto the camera to help prevent unwanted material from entering the camera.

Nikon offers a variety of lenses to suit nearly all types of shooting and a wide range of budgets.

To mount a lens, align the two white index marks – one on the camera the other on the lens – before entering the lens-mount flange in to the camera body, and then twist the lens counter-clockwise until it locks into place.

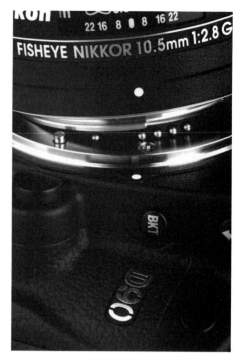

Note: When using a CPU lens with an aperture ring (G-type lenses lack a conventional aperture ring), ensure it is set and locked to its minimum aperture value (highest f/-number). If "fEE" appears and blinks in the control panel and viewfinder, the lens has not been set to its minimum aperture value. In this state, the shutter release is disabled and the camera will not operate.

Demystifying Nikkor Lenses

The designations of Nikkor lenses, particularly modern auto-focus types, are peppered with initials. Here is an explanation of what some of these stand for:

AF D-type: These lenses have a conventional aperture ring and an electronic chip (CPU) that communicates information

330

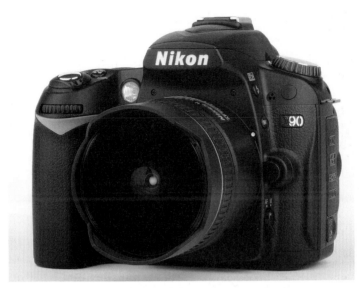

The AF Fisheye 10.5mm f/2.8G ED is one of a number of Nikkor lenses designed specifically for the DX-format of the D90.

about lens aperture and focus distance between the lens and the camera body. A "D" appears on the lens barrel.

AF G-type: These lenses have no aperture ring and are only compatible with Nikon cameras that allow the aperture value to be set from the camera body. They contain an electronic chip (CPU) that communicates information about lens aperture and focus distance between the lens and the camera body, similarly to the D-type lenses. A "G" appears on the lens barrel.

AF-type: These lenses are the predecessors to the later D- and G-type designs. They have a conventional aperture ring and do not communicate focus distance information to the camera.

AF-S: These lenses use a silent-wave motor (SWM) for focusing; alternating magnetic fields drive the motor, which moves the lenses' elements to shift focus. This system offers the fastest autofocusing of all AF Nikkor lenses. Most AF-S lenses have an additional feature that allows you to switch between autofocus and manual focus, without adjusting any camera controls, by simply taking hold of and turning the focus ring. "AF-S" appears on the lens barrel.

AF-I: The predecessor to the AF-S lens type; these lenses also have an internal focusing motor, but not a silent-wave motor (SWM).

DX: These lenses have been specially designed for use on Nikon DX-format digital SLR cameras. They project a smaller image circle than lenses designed for 35mm and FX-format cameras, and the light exiting their rear element is more collimated (actually parallel to one another) to improve the efficiency of the photo diodes (pixels) on the camera's sensor. "DX" appears on the lens barrel.

ED: To reduce the effect of chromatic aberration, Nikon developed a special type of glass known as Extra-low Dispersion to bring various wavelengths of light to a common point of focus.

IF: To speed up focusing, particularly with long focal length lenses, Nikon developed their internal focusing (IF) system. This moves a group of elements within the lens (as opposed to the entire lens barrel) so that it does not alter the length of the lens during focusing, and prevents the front filter mount from rotating; this also better facilitates the use of filters whose positions must remain stationary in order to be effective, such as polarizers and graduated filters.

N (Nano Crystal Coat): A specialized lens coating that is applied to the surface of some lens elements to help reduce the level of light reflection, improving overall image quality. An "N" appears on the lens barrel.

Non-CPU: Nikon uses the term "non-CPU" to describe any Nikkor lens lacking the electrical connections and components that communicate information about the lens to the camera. (With the exception of the PC-E 24mm f/3.5D, PC-E Micro 45mm f/2.8D, PC-E Micro 85mm f/2.8D, PC-Micro 85mm f/2.8D lens, and Ai-P type Nikkor lenses, all manual focus Nikkor lenses are non-CPU types.)

Micro-Nikkor: The name given to specialized lenses designed specifically for close-up and macro photography; the optical formula of these lenses is optimized for close focusing.

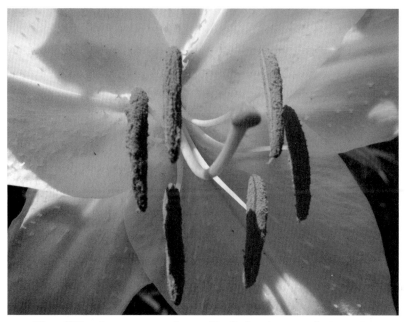

Micro-Nikkor lenses are made specifically for close-up photography.
©Kevin Kopp

PC-E: A special type of lens that offers the ability to shift and tilt the lens relative to the plane of the sensor in the camera to control perspective and depth-of-field. "PC-E" appears on the lens barrel.

VR: Vibration Reduction (VR) is Nikon's name for a sophisticated technology that enables a lens to counter the effects of camera shake and other vibrations. A set of built-in motion sensors that cause micro-motors to shift a dedicated set of lens elements are used to improve the sharpness of pictures. "VR" appears on the lens barrel.

Lens Compatibility

The following table provides details of the compatibility of CPU-type Nikkor lenses with the D90:

Camera setting / Lens/accessory	Focus AF	M (with electronic rangefinder)	M	Mode ⌖,⊕,✿,🏔, / ⚘,🌷,📷, P, S, A	M	Metering 3D	Color	⊙
Type G or D AF Nikkor[2], AF-S, AF-I Nikkor	✔	✔	✔	✔	✔	✔	—	✔[3]
PC-E NIKKOR series[4]	—	✔	✔	✔	✔	✔	—	✔[3]
PC Micro 85mm f/2.8D[5]	—	✔[4]	✔	—	✔	✔	—	✔[3]
AF-S / AF-I teleconverter[6]	✔[7]	✔[7]	✔	✔	✔	✔	—	✔[3]
Other AF Nikkor (except lenses for F3AF)	✔[8]	✔[8]	✔	✔	✔	—	✔	✔[3]
AI-P Nikkor	—	✔[9]	✔	✔	✔	—	✔	✔[3]

1. *IX Nikkor lenses can not be used.*
2. *Vibration Reduction (VR) supported with VR lenses.*
3. *Spot metering meters selected focus point.*
4. *Can not be used with shifting or tilting.*
5. *The camera's exposure metering and flash control systems may not function as expected when the lens is shifted and/or tilted or an aperture other than the maximum aperture is used.*
6. *AF-S or AF-I lens required (see below).*
7. *With maximum effective aperture of f/5.6 or faster.*
8. *When AF 80-200 mm f/2.8, AF 35-70 mm f/2.8, AF 28-85 mm f/3.5-4.5 (New), or AF 28-85 mm f/3.5-4.5 lenses are zoomed all the way in at the minimum focus distance, the in-focus indicator may be displayed when the image on the matte screen in the viewfinder is not in focus. Focus manually until image in viewfinder is in focus.*
9. *With maximum aperture of f/5.6 or faster.*

Using Nikon AF-S/AF-I Teleconverters

The Nikon AF-S/AF-I teleconverters can be used with the following AF-S and AF-I lenses:

AF-S VR Micro 105mm f/2.8G ED [1]	AF-I 500mm f/4D ED [2]
AF-S VR 200mm f/2G ED	AF-S 600mm f/4D ED II [2]
AF-S VR 300mm f/2.8G ED	AF-S 600mm f/4D ED [2]
AF-S 300mm f/2.8D ED II	AF-I 600mm f/4D ED [2]
AF-S 300mm f/2.8D ED	AF-S VR 70–200mm f/2.8G ED
AF-I 300mm f/2.8D ED	AF-S 80–200mm f/2.8D ED
AF-S 300mm f/4D ED [2]	AF-S VR 200–400mm f/4G ED [2]
AF-S 400mm f/2.8D ED II	AF-S 400mm f/2.8G ED VR
AF-S 400mm f/2.8D ED	AF-S 500mm f/4G ED VR [2]
AF-I 400mm f/2.8D ED	AF-S 600mm f/4G ED VR [2]
AF-S 500mm f/4D ED II [2]	AF-S 500mm f/4D ED [2]

1. *Autofocus is not recommended; at close focus distances, the maximum effective aperture is likely to be less than f/5.6.*
2. *Autofocus is not guaranteed when used with TC-17E II/TC-20 E II teleconverter, as maximum effective aperture is less than f/5.6; although in bright conditions, or with good levels of contrast in the subject, it will often work quite well, if a little more slowly.*

Using Non-CPU Lenses

Although the Nikon 'F' mount has remained largely unchanged for almost fifty years, the design of modern cameras has progressed considerably. The introduction of electronic communication between the lens and camera for the purposes of exposure metering and autofocus has meant a number of changes have been introduced, such that older non-CPU type lenses offer a very restricted level of compatibility with the D90. In this case, the camera can only be used in manual exposure mode (if you select another exposure mode, the camera disables the shutter release automatically). The lens aperture must be set using the aperture ring on the lens, with no function available from the autofocus system, TTL metering system, electronic analogue exposure display, and TTL flash control. However, the electronic rangefinder does operate, provided the maximum effective aperture is f/5.6 or larger (faster), unless otherwise stated, with the following non-CPU type lenses.

The following non-CPU type lenses can be used as described with the D90:

- Ai-modified, Ai, Ai-S, and E-series Nikkor lenses
- Medical Nikkor 120mm f/4 (Only shutter speeds slower than 1/180 second can be used.)
- Reflex Nikkor lenses (The electronic rangefinder does not operate.)
- PC Nikkor lenses (The electronic rangefinder does not operate if lens is shifted.)
- Ai-type teleconverters (The electronic rangefinder requires an effective aperture of f/5.6 or larger to operate.)
- PB-6 Bellows focusing attachment
- Extension rings PK-11A, PK-12, PK-13, and PN-11

Incompatible Lenses and Accessories

The following accessories and lenses are incompatible with the D90. If you attempt to use them it may damage the equipment.

- TC-16A AF teleconverter
- Non-Ai lenses
- Lenses that require the AU-1 focusing unit (400mm f/4.5, 600mm f/5.6, 800mm f/8, 1200mm f/11)
- Fisheye (6mm f/5.6, 7.5mm f/5.6, 8mm f/8, OP 10mm f/5.6)
- 21mm f/4 (old type)
- K2 rings

336

- ED 180–600mm f/8 (serial numbers 174041–174180)
- ED 360–1200mm f/11 (serial numbers 174031–174127)
- 200–600mm f/9.5 (serial numbers 280001–300490)
- Lenses for the F3AF (AF80mm f/2.8, AF ED200mm f/3.5, TC-16S teleconverter)
- PC 28mm f/4 (serial number 180900 or earlier)
- PC 35mm f/2.8 (serial numbers 851001–906200)
- PC 35mm f/3.5 (old type)
- 1000mm f/6.3 Reflex (old type)
- 1000mm f/11 Reflex (serial numbers 142361–143000)
- 2000mm f/11 Reflex (serial numbers 200111–200310)

Depth of Field

When a lens brings light to focus on a camera's sensor, there is only one plane of focus that is critically sharp. However, in the two-dimensional picture produced by the camera, there is a zone in front of and behind the plane of focus that is perceived to be sharp. This area of apparent sharpness is often referred to as the depth of field, and its extent is influenced by the camera-to-subject distance together with the focal length and aperture of the lens in use.

If the focal length and camera-to-subject distance are constant, depth of field will be shallower with large apertures (low f/numbers) and deeper with small apertures (high f/numbers). If the aperture and camera-to-subject distance are constant, depth of field will be shallower with a long focal length (telephoto range) and deeper with shorter focal length (wide-angle range). If the focal length and aperture are constant, depth of field will be greater at longer camera-to-subject distances and shallower with closer camera-to-subject distances. Depth of field is an important consideration when deciding on a particular composition, as it has a direct and fundamental effect on the final appearance of the picture.

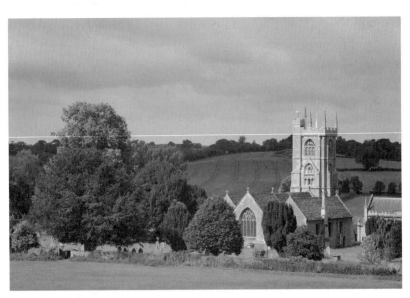

Use the Depth-of-Field Preview button to see the effect of the taking aperture on the image's depth of field before actually taking the picture.

Depth-of-Field Preview

In order for the viewfinder image to be as bright as possible for composing, focusing, and metering, the D90 operates with the lens automatically set to its maximum aperture (lowest f/number). The iris of the lens does not close down to the shooting aperture until after the shutter release has been pressed and the reflex mirror has lifted, just a fraction of a second before the shutter opens. However, this means that the image you see in the viewfinder appears as it would if the photograph were to be taken at the maximum aperture of the lens. To assess the depth of field visually, you must close the lens iris down to the shooting aperture.

The D90 has a Depth-of-Field Preview button (the lower of the two buttons on the front of the camera located next to the lens mount) that stops the lens down to the selected shooting aperture when pressed, allowing you to see the effect that the

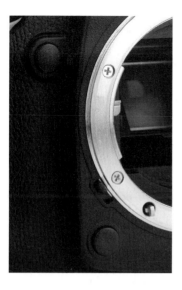

The Depth-of-Field Preview button on the D90 is located beside the lens mount flange.

lens aperture has on the depth of field. The viewfinder image will become darker as less light passes through the lens when the aperture iris in the lens is closed down.

Hint: At apertures of f/11 or smaller (higher f/number), the viewfinder image will become very dark and difficult to see, even with brightly lit scenes. It is often better to make a general assessment of depth of field at f/8, and then change the aperture value to the one required for shooting.

Depth of Field Considerations

The smaller the imaging medium (sensor or film plane) is, the shallower the depth of field will be in the images it produces. So, depth of field is slightly less for images shot using the DX-format (23.6 x 15.8 mm; used in the D90) compared with those taken on the FX- or 35mm-format (approximately 36 x 24 mm). Due to the smaller size of the imaging area, the DX-format picture must be magnified by a greater amount compared with the larger format in order to achieve any given identical print size. Therefore, at normal viewing distances, detail that appears to be sharp in a print made from a larger format sensor may no longer look sharp in a print of the same dimensions made from one recorded in the DX-format. If you use the depth-of-field values given in tables for 35mm film or larger sensors, you will find they do not correspond to images shot on the DX-format, assuming the same camera-to-subject distance and focal length apply. To guarantee that the depth of field in pictures taken on the DX-format is sufficiently deep, use the values for the next larger lens aperture. For example, if set your lens to f/11, refer to depth of field values for f/8.

Diffraction

Diffraction is an optical effect that, under certain circumstances, will limit the resolution you can achieve in a photograph. Assuming conditions of a uniform atmosphere (i.e., still, clear air), light waves will travel in straight lines. However, if those same light waves have to pass through a small hole, such as the aperture in the iris diaphragm of a camera lens, they become dispersed, or diffracted. At wide apertures, the number of diffracted light waves is very small compared to the total number that pass through the aperture; therefore the diffraction effect is negligible. But the proportion of diffracted waves to non-diffracted ones increases as the size of the aperture is reduced, to the point where it becomes significant. After passing through a small aperture, the previously parallel light waves become diverged (i.e., they spread out in different directions) and consequently travel different distances between the iris diaphragm and the digital sensor, causing some light waves to shift out of phase and interfere with others. This process of interference creates a diffraction pattern that is manifest as a general softening of detail in the image.

At a certain lens aperture, the loss of resolution (softening) that occurs due to the effects of diffraction cancels any gain in perceived sharpness due to increased depth of field. At this point, the camera lens is said to have become "diffraction limited." It is essential to know the diffraction limit for your lens(es) and different cameras, since there is no

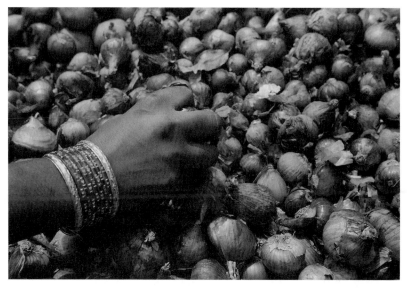

Diffraction is an important consideration, as it will often negate any increase in perceived sharpness achieved when shooting at small lens apertures.

point in selecting aperture values beyond the diffraction limit, as image resolution will become increasingly degraded and exposure times will be extended with the risk of further loss of resolution through camera or subject movement.

I recommend you test each of your lenses with your D90 to determine the diffraction limit for your own equipment. As a general rule, I find diffraction limit for Nikon DX-format models to be around f/11 to f/13. Keep this in mind when you are looking to maximize depth of field by choice of lens aperture, and avoid using smaller values.

Shutter Speed Considerations

If you handhold your camera, it is worth remembering a rule of thumb concerning the minimum shutter speed that is generally sufficient to prevent a loss of sharpness due to camera shake. For the DX-format, multiply the focal length of the lens by 1.5x, and then take the reciprocal value of the focal length and use this as the slowest shutter speed with that lens while hand-holding the camera (as opposed to using a tripod). For example, a focal length of 300mm would require a minimum shutter speed of 1/450 second (300 x 1.5); the closest value available on the D90 is 1/500-second.

The shutter speed can, however, be used for creative effect, because it controls the way the motion of the subject or camera is depicted in a photograph. Conventionally, a fast shutter speed is used to freeze motion in sports or action photography; however, slower shutter speeds can be used to introduce a degree of blur that will often evoke a greater sense of movement compared with a subject that is rendered pin-sharp. The panning technique is an example: Using a slow shutter speed while moving the camera to track the subject so that it appears relatively sharp against an increased level of blur in the background. Or, if you simply hold the camera still and use a slow shutter speed for a moving subject, the subject will appear to blur across the image frame; the slower the shutter speed and/or the faster the subject's movement, the more dramatic the blur.

I used a relatively slow shutter speed here—1/30 second. That was slow enough to show that the snake was moving, but not so slow that the rest of the image lost any clarity. ⇨

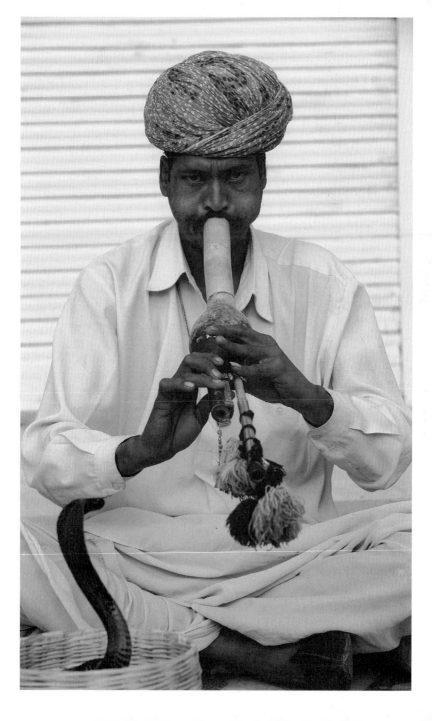

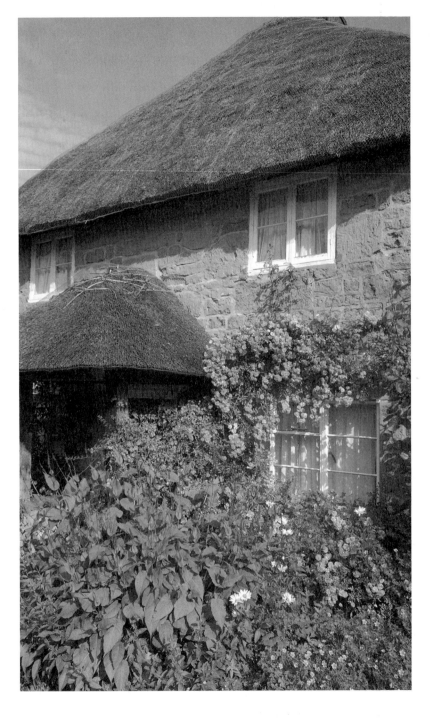

Working Digitally

In addition to image data, the picture files generated by the D90 contain a wealth of other information, including the shooting parameters and instructions about printing pictures. This information is tagged to the image file using a number of common standards, depending on the sort of information to be saved with the image file. The following standards are supported by the D90:

DCF (v 2.0): Design Rule for Camera File System (DCF) is a standard in the digital imaging industry to ensure compatibility across different makes of cameras.

DPOF: Digital Print Order Format (DPOF) is a standard that allows pictures to be printed from a print order saved on a memory card.

EXIF (v 2.21): The D90 supports Exchangeable Image File Format for Digital Still cameras (EXIF), which allows information stored with image files to be read by software, and helps ensure image quality when an EXIF-compliant printer is used.

PictBridge: A standard that permits an image file stored on a memory card to be outputted directly to a printer without the need to connect the camera to a computer, or download the image file from a memory card to a computer first.

The D90 supports a number of digital information standards, making it compatible with many other devices and technologies.

Metadata

Metadata is any data that helps to describe the content or characteristics of a file. You may be familiar with viewing and perhaps adding some basic metadata through the File Info or Document Properties box found in many software applications and some operating systems. You may also use a digital image management application that can search file properties and display them for you.

EXIF Data

The D90 uses the EXIF standard (see page 345) to tag additional information to each image file it records. Most popular digital imaging software is able to read and interpret the EXIF tags, so the information can be displayed; but other, non-imaging or off-brand software may not be as capable, in which case, some or all of the EXIF data values may not be available. The information recorded includes:

- Nikon (the name of the camera manufacturer)
- D90 (the model number)
- Camera firmware version number
- Exposure information, including shutter speed, aperture, exposure mode, ISO, Ev value, date/time, exposure compensation, flash mode, and focal length
- Thumbnail of the main image

Examining EXIF data, by either viewing the image information pages on the camera's monitor or accessing the shooting data in appropriate software, is a great teaching aid because you can see exactly what the camera settings were for each shot. By comparing pictures with their shooting data, you can quickly learn about the technical aspects of exposure, focusing, metering, and flash exposure control.

IPTC (DNPR)/XMP Metadata

Other metadata that can be tagged to an image file includes the use of a standard developed by the International Press Telecommunications Council (IPTC). Known as Digital Newsphoto Parameter Record (DNPR), it can append image

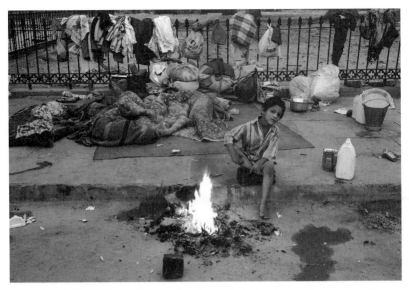

Digital Newsphoto Parameter Record technology allows you to attach copyright information to your photos. If you do any photojournalism, it is highly recommended, and sometimes required, that copyright and origin data accompany your image files.

information to include details of the origin, authorship, copyright, caption details, and keywords for searching purposes. Any application that is DNPR-compliant will show this information and allow you to edit it. If you are considering submitting any pictures you shoot with the D90 for publication, you should make use of DNPR (IPTC) metadata, as most publishing organizations require it to be present before accepting a submission.

Adobe's Extensible Metadata Platform (XMP) is an open-standard, digital labeling technology that allows metadata to be embedded into an image file. Any XMP-enabled software application allows descriptions and titles, searchable keywords, plus author and copyright information, to be stored in a format that is easily understood by other software applications, hardware devices, and even file formats. Since XMP is extensible, it can accommodate existing metadata schemes.

The EXIF metadata recorded by the D90 is not saved as standard IPTC/XMP metadata; however, standard IPTC/XMP metadata can be embedded automatically in images recorded by the D90 during transfer by completing the appropriate IPTC/XMP data fields under the [Embedded info] tab in Nikon Transfer software. Nikon View NX and Nikon Capture NX2 also support the EXIF, IPTC, and XMP standards.

Camera Connections

The external connection ports for the D90 are located under a rubber cover on the left side of the camera.

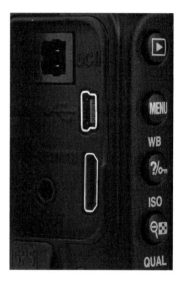

The D90 can be connected to many different devices for the purpose of image display and image transfer using ports located on the left side of the camera. This section outlines the various processes.

AV (Video) Out
The D90 can be connected to a television set or LCD screen for playback, or alternatively, to a VCR or DVD player for recording of saved images. In many countries, the camera is supplied with the EG-D2 video cable for this purpose. First you need to select the appropriate video standard. To do

this, open the Setup menu, navigate to the [Video Mode] item, and press ⊚ . Highlight the desired option, [NTSC] or [PAL], and then press ⊚ again to confirm the selection. NTSC is the video standard used in the USA, Canada, and Japan, while PAL is used in most European countries.

Before connecting the camera to the video cord, make sure the camera power is switched off. Open the rubber cover on the left end of the camera body to reveal the AV-out port. Connect the narrow jack-pin of the EG-D2 to the camera and the other end to the TV, LCD screen, VCR, or DVD player (the yellow plug goes to the video input and the white plug to the audio input). Tune the TV to the video channel, then turn on the camera and press the ▶ button. The image that would normally be displayed on the LCD monitor will be shown on the television screen and can now be recorded to video or DVD. The LCD monitor can still be used to display camera menus and all other camera operations will function normally. This means that you can take pictures with the camera connected to a TV set and carry out review / playback functions simply by looking at the TV screen. It is probably best to use the EH-5/EH-5a AC adapter if you intend to use the camera for an extended period for image playback via a television screen.

Connecting via HDMI
The D90 can be connected to an HDMI device using a type-C mini-pin HDMI cable. Check the HDMI format options in the Setup menu under the [HDMI] item; the [Auto] option is the default. Then, switch the camera off and connect the HDMI cable to the HDMI port (it is located next to the video out [AV Out] connector). Tune the device to the HDMI channel. Then turn the camera on and press the ▶ button. The camera's LCD monitor will remain blank, as the display of images or menus is not supported when the camera is connected via the HDMI output; however, all other camera operations will function normally.

Connecting to a Computer

The D90 can be connected directly to a computer via the supplied UC-E4 USB cable. The camera supports the high-speed USB (2.0) interface that offers a maximum transfer rate of 480Mbps. You can download images from the camera using the supplied Nikon Transfer software. Images can be viewed and organized using the supplied Nikon View NX software, while the optional Nikon Capture NX2 can be used enhance images recorded by the D90. Alternatively, the D90 can be controlled from the computer using the optional Nikon Camera Control Pro 2 software.

Hint: If you use the D90 tethered to a computer for any function, ensure that the installed camera battery is fully charged. Or preferably, use the EH-5 or EH-5a AC adapter in conjunction with an installed battery to prevent interruptions to data transfer by loss of power.

Before connecting the D90 to a computer, check that one of the following operating systems is running:

- Windows Vista (32-bit Home basic/Home Premium/Business/Enterprise/Ultimate Edition, with SP1), or Windows XP (Home, or Pro, with SP3)
- Macintosh OS X (version 10.3.9, 10.4.11, 10.5.3 or 10.5.4)

Also make sure that the appropriate Nikon software (Nikon Transfer and Nikon View NX) is installed.

Direct USB Connection

To connect the camera to a computer, start by turning the camera off, then turn the computer on and wait for it to start up. Connect the USB cable to the USB port of the camera (also located under the large rubber cover on the left side) and to the computer. Turn the camera on.

Nikon Transfer should start automatically. I recommend you set the preferences by clicking on the [Preferences] tab before clicking on the [Transfer] button to initiate data trans-

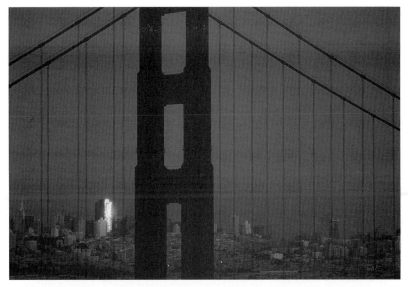

Although connecting the camera directly to a computer to transfer photos can be very convenient, because it eliminates the need to carry any additional equipment, a card reader can be simpler and will save wear and tear on the camera. Card readers are also fairly inexpensive and compact.

fer the first time you use the application. The camera can be turned off as soon as the data transfer is complete.

Memory Card Readers

Although the D90 can be tethered directly to a computer for transferring image data, there are several reasons why you should consider using a dedicated memory card reader as an alternative:

- If you use the tethered camera method, you will drain battery power and risk data being lost or corrupted if the power fails.
- Using a card reader allows you to run software to recover lost or corrupted image files as well as diagnose problems with the memory card.

- You can leave a card reader permanently attached to your computer, which further reduces the risk of losing or corrupting files as a result of a poor connection due to the wear and tear caused by constantly connecting the camera.

Direct Printing

As mentioned previously, the D90 supports a standard that allows either individual or multiple pictures to be printed directly from the camera via a USB connection without the aid of a computer. Alternatively, you can use the camera to select specific images on the memory card, using Digital Print Order Format feature ([Print set DPOF] in the Playback menu), and print those selections directly from the card. Regardless, this feature is only compatible with JPEG image files and a printer that supports the PictBridge standard (see page 345).

Note: Nikon recommends that images destined for direct printing should be recorded in the sRGB color space (use the [Color Space] item in the Shooting menu).

Direct Printer Link

The D90 can be connected to a PictBridge compatible printer to print pictures directly from the camera. Start by turning the camera off, and then turn the printer on before connecting the printer to the camera via the supplied UC-E4 USB lead; do not connect the camera and printer via a USB hub. Turn the camera on and a welcome message will show on the camera's LCD screen, followed by the PictBridge playback display.

Note: It is essential that you make sure the camera battery is fully charged or use the EH-5/EH-5a AC adapter.

Printing a Single Picture

To select a picture for printing from the PictBridge playback display, scroll through the images saved on the memory card, using ▲ and ▼. To view an enlarged section of the image, press ⊕ button; press ▶ to return to the normal full-frame view. To view up to six thumbnail images at a time, press ⊖∙∙ . Use the multi selector button to highlight an individual thumbnail picture. Again, you can press ⊕ to display the selected thumbnail image in full frame.

To print a single image selected in the PictBridge playback display, press and release the ⊛ button. The PictBridge printing menu will appear. Use ▲ or ▼ to select the required option and press ▶ to select it:

Option	Description
Page Size	Press ▲ and ▼ to select the appropriate paper size from the [Printer Default] item: [3.5 x 5in], [5 x 7in], or [A4]. Then press ⊛ to select the option and return to the main print menu.
Number of Copies	Press ▲ and ▼ to select the number of copies of the highlighted image to be printed (maximum 99), and then press ⊛ to select the option and return to the main print menu.
Border	Press ▲ and ▼ to select [Printer Default] (uses default setting of current printer), [Print with Border] (white border), or [No Border]. Then press ⊛ to select option and return to the main print menu.
Time Stamp	Press ▲ and ▼ to select [Printer Default] (uses default setting of current printer), [Print Time Stamp] (date and time images were recorded will be printed), or [No Time Stamp]. Use ⊛ to select the option and return to the main print menu.
Cropping	Press ▲ and ▼ to select [Crop] (picture can be cropped in-camera), or [No Cropping] (printed full frame). Selecting [No Cropping] and pressing ⊛ returns you to the main print menu. Selecting [Crop] and then pressing ▶ displays a dialog box; press ⊕ to increase the size of the crop, and press ⊖∙∙ to reduce the crop. Use ⊕ to position the crop frame. Press ⊛ to return to the main print menu.
Start Printing	Select [Start printing] and press ⊛ to print the image highlighted in the PictBridge display. To cancel the process before all copies have been printed, press ⊛ button.

Printing Multiple Pictures

Multiple pictures can be printed either directly from the camera by connecting it to a compatible printer, or by using the DPOF feature; in the case of the latter option, either the camera or memory card can be connected directly to the printer.

To print directly from the camera, connect it to a compatible printer as described above, and make sure the PictBridge playback display is shown on the LCD monitor. Now press the **MENU** button to display the available options (a description of these four options is set out below), highlight the required option and press ▶ :

Option	Description
Print Select	The selected images are printed.
Select date	Print one copy of all the pictures taken on the selected date.
Print (DPOF)	The current DPOF print order set is printed (DPOF date and information options are not supported).
Index Print	Creates an index print of all images saved in the JPEG format. (If the memory card contains more than 256 JPEG images, only the first 256 will be printed.) Press the ⊙ button to display a sub-menu with three further options: [Page Size], [Border], and [Time Stamp]. These have the same options as described in the table for single-image printing (see above).

Print Select

If the [Print Select] option is chosen from the PictBridge menu and ▶ pressed, six thumbnail images will be displayed on the monitor. Use the multi selector button to scroll through the images, and press ⊕ to see the highlighted image full frame. To select the image highlighted currently for printing, press ◉▦ and ▲ ; the image is marked with 凸 and the number of copies to be printed is set to one [1]. To specify the number of copies of each image selected for printing, keep the ◉▦ button pressed then use ▲ and ▼ to increase or decrease the number respectively. Repeat this process for each image to be printed. To deselect a picture for printing, press ▼ when the number of prints is set to [1]. Press ⓞⓚ to display the print options for multiple printing and set [Page size], [Border type], and [Time stamp] options as required according to the instructions previously described under "Printing a Single Picture." To print selected images, highlight [Start Printing] and press ⓞⓚ .

Images saved in the NEF format will be displayed in the Print Selected menu, but it is not possible to select them for printing. However, it is possible to create a JPEG copy of an NEF file by using the [NEF (RAW) processing] item in the Retouch menu.

Select Date
To print all the pictures taken on a specific date, highlight the [Select date] option from the PictBridge menu and press ▶ ; a list of the dates recorded in the EXIF data of image files stored on the installed memory card will be displayed. Press ▲ or ▼ to selected the desired date, and then press ▶ to select it. To view the pictures taken on a specific date, highlight the date and press ⊖▧ ; use ⊖▧ to scroll through the pictures or press ⊕ to view the highlighted picture at full screen. Once a specific date is selected, press ⓞⓚ to display the print options for multiple printing and set [Page size], [Border type], and [Time stamp] options as required according to the instructions detailed previously under "Printing a Single Picture." To print selected images, highlight [Start Printing] and press ⓞⓚ .

Print (DPOF)
The D90 supports the Digital Print Order Format (DPOF) standard that embeds an instruction set in the appropriate EXIF data fields of an image file. This allows you to insert the memory card into any DPOF-compatible home printer or commercial minilab printer, and automatically get a set of prints of only those images you wish to print. Apart from the fact that you do not have to attach the camera to a compatible printer through a USB connection, this feature can be

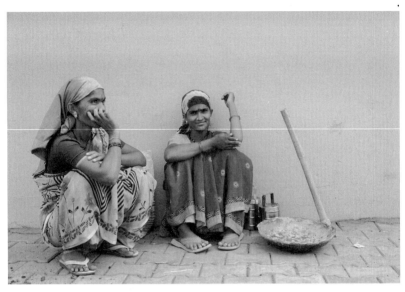

DPOF technology enables you to make a print order in your camera, save it to your memory card, and make prints from it without ever using a computer. This is particularly useful for when you are traveling and do not have access to a computer.

particularly useful if, for example, you are away from home, as you can still produce prints from your digital files even if you do not have access to your own printer; DPOF prints can be made by any DPOF compatible printer.

To select images for printing using the DPOF feature, it is necessary to create a DPOF print order from the images saved to the memory card. Start by highlighting [Print set (DPOF)] from the Playback menu of the D90; the [Select/Set] option will be highlighted. Press ▶ to select it, and the camera will display a thumbnail of all the images stored on the inserted memory card, in groups of up to six. Use the same procedure as previously described under the Print Select section to select the desired pictures and the number of copies to be printed. Once all images to be printed have been selected, press the ⓞⓚ button to save the selected group of images.

To print the current DPOF print set when the camera is connected to a compatible PictBridge printer, highlight [Print (DPOF)] from the PictBridge playback display and press ▶ to select it. The camera will display a thumbnail of all the images in the current DPOF print set in groups of up to six at a time. If desired, the current print set can be modified using the same procedure as described in the "Print Multiple Pictures" section above, to change the number of copies of each picture to be printed and set [Page size], [Border type], and [Time stamp] under the printing options as required. To print the existing print set without modification or print it once any modifications have been completed, highlight [Start Printing] and press ⓞⓚ .

Note: If the current print set is modified by deleting images from it using a computer (or other device) after the print set has been created and saved, it may not print correctly.

Print set selections can only be made from JPEG format images stored on the memory card; if an image was shot using the NEF+JPEG option, only the JPEG image can be selected for printing. However, it is possible to create a JPEG copy of an NEF file by using the [NEF (RAW) processing] item in the Retouch menu.

Note: There are subtle differences in the functionality between the direct printing routes. For example, direct printing of a single image with the D90 connected to a PictBridge compatible printer allows you to perform cropping before printing, whereas multiple printing from the camera or memory card, the latter using a print set created using the DPOF standard, allows images to be printed only as full frame.

To imprint shooting data on the image, highlight [Data Imprint] and press ▶ to switch the option on or off. To print the date/time the image was recorded on the image, highlight [Imprint Date] and press ▶ to switch the option on or off. To finish, save the print set order by highlighting [Done] and pressing ⓞⓚ . However, information entered via the [Data Imprint] and [Imprint Date] options is not printed when the DPOF print set is printed using a direct USB connection between the camera and printer, but only when the memory card is inserted directly into a PictBridge compatible printer.

To deselect the entire print set, highlight [Print Set (DPOF)] from the Playback menu and press ▶ , then highlight [Deselect all?]. Then press ▶ , highlight [Yes], and press 🆗 to confirm the selection.

Index Print
To make an index print (or a contact sheet, with multiple images on the same page), connect the camera to a compatible printer as described above. Once the PictBridge playback display is open, it is possible create an index print of all the JPEG files on the memory card. Start by pressing the **MENU** button, select the [Index print] option, and then press ▶ . Next, press 🆗 to display the PictBridge printing options and set page size, border type, and time stamp options as required according to the instructions described previously (see pages 353-357—note that if the selected page size is too small, a warning will be displayed). To print, highlight [Start Printing] and press 🆗 . To cancel the operation before printing is complete, press 🆗 .

Digital Workflow

For those photographers who shoot with film, their direct involvement in the production of their pictures usually ends when they hand over the exposed film to be processed and printed by someone else. The digital photographer can exercise a far greater level of control over every stage of image processing, from initial capture in the camera to the output of an image as a print or for electronic display.

It is essential to develop a routine to make sure you work in an efficient and effective manner. You may wish to consider the following seven-point workflow as a foundation for establishing one of your own, built around your specific requirements.

Preparation

- Familiarize yourself with your camera. The more intuitive you become with your equipment, the more time you are able to spend concentrating on the scene/subject being photographed.
- Make sure the camera battery is charged and always carry a spare.
- Rather than saving all your pictures to a single, high-capacity memory card, reduce the risk of a catastrophic loss due to card failure or loss by spreading your images over several memory cards.
- Always clean the low-pass filter array in front of the sensor before you begin a shoot to reduce the level of post-processing work (see pages 363-369).
- Format the memory card in the camera each time you insert the card.

Shooting

- Adjust the camera settings to match the requirements of your shoot. Choose an appropriate image quality, image size, ISO, color space, and white balance.
- Set other camera controls such as metering and autofocus according to the shooting conditions.
- Use the Image Comment feature (see Setup menu) to assign a note about the authorship/copyright of the images you shoot.
- Review images and make any adjustments you deem necessary. Use the histogram display to check the exposure level and use the magnification feature to check image sharpness. However, do not rely on this display to assess color, contrast, or hue; remember, even if you shoot NEF (RAW) you only see a JPEG version of the image displayed on the LCD monitor.
- Do not be in too much of a hurry to delete pictures unless they are obvious failures. It is often better to edit after shooting is completed, rather than "on-the-fly." Memory cards are relatively cheap; so do not skimp on memory capacity.

Transfer

- Before transferring images to your computer, designate a specific folder or folders in which the images will be stored so that you know where to find them.
- Rather than connecting the camera directly to the computer, use a card reader. It is much faster, more reliable, and reduces the wear and tear on the camera.
- If the application used to transfer the image files from the memory card to a computer permits you to assign general information to the image files during transfer (e.g., XMP or DNPR (IPTC) metadata) make sure you at least complete the appropriate fields for image authorship and copyright.
- Consider renaming files and assigning further information and keywords to facilitate searching and retrieving images at a later date.

Edit and File

- Use a browsing application to sort through your pictures. Again, do not be in too much of a hurry to edit out pictures. It is often best to take a second look at images a few days, or even weeks, after they were shot—your opinions about your images will often change.
- Print a contact sheet of small thumbnail images to help you decide which images to retain.

Processing

- Make copies of RAW files and save them to a working file format such as TIFF (RGB) or PSD (Adobe Photoshop).
- Do not use the JPEG format for processing. Each time you modify file data and resave it as a JPEG, compression will be applied to the altered data. The effects of repeated compression are cumulative.
- Make adjustments in an orderly and logical sequence, starting with overall brightness, contrast, and color. Then make more local adjustments to correct problems or enhance the image.
- Save your adjusted file as a master copy to which you can then apply a crop, resizing, unsharp mask, and any other finishing touches appropriate to your output

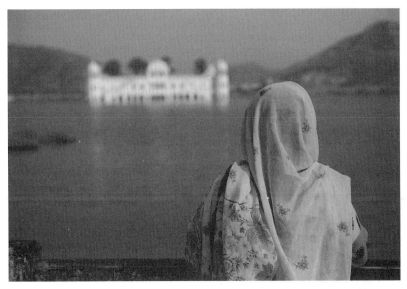

Stay on top of keeping your picture files organized and manageable. This will make your life much easier—especially if you do any professional shooting like photojournalism, stock, wedding, or commercial photography.

requirements. The maxim to follow here is: Process once; output many times.

Archive
- Data can become lost or corrupted at any time for a variety of reasons—always make multiple backup copies of your original files and the edited master copies.
- If you shoot in NEF format, consider creating a copy of all your NEF files in Adobe's open Digital Negative (DNG) format to help ensure compatibility with future iterations of software.
- CDs have a limited capacity, so consider using DVDs or an external hard drive. No electronic storage media is guaranteed 100% safe, nor does it have an infinite lifespan—always check your backup copies regularly and repeat the back-up process as required.

Display

- We all shoot pictures to share with others. Digital technology has expanded the possibilities of image display considerably: We can e-mail pictures to family, friends, colleagues, and clients; prepare digital slideshows; or post images to a website for pleasure or profit.

- Home printing in full color is now reliable, cost effective, and above all, attainable. Spend some time to set up your system properly and work methodically: Calibrate your monitor and printer, use an appropriate resolution for the print size you require, and choose paper type and finish accordingly.

- Once you have a high-quality print, ensure you present it in a manner befitting its status; make sure to frame or mount it securely. This will also help to protect it from the effects of light and atmospheric pollutants.

Care for Body and Lenses

Obviously, keeping your camera and lens(es) in a clean and dry environment is very important. But regardless of how scrupulous you are about doing this, dust and dirt will eventually accumulate on or inside your equipment.

Since prevention is better than a cure, always keep the body and lens caps in place when not using your equipment. Always switch the D90 off before attaching or detaching a lens to prevent particles from being attracted to the optical low-pass filter by the electrical charge in the camera's electronics. Remember, gravity is your friend! Whenever you change lenses, get in to the habit of holding the camera body with the lens mount facing downwards. For the same reason, do not carry or store your D90 on its back, as particles already inside the camera will settle on the optical low-pass filter. Periodically, vacuum-clean the interior of your camera bag/case; it is amazing how much debris can collect there! Sealing you camera body in a clear plastic bag, which you then keep within your camera case will add another valuable layer of protection in very dusty or damp conditions. In the latter situation, keep some sachets of silica gel inside the bag to absorb any moisture. Putting together a basic cleaning kit is important. You should consider the following:

- 1/2-inch (12mm) artist's paintbrush made from soft sable hair for general cleaning
- Micro-fiber lens cloth for cleaning lens elements
- Micro-fiber towel (available from any good camera store or outdoors store) for absorbing moisture when working in damp conditions (I find these towels invaluable in all sorts of conditions, and they are soft enough to use for cleaning lenses and filters)
- Rubber-bulb blower made for cleaning lenses and the low-pass filter

Always brush or blow as much material off of your equipment as possible before wiping it with a cloth. For lens elements and filters, use a micro-fiber cloth and wipe surfaces in short strokes, not a sweeping circular motion. Turn the cloth frequently to prevent depositing the dirt you have just removed back onto the same surface! For any residue that cannot be removed with a dry cloth, you will need a lens cleaning fluid suitable for photographic lenses. Apply a small amount of fluid to the cloth—never directly to the lens, as it may seep inside and cause damage. Wipe the residue away and then buff the glass with a dry area of the cloth. Any lens cloth should be washed on a regular basis to keep it clean, although it is not recommended to dry them in the dryer, as static electricity can attract dust to an otherwise clean cloth.

Cleaning the Low-Pass Filter

Unwanted material such as dust or particles of lint can accumulate inside the D90 and may settle on the surface of the optical low-pass filter (OLPF). This is an unfortunate problem that can afflict any digital camera, especially those with interchangeable lenses, because foreign matter can enter the camera when a lens is removed or exchanged. Focusing or adjusting the zoom ring of a lens causes groups of lens elements to shift inside the lens barrel, creating very slight changes in air pressure. This can cause dust in the atmosphere to be drawn through the lens into the camera. Furthermore, the operation of internal camera mechanisms such as the shutter and reflex mirror can generate minute particles due to the wear and tear of the moving parts. During the manufacture of the D90, Nikon has attempted to reduce the incidence of such problems by cycling the shutter mechanism many hundreds of times before it is installed in the camera.

Any dust or other material that settles on the low-pass filter will often appear as dark spots in your pictures; they cast a shadow on the camera's sensor that is located behind this filter. The exact nature of the appearance of these shadows will depend on the size of the particle and the lens aperture you use. At very large apertures (f/1.4), it is likely that most very small dust specks will not be visible. However, at small apertures (f/22), they will probably show up with well-defined edges.

Self-Cleaning

The D90 incorporates a self-cleaning function that vibrates the OLPF at four different frequencies using a piezoelectric oscillator. The cleaning process can be set to activate automatically when the camera is turned on, turned off, or both. Alternatively, it can be activated at any time you deem it necessary.

Make sure the camera is placed base-down on a solid surface whenever you use the self-cleaning feature. There are two good reasons for this: First, the effect of vibrating the low-pass filter will be most efficient when the camera is supported firmly; and second, there is a strip of adhesive material located along the bottom edge of the low-pass filter that is designed to capture and retain any dislodged material.

To configure the self-cleaning feature, open the Setup menu and navigate to the [Clean image sensor] option and press ⊛ to display two options: [Clean now] and [Clean at startup/shutdown]. [Clean now] is highlighted by default, and pressing ⊛ will initiate the process during which the message, "Cleaning image sensor" is displayed. The message "Done" is displayed once cleaning is completed. This option can be used at any time during camera operation.

Hint: It worth getting into the habit of checking images periodically as you shoot for any telltale particle shadows; use the zoom function in image playback by pressing the ⊕ button. I have added the [Clean image sensor] item to the listing under [My Menu] on my D90, so I can access it quickly and effectively at any time, should the need to use it arise.

To have the cleaning process commence automatically on a regular basis, open the Setup menu and navigate to the [Clean image sensor] option and press ⊛ , then highlight the [Clean at startup/shutdown] option and press ⊛ to display four options:

- ⦿ON [Clean at startup]: Cleaning is only performed when you turn the camera on.
- ⦿OFF [Clean at shutdown]: Cleaning is only performed when you turn the camera off.
- ⦿ON OFF [Clean at startup and shutdown] (default): Cleaning is performed at both startup and shutdown.
- ⦸ [Cleaning off]: Automatic cleaning function is off.

[Clean at startup] would appear to be the most logical selection, as it will help remove any unwanted material before you start shooting. Having the function operate at camera shutdown will bring no benefit to images that have already been recorded and will have no effect on any material that settles on the low-pass filter while the camera is dormant; therefore, I can see little advantage in running the process at this point.

Any of the following functions will interrupt the sensor cleaning process: raising the built-in Speedlight; pressing the shutter release, Live View (Lv), Depth-of-Field Preview, or AF buttons; using the AE-L/AF-L button to activate focus; or using the Fn button for the FV Lock feature. When operating the sensor cleaning function, a short sequence of very faint high-pitch squeaks may be heard; this is normal and not an indication of malfunction.

Note: If the sensor cleaning process is repeated several times in rapid succession, the D90 may disable the function to protect the camera's electrical circuitry. If this occurs, wait a few minutes before attempting to use the function again.

Manual Cleaning

Nikon expressly recommends that you should leave manual cleaning of the optical low-pass filter to an authorized service center. However, in recognition of the fact that this is likely to be impractical for a variety of reasons, the D90 has a feature that enables the reflex mirror to be locked up in its raised position and the shutter opened to provide access to the front surface of the OLPF.

Caution: Nikon states that under no circumstances should you touch or wipe the low-pass filter. Any manual cleaning process you perform is done entirely at your own risk; any damage caused to the low-pass filter, or any other part of your camera, as a result of manual cleaning by the user will not be covered by warranties provided by Nikon.

To inspect and/or clean the low-pass filter, you need to perform a few preparatory steps. First, ensure the camera has a fully charged battery installed or is powered by the optional EH-5/EH-5a AC adapter. Second, remove the lens or body cap and keep the camera facing downwards. Now switch the camera on, navigate to the [Lock mirror up for cleaning] option in the Setup menu, and press ⊚ to display [Start—OK]. Press ⊛ and a dialog box will appear with the following instruction: "When shutter button is

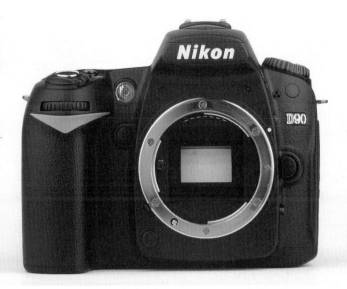

Access to the OLPF for cleaning is via the lens opening; here, the reflex mirror is shown in its lowered position; it must be raised and the shutter opened to reveal the front surface of the OLPF using the [Lock mirror up for cleaning] item in the Setup menu.

pressed, the mirror lifts and shutter opens. To lower mirror, turn camera off." At the same time, a series of dashes will appear in the control panel and viewfinder displays; all other information will disappear. Once the shutter release is pressed all the way down, the mirror will lift and remain in its raised position and the series of dashes in the control panel and viewfinder will begin to blink. Keep the camera facing down so any debris falls away from the filter; look up in to the lens mount to inspect the low-pass filter surface (it is probably helpful to shine a light onto it).

Note: Because the photosites on the CMOS sensor of the D90 are just 5.9 microns (mm) square (one micron = 1/1000 of a millimeter), offending particles are often very, very small, and it is unlikely you will be able to resolve them by eye.

With the camera facing down, use a rubber bulb blower to gently puff air towards the low-pass filter surface. Take care that you do not enter any part of the blower into the camera. Never use an ordinary blower brush with bristles, which can damage the surface of the low-pass filter, or an aerosol-type blower, which might emit propellant agent or cause condensation and leave a residue. Once you have finished cleaning, switch the camera off to return the mirror to its down position. If the blower bulb method fails to remove any stubborn material, I recommend you have the sensor cleaned professionally.

Note: If [icon] or a lower battery level is displayed in the control panel the [Lock mirror up for cleaning] option will be grayed out in the Setup menu.

Caution: *The shutter will close and the mirror will return to its down position if the power supply fails during the cleaning process. This has potentially dire consequences if you have any cleaning utensils in the camera at that time! Therefore, always use a fully charged EN-EL3e battery. If you use an AC adapter, I recommend you also keep a fully charged battery in the camera in case the AC power supply is interrupted during inspection/cleaning of the low-pass filter.*

Also, make sure you never use any alcohol based (e.g., ethanol or methanol) cleaning fluid. The low-pass filter of the D90 has a special anti-static coating made from indium tin oxide that can be damaged by such chemical compounds.

Note: If power from the installed battery begins to run low while the mirror is locked up for cleaning, the camera will emit an audible warning and the self-timer lamp will begin to flash, indicating the mirror will be automatically lowered in approximately two minutes.

For users with plenty of confidence, there is a range of proprietary sensor cleaning materials that can be used to clean stubborn and tenacious material from the low-pass filter. These include brushes, swabs, and fluids that are avail-

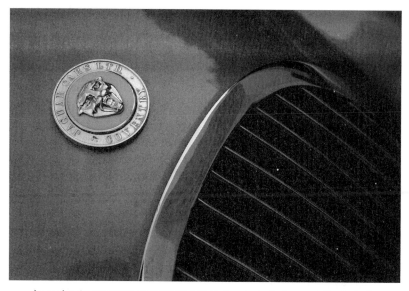

In order to prevent unwanted spots in your photos, particularly in continuous-tone pictures taken at smaller apertures, clean the optical low-pass filter, or have it cleaned professionally, on a regular basis.

able from a number of manufacturers (see the list of resources on pages 390-391). It must be stressed that if you use any such materials or implements, it is done entirely at your own risk. Remember, it is essential that the camera's battery be fully charged before you attempt any manual cleaning procedure (preferably, use the EH-5/EH-5a AC adapter with a fully charged battery installed in the camera at the same time to ensure a continuous power supply).

Finally, if you have Nikon Capture NX2 software, you can use the Dust Reference Photo feature with NEF files shot using the D90 to help remove the effects of dust particles on the low-pass filter by masking their shadows electronically (see pages 246-248 for more details).

Troubleshooting

On occasion, the D90 may not operate as you expect. This may be due to an alternative setting that has been made (often inadvertently), or for some other reason. Many of the reasons for these problems are simple and the solutions are set out in the table below:

Problem	Solution
Display	
Viewfinder appears out of focus	• Adjust viewfinder focus • Use diopter adjustment lens
Viewfinder display is dark	• Battery not inserted • Battery exhausted
Displays turn off unexpectedly	Set longer delay for [auto meter off] CS-c2 / [monitor-off] CS-c4
Unusual characters displayed in control panel	See page 378 information about electrostatic interference
Displays in LCD panels appear slow to react and are dimmed	Effect of high or low temperature
Fine lines visible around the active AF point, or display turns red when AF point is highlighted	Normal behavior for this type of viewfinder; these are not malfunctions.
Shooting (All Modes)	
Camera takes longer than expected to turn on	Delete files / folders
Shutter release disabled	• CPU lens aperture ring not set to minimum value • Memory card not installed, or full • $bu\,L\,b$ selected as shutter speed in S exposure mode
Image shows more than displayed in viewfinder	• Viewfinder coverage is only 96% i in both horizontal and vertical directions—not a malfunction

Problem	Solution
Pictures out of focus	• Set focus mode selector to AF • AF unable to operate; use manual focus
Focus does not lock when shutter release is depressed halfway	Camera in AF-C focus mode: use AF-L/AE-L button to lock focus
Image size cannot be altered	NEF (RAW) selected for image quality
Cannot select focus point	• Unlock focus area selector • Auto-area AF selected for focus mode • Monitor is on: Press shutter release halfway down
Camera is slow to record photos	Turn long exposure noise reduction off
Randomly spaced, bright pixels appear in photos ("noise")	• Select lower ISO setting, or use high ISO noise reduction • Shutter speed exceeds 8 seconds; use long exposure noise reduction
AF-assist illuminator does not light	• AF-C focus mode selected • Center focus point is not selected for Single-point, Dynamic-area, or 3D-tracking AF • [Off] selected for CS-a3 • Illuminator is shut down automatically due to overheating
No picture is taken when remote control shutter release button is pressed	• Remote control battery exhausted • Select remote control mode • Flash is charging • Duration set at CS-c5 has elapsed • Bright light interfering with remote
Photos are blotched or smeared	• Clean lens • Clean low-pass filter
Menu item cannot be selected	Some menu items not available in all exposure modes

Problem	Solution
Shooting (P, A, S, M modes only)	
Shutter-release disabled	• Flash charging • Non-CPU lens attached: select M mode • ᏏuᏞᏏ or (- -) selected in M mode and then mode dial set to S mode: Choose new shutter speed
Full range of shutter speeds not available	• Flash in use. • Select CS-e1 to set [Flash shutter speed] • Select [On] at CS-e5 [Auto FP]
Colors appear unnatural	• Adjust white balance • Adjust Set Picture Control settings
Cannot measure preset white balance	Test target too dark or too bright
Image cannot be selected as source for preset white balance	Image not created with D90
White balance bracketing unavailable	• NEF or NEF + JPEG selected for image quality • Multiple exposure mode is active
Results with Picture Control vary from image to image	Avoid A (auto) for sharpening, contrast, or saturation when shooting a sequence of pictures.
Metering cannot be changed	• Autoexposure Lock is active • Camera is in Live View mode
Exposure compensation cannot be used	Select P, A, or S exposure modes
Only one shot taken when shutter release button is pressed in continuous shooting mode	Lower the built-in flash
Reddish areas and/or uneven textures appear in photos	May occur with long time exposures. Use long exposure noise reduction when shooting with shutter speed set to Bulb

Problem	Solution
Playback	
• Flashing areas appear in images • Shooting data appear on images • A graph appears during playback	Press ⓖ to select photo information displayed, or change settings for Display mode
NEF (RAW) image is not played back	Photo taken at NEF + JPEG image quality
Some photos not displayed in playback mode	Select [All] for [Playback Folder]
"Tall" (portrait) orientation photos are displayed in "Wide" (landscape) orientation	• Select ON for Rotate Tall • [Off] selected for Auto Image Rotation • Camera orientation was altered while shooting in continuous mode • Camera was pointed up/down when shooting
Cannot delete a photo	Photo is protected; remove protection
No images available for display in playback mode	Select [All] for [Playback Folder]
Cannot change print order	• Memory card is full: Delete images • Memory card is locked
Cannot select image for direct printing	• Photo saved in NEF format • Create JPEG copy using [NEF RAW processing] item • Transfer to computer and print using Nikon View NX or Capture NX2
Photos not displayed on TV	Select correct video mode
Photo is not displayed on high-definition video device	Confirm that HDMI cable is connected
NEF photos not displayed in Capture NX	Update software to Capture NX 2 or later

Problem	Solution
Image Dust Off option in Nikon Capture NX 2 is ineffective	Dust off reference data recorded before image sensor cleaning is performed cannot be used with images recorded after image sensor cleaning is performed. Dust off reference data recorded after image sensor cleaning is performed cannot be used with photographs taken before image sensor cleaning is performed.
Computer displays NEF images differently from camera display	Off-brand software does not display effects of Picture Controls, Active D-Lighting, or Vignette Control: Use Capture NX2
Miscellaneous	
Date of recording is not correct	Reset camera clock
Menu item cannot be selected	Some options are not available at certain combinations of settings or when no memory card is inserted [Battery info] is not available when EH-5 / EH-5a is used to power camera.

Error Messages and Displays

The D90 is a sophisticated electronic device capable of reporting a range of malfunctions and problems through indicators and error messages that appear in the displays of the viewfinder, control panel, and monitor. The following table will assist you in finding a solution should one of these indicators or messages be displayed.

Indicator			
Control Panel	**Viewfinder**	**Problem**	**Solution**
FE E (blinks)		Lens aperture ring is not set to minimum aperture.	Set ring to minimum aperture (largest f number).
		Low battery.	Ready a fully charged spare battery.
▭◢ (blinks)	◼▭ (blinks)	• Battery exhausted. • Battery can not be used. • An extremely exhausted rechargeable Li ion battery or a third party battery is inserted either in the camera or in the optional MB D80 battery pack.	• Recharge or replace battery. • Use Nikon approved battery, or contact Nikon authorized service representative. • Replace the battery, or recharge the battery if the rechargeable Li ion battery is exhausted.
CLOCK (blinks)	—	Camera clock is not set.	Set camera clock.
F - - (blinks)		• No lens attached. • Non CPU lens attached.	• Attach non IX Nikkor lens. • Select mode M.
—	● (blinks)	Camera unable to focus using autofocus.	Focus manually.
H I		Subject too bright; photo will be overexposed.	• Use a lower ISO sensitivity • Use optional ND filter • In exposure mode: **S** Increase shutter speed **A** Choose a smaller aperture (larger f-number)

Indicator			
Control Panel	Viewfinder	Problem	Solution

Lo		Subject too dark; photo will be underexposed.	• Use a higher ISO sensitivity
			• Use flash
			• In exposure mode:
			  S Lower shutter speed
			  A Choose a larger aperture (smaller f-number)

buLb (blinks)		buLb selected in exposure mode **S**.	Change shutter speed or select manual exposure mode.
- - (blinks)		selected in exposure mode **S**.	Change shutter speed or select manual exposure mode.
⚡ (blinks)	⚡ (blinks)	Optional flash unit that does not support i-TTL flash control attached and set to TTL.	Change flash mode setting on optional flash unit.
—	⚡ (blinks)	If indicator blinks for 3 s after flash fires, photo maybe underexposed.	Check photo in monitor; if underexposed, adjust settings and try again.
FuLL (blinks)	FuL (blinks)	Memory insufficient to record further photos at current settings, or camera has run out of file or folder numbers.	• Reduce quality or size. • Delete photographs. • Insert new memory card.
(-E-)	🔲 (-E-)	No memory card.	Insert memory card.
Err (blinks)		Camera malfunction.	Release shutter. If error persists or appears frequently, consult Nikon authorized service representative.

Indicator			
Monitor	**Control Panel Viewfinder**	**Problem**	**Solution**
No memory card.	$(-E-)$/ $\boxtimes(-E-)$	Camera cannot detect memory card.	Turn camera off and confirm that card is correctly inserted.
This memory card cannot be used. Card may be damaged. Insert another card.	$[HR,$ $(\quad \boxdot]$ (blinks)	Error accessing cannot beused.	• Use approved card. • Check that contacts are clean. If card is damaged, contact retailer or Nikon representative.
		Unable to create new folder.	Delete files or insert new memory card.
This card is not formatted. Format the card.	For (blinks)	Memory card has not been formatted for use in camera.	Format memory card or insert new memory card.
Folder contains no images	—	No images on memory card or in folder(s) selected for playback	Select folder containing images from Playbackfolder menu or insert different memory card.
All images are hidden.	—	All photos in current folder are hidden.	No images can be played back until another folder has been selected or Hide image used to allow at least one image to be displayed.
File does not contain image data.	—	File has been created or modified using a computer or different make ofcamera, or file is corrupt.	File can not be played back on camera.
Memory card is locked. Slide lock to "write" position.	$[HR,$ $(\quad \boxdot]$ (blinks)	Memory card is locked. (write protected).	Slide card write-protect switch to "write" position.

Indicator		Problem	Solution
Monitor	Control Panel Viewfinder		
Cannot select this file.	—	Memory card does not contain images that can be retouched.	Images created with other devices can not be can be retouched.
No images available for processing.	—	Memory card does not contain NEF (RAW) images.	Take NEF (RAW) photographs.
Check printer.	—	Printer error.	Check printer. To resume, select Continue (if available).
Check paper.	—	Paper in printer is not of selected size.	Insert paper of correct size and select Continue
Paperjam	—	Paper is jammed in printer.	Clear jam and select Continue.
Out of paper.	—	Printer is out of paper.	Insert paper of selected size and select Continue.
Check ink supply.	—	Ink error.	Check ink. To resume, select Continue.
Out of ink.	—	Printer is out of ink.	Replace ink and select Continue.

Electrostatic Interference

Operation of the D90 is totally dependent on electrical power. Occasionally, the camera may stop functioning properly, or display unusual characters or unexpected messages in the viewfinder and LCD displays. Such behavior is generally due to the effects of a strong external electrostatic charge. If this occurs, try switching the camera off, disconnecting it from its power supply (remove the installed EN-EL3e battery or unplug the EH-5/EH-5a AC adapter), then reconnecting the power and switching the camera back on. If the symptoms persist, the camera will require inspection by an authorized technician.

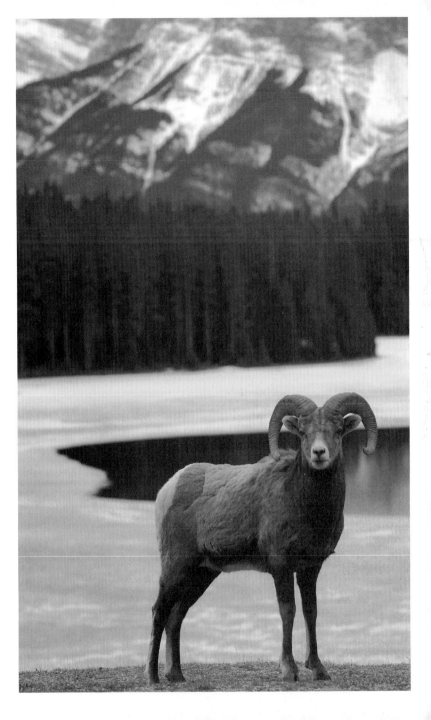

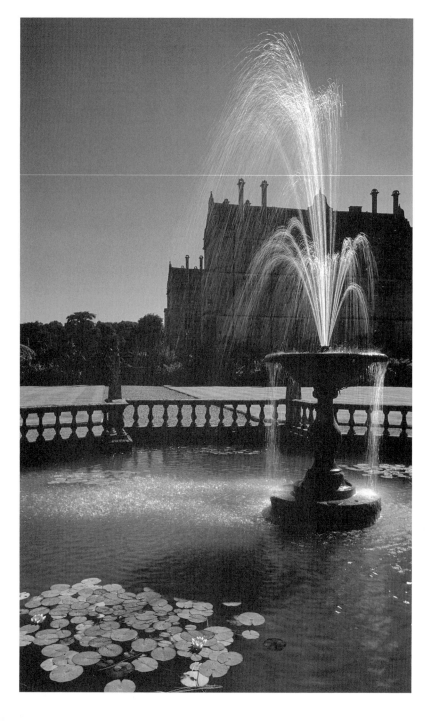

Accessories & Resources

Nikon produces a range of software applications and camera accessories for the D90, together with a vast amount of information and assistance on-line. A wide range of other useful off-brand accessories is available from other sources (see the Resources section below).

Nikon Software

It is beyond the scope of this book to describe fully the features and functions of Nikon's dedicated software, but details can easily be obtained from the technical support sections of the websites maintained by the Nikon Corporation. The D90 is supplied with copies of Nikon Transfer and Nikon View NX (in some regions, a trial version of Nikon Capture NX2 is included). The following section is intended to provide a brief overview of the six principal Nikon software applications in their current versions at the time of this writing:

- Nikon Transfer (version 1.2.0)
- Nikon View NX (version 1.2.0)
- Nikon Capture NX2 (version 2.1.0)
- Nikon Camera Control Pro (version 2.3.0)

For Windows, the following operating systems are supported:

- Microsoft Windows XP Professional (Service Pack 3)
- Microsoft Windows XP Home Edition (Service Pack 3)
- Microsoft Windows Vista (Service Pack 1, 32 bit version)

↺ *Nikon offers a range of software to help you manage your workflow. A suite of software, which can vary according to region and time of purchase, is included with the D90, and other software is available for download from nikonusa.com.*

For Macintosh, the following operating systems are supported:

- Mac OSX 10.4.11 to 10.5.4 (Note that the latest iterations of Nikon Transfer, View NX, and Camera Control Pro2 are also supported by Mac OS 10.3.9.)

Note: For information about Nikon software and to download updates to existing application updates, I recommend you visit the various technical support websites maintained by Nikon, which can be accessed via: www.nikon.com.

Note: At the time of writing, a number of third party RAW file converters that enable NEF files from the D90 to be opened have become available; examples include Adobe Camera RAW 4.6 for Adobe Photoshop CS3, Photoshop Elements 6, or alternatively, Adobe Camera RAW 5.1 for Adobe Photoshop CS4, Photoshop Elements 6, or Elements 7. No doubt other software manufacturers will add support for NEF files from the D90 in due course. Most manufacturers offer their software for a free trial period, so I recommend you try a few to see which meets your requirements before you commit to a licensed purchase.

Nikon Transfer

Nikon Transfer is Nikon's new utility for downloading images from camera or memory card to your computer. Nikon Transfer provides a simple intuitive workflow suitable for all users from beginners to professionals. It is included with the latest Nikon cameras and can also be downloaded for free from Nikon websites. Features include:

- Automatic recognition / auto-start after camera connection or inserting CF/SD card
- Transfers images from CD, external hard drive or other removal media
- Transfers images to computer's hard drive
- Easy selection and viewing of images on up to five external devices before transfer
- Transfer image data, not only to a primary destination, but also to a backup location simultaneously

- Add metadata during transfer; both XMP/IPTC standards are supported
- Select the application the images are displayed in after transfer

Nikon View NX

View NX offers photographers a fast solution to the organization and classification of their digital images. This software uses your computer's file directory to display and browse images. Nikon View NX is included with the latest Nikon D-SLR cameras and can be downloaded for free from Nikon websites. Features include:

- High-speed thumbnail and preview display
- A simple way to choose images; operation similar to Explorer/Finder
- Fast sorting using image rating and labeling classification system
- Includes Picture Control Utility (including sharpening, contrast, saturation, hue, brightness, black-and-white conversion)
- Batch processing to convert file format, resize, rename, change settings, multiple destinations
- Integration with Capture NX2
- Integration with Nikon Transfer
- Printing and email transmission
- IPTC/XMP data compatible (user settings retained when image opened in other supported applications)
- Quick Adjustment features for NEF (RAW) images including white balance, exposure, and creating custom curves

Nikon Capture NX 2

In mid-2008, Nikon released an updated version of Capture NX, which although not an extensive re-working, does introduce some key improvements. As a general-purpose image editing application, Nikon Capture NX2 is really quite good, since all the adjustment features work with JPEG and TIFF files, as they do with NEF files. It incorporates the same unique U-point technology that permits complex selections of an area (or areas) within an image to be made with accuracy and speed, which is far better than can be achieved using current digital imaging software. You have an extensive toolbox available to enhance and modify any image file, regardless of whether it was saved in the NEF RAW, TIFF, or JPEG format.

Capture NX 2 applies non-destructive image processing to NEF RAW files, which means that the original image data is never compromised. Each enhancement that is made is saved in an edit list with the original data and thumbnail. However, changes made to JPEG or TIFF files will alter the data of the original image. To prevent this from occurring, the image can be saved using a different file name or converted into the NEF format. Parameters set on any Nikon camera-produced NEF RAW file, such as white balance, sharpening, color mode, and saturation are applied to the image when it is opened in Nikon Capture NX 2 for editing, so the camera settings are preserved. Established key features include:

- Advanced white balance control with the ability to select a specific color temperature or sample from a gray point.
- Advanced NEF file control that permits attributes such as exposure compensation, sharpening, contrast, color mode, saturation, and hue to be modified after the exposure has been made, without affecting the original image data.
- The Image Dust Off feature, which compares an NEF file with a reference image taken with the same camera to help reduce the effects of any dust particles on the low-pass filter.
- The D-Lighting tool, which emulates the dodge & burn techniques of traditional photographic printing that control highlight and shadow areas to produce a more balanced exposure.
- A Color Noise Reduction tool, which minimizes the effect of random electronic noise that can occur, especially at high sensitivity settings.
- An Edge Noise Reduction tool that accentuates the boundary between areas of the image to make them more distinct.

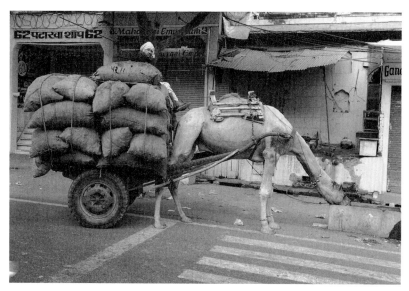

Capture NX/NX2 features editing tools such as white balance adjustment, noise reduction, vignette control, and fisheye effect.

- The Color Moiré Reduction feature helps to remove the effects of moiré, which can occur when an image contains areas with a very fine repeating pattern.
- LCH Editor allows for control of luminosity (overall lightness), chroma (color saturation), and hue in separate channels.
- Lens Vignette control to correct for uneven illumination across an image, particularly near the corners.
- Fisheye Lens tool converts images taken with the AF Fisheye-Nikkor DX 10.5mm f/2.8G lens so they appear as though they were taken using a conventional rectilinear lens with a diagonal angle-of-view equivalent to approximately 120°.

NX2 is without a doubt the most effective and efficient iteration of the application to date making it a pleasure to work with. New key features include:

- A new Workspaces option provides four pre-defined palette and toolbar configurations (Browser, Metadata, Multi-Purpose, and Edit) with support for two monitors; plus you can create your own custom Workspace (desktop layout), which can be supported across one or two displays. The pre-defined and custom Workspaces can be assigned a keyboard shortcut to help improve efficiency (Option/Alt plus keys 1 through 9 are assignable for this purpose).
- An improved browser palette with an extended feature set that should obviate the need to switch to and fro between Capture NX and View NX for thumbnail viewing. The new Workspaces makes it more straightforward to move in and out of the browser where there is ready access to labels, ratings, primary and secondary sort and filter options, the ability to display NEF files, JPEG files (or both), as well as TIFF files. There is also a new Favorite Folders option that makes accessing frequently used folders very quick. The time it takes to open an image from the browser has been reduced significantly.
- New Quick Fix and Adjust sections of the Edit List improve the general layout and access to key tools such Exposure Compensation, levels and curves adjustments, Contrast, Saturation, and the new Highlight Protection and Shadow Protection controls.
- The U-Point technology of Capture NX, which is the key to its image editing simplicity, has been extended to almost all photo adjustment tools, including Noise Reduction and Unsharp Mask, to enhance an already powerful feature for applying local changes to an image.
- There is a new Auto Retouch Brush that provides a one-click tool to remove the effects of dust spots and other blemishes in an image.

However, it still lacks one important attribute – the ability to batch process a large number of files in a reasonable amount of time; in this respect, Nikon Capture NX2 lags behind its competitors, such as Lightroom 2.1 from Adobe.

Camera Control Pro 2

Camera Control Pro 2 enables remote control of the key shooting functions of the D90 from a computer that is connected via USB cable; however, unlike some other Nikon camera models such as the D300, D700, and D3, the D90 does not allow connection though either a wired (Ethernet) or wireless LAN using a wireless transmitter. Features and functions of the D90 such as Live View and the Picture Control System are supported. The Viewer feature in the application enables the preview and selection of images prior to transfer to a computer. It also integrates with Nikon View NX and Nikon Capture NX2 software. Key features include:

- Most settings of Nikon D-SLR cameras, such as exposure mode, shutter speed, and aperture can be controlled remotely.
- Images in a camera buffer can be confirmed with thumbnail or preview display on a computer prior to transferring, enabling deletion of unwanted images.
- Support of the Live View function of the D90; it permits adjustment and confirmation of focus point via the image displayed on a computer monitor and control of the shutter release mode; it is also possible to control the contrast-detect AF system in the Live View Tripod mode from a computer monitor.
- Supports Picture Control System of the cameras. Picture Control parameters can be selected and adjusted on a computer, and custom curves (to modify contrast) can be created and saved.
- Multiple-point AF systems can be controlled and displayed on a computer monitor.
- Fine-tuning of White Balance is available.

General Nikon Accessories

The MC-DC2 remote release cable for the D90.

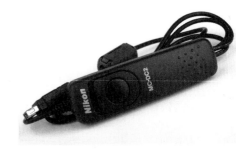

AS-15: Accessory shoe adapter that has a standard PC sync socket for connecting the D90 to a non-dedicated flash unit via a PC sync cable.

BF-1A: The body cap that will help prevent dust from entering the camera. Keep it in place at all times when a lens is not mounted on the camera. A BF-1A is supplied with the D90.

Note: The earlier BF-1 body cap cannot be used. It may damage the lens mount of the D90.

BM-10: Monitor screen cover for D90

DG-2: This viewfinder eyepiece magnifier provides an approximate 2x magnification of the central area of the viewfinder field.

Note: The DG-2 requires the DK-22 eyepiece adapter to be fitted.

DK-20C: An optional viewfinder eyepiece lens available in a range of strengths to facilitate viewing without wearing your normal eyeglasses.

DK-21: The standard viewfinder eyepiece for the D90; one is supplied with the camera.

DK-21M: An optional viewfinder eyepiece lens that magnifies the viewfinder image by approximately 1.2x.

DK-22: An optional viewfinder eyepiece adapter for attaching the DG-2 eyepiece magnifier.

DR-6: A right angle viewer that can attach directly to the circular frame of the viewfinder eyepiece on the D90. It is useful for when the camera is at a low shooting position.

EH-5a: The multi-voltage AC adapter used to power the D90.

EN-EL3e: The dedicated lithium ion battery.

GP-1: Dedicated Global Positioning System (GPS) device that enables the D90 to record longitude, latitude, altitude, and time information within the EXIF data of an image file; it connects via the accessory terminal.

MB-D80: The battery-pack for the D90; accepts one or two EN-EL3e(s), or 6x AA batteries, and provides a second shutter release button, an AE-L/AF-L button, and a pair of command dials.

MC-DC2: The standard remote shutter release cord (39-inch/1.0m) that connects to the accessory terminal on the D90.

MH-18a: The multi-voltage AC charger for a single EN-EL3e battery; the MH-18a is supplied with the D90.

ML-L3 Remote Control: An infrared remote release for the D90 that requires a single 3V CR2025 battery.

SB-400: An external Speedlight (flash unit) for the D90. It can be attached to the camera's accessory shoe or via the SC-28/SC-29 TTL flash cord.

SB-600: An external Speedlight (flash unit) for the D90. It can be attached to the camera's accessory shoe or via the SC-28/SC-29 TTL flash cord.

SB-800: An external Speedlight (flash unit) for the D90. It can be attached to the camera's accessory shoe or via the SC-28/SC-29 TTL flash cord.

SB-900: An external Speedlight (flash unit) for the D90. It can be attached to the camera's accessory shoe or via the SC-28/SC-29 TTL flash cord.

SB-R200: An external Speedlight (flash unit) for the D90 intended for close-up and macro photography. It cannot be attached to camera's accessory shoe; it requires the use of the optional SU-800 Speedlight Commander unit or an SB-800 / SB-900 Speedlight used in its Commander mode.

SC-28: A TTL flash cord that maintains full functionality between a compatible external Speedlight and a D90.

SC-29: A TTL flash cord that maintains full functionality between a compatible external Speedlight and a D90; the terminal unit that attaches to the camera has a built-in AF-assist lamp.

SD-8a: External battery pack for SB-900 or SB-800 Speedlight (flash unit).

SD-9: External battery pack for SB-900 Speedlight (flash unit).

SK-6 / SK-6a: Power bracket for SB-900 or SB-800 Speedlight (flash unit); it attaches to the base of the D90, allowing the flash to be mounted farther from the central axis of the lens.

UC-E4: USB cable for connecting the D90 to another USB compliant device; a cable is supplied with the camera.

WG-AS3: Cover for the foot of the SB-900 Speedlight to protect the camera accessory shoe from water.

The MB-D80 Multi Battery Pack is pictured here with two EN-EL3e batteries installed.

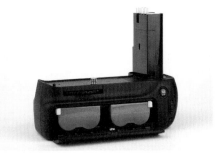

Resources

A number of other manufacturers and suppliers provide equipment to compliment and enhance the performance of the cameras and flash accessories produced by Nikon. The following is a list of some that you may find useful:

B+W: Manufacturers of filters and accessories; http://www.schneideroptics.com

Gitzo: Manufacturers of tripods, monopods, and general camera support accessories; http://www.gitzo.com

HDRsoft: Authors of the popular Photomatix high-dynamic range software; http://www.hdrsoft.com

Kirk Enterprises: Manufacturers of camera and flash accessories, including flash brackets; http://www.kirkphoto.com

Lastolite: Manufacturers of lighting accessories for portable flash units and a wide range of reflectors, diffusers, and other light modifying devices; http://www.lastolite.com

Lee Filters: Manufacturers of both lens and lighting filters, including graduated filters; http://www.leefilters.com

Lexar Media: Manufacturers of flash memory cards, including Secure Digital (SD) and high-capacity Secure Digital (SDHC) cards compatible with the D90; http://www.lexar.com

Lightshpere: A range of flash diffusion devices designed by photographer Gary Fong; http://www.garyfong.com

Lumiquest: Manufacturers of flash modifiers and diffusers; http://www.lumiquest.com

Manfrotto: Manufacturers of tripods, lighting stands, and flash support accessories; http://www.manfrotto.com

Really Right Stuff: Manufacturers of an extensive range of camera, flash, close-up, and panoramic photography accessories; http://www.reallyrightstuff.com

SanDisk: Manufacturers of flash memory cards, including Secure Digital (SD) and high-capacity Secure Digital (SDHC) cards compatible with the D90; http://www.sandisk.com

Singh-Ray: Manufacturers of camera lens filters, including graduated filter types; http://www.singh-ray.com

Web Support

Nikon maintains product support and provides further information online at the following sites:

http://www.nikon.com/ - global gateway to Nikon Corporation

http://www.nikonusa.com/ - for continental North America

http://www.europe-nikon.com/support - for most European countries

http://www.nikon-asia.com/ - for Asia, Oceania, Middle East, and Africa

Glossary

AI
Automatic Indexing.

angle of view
The area that can be recorded by a lens, usually measured in degrees across the diagonal of the film frame. Angle of view depends on both the focal length of the lens and the size of its image area.

anti-aliasing
A technique that reduces or eliminates the jagged appearance of lines or edges in an image by filling in nearby pixels with intermediate values.

aperture
The opening in the lens that allows light to enter the camera. Aperture is usually described as an f/number. The higher the f/number, the smaller the aperture; the lower the f/number, the larger the aperture.

bit depth
The number of bits per pixel that determines the number of colors the image can display. Eight bits per pixel is the minimum requirement for a photo-quality color image.

buffer
Temporarily stores data so that other programs, on the camera or the computer, can continue to run while data is in transition. Also called a memory buffer.

card reader
A device that connects to your computer and enables the quick and easy download of images from memory card to computer.

CMOS
Complementary Metal-Oxide Semiconductor. Like CCD sensors, this sensor type converts light into an electrical impulse. Unlike CCDs, CMOS sensors allow individual processing of pixels, are less expensive to produce, and use less power. See also, CCD.

color cast
A colored hue over the image often caused by improper lighting or incorrect white balance settings. Can be produced intentionally for creative effect.

color space
A mapped relationship between colors and computer data about the colors.

compression
A method of reducing file size through removal of redundant data. Comes in two forms: lossy (i.e., JPEG) and lossless (i.e., TIFF).

contrast
The difference between two or more tones in terms of luminance, density, or darkness.

depth of field (DOF)
The image space in front of and behind the plane of focus that appears acceptably sharp in the photograph. Determined by aperture, focal length, and camera-to-subject distance.

Ev
Exposure value. A number that quantifies the amount of light within a scene, allowing you to determine the relative combinations of aperture and shutter speed to accurately reproduce the light levels of that exposure.

firmware
Software that is permanently incorporated into a hardware chip. All computer-based equipment, including digital cameras, uses firmware of some kind.

focal length
When the lens is focused on infinity, it is the distance from the optical center of the lens to the film or sensor plane.

focal plane
The plane perpendicular to the axis of the lens that is the sharpest point of focus. Also, it may be the film plane or sensor plane.

FP high-speed sync
Focal Plane high-speed sync. An FP mode in which the output of an electronic flash unit is pulsed to match the small opening of the shutter as it moves across the sensor, so that the flash unit can be used with higher shutter speeds than the normal flash sync limit of the camera. In this flash mode, the level of flash output is reduced and, consequently, the shooting range is reduced.

f/stop
The size of the aperture or diaphragm opening of a lens, also referred to as f/number or stop. The term stands for the ratio of the focal length (f) of the lens to the width of its aperture opening. (f/1.4 = wide opening, and f/22 = narrow opening.) Each stop up (lower f/number) doubles the amount of light reaching the sensitized medium. Each stop down (higher f/number) halves the

amount of light reaching the sensitized medium.

gray card
A card used to take accurate exposure readings. It typically has a white side that reflects 90% of the light and a gray side that reflects 18%.

grayscale
A successive series of tones ranging between black and white, which have no color. Also, an image with purely luminance data and no chroma information.

guide number (GN)
A number used to quantify the output of a flash unit. It is derived by using this formula: GN = aperture x distance. Guide numbers are expressed for a given ISO film speed in either feet or meters.

histogram
A two-dimensional graphic representation of image tones. Histograms plot brightness along the horizontal axis and number of pixels along the vertical axis, and are useful for determining if an image will be under- or overexposed.

infinity
In photographic terms, the theoretical most distant point of focus.

ISO
From ISOS (Greek for equal), a term for industry standards from the International Organization for Standardization. When an ISO number is applied to film, it indicates the relative light sensitivity of the recording medium. Digital sensors use film ISO equivalents, which are based on enhancing the data stream or boosting the signal.

JPEG
Joint Photographic Experts Group. This is a lossy compression file format that works with any computer and photo software. JPEG examines an image for redundant information and then removes it. It is a variable compression format because the amount of left-over data depends on the detail in the photo and the amount of compression. At low compression/high quality, the loss of data has a negligible effect on the photo. However, JPEG should not be used as a working format—the file should be reopened and saved in a format such as TIFF, which does not compress the image.

latitude
The acceptable range of exposure (from under to over) determined by observed loss of image quality.

lithium-ion (Li-ion)

A popular battery technology that is not prone to the charge memory effects of nickel-cadmium (Ni-Cd) batteries, or the low temperature performance problems of alkaline batteries.

Manual exposure mode

A camera operating mode that requires the user to determine and set both the aperture and shutter speed. This is the opposite of automatic exposure.

middle grey

Halfway between black and white, it is an average gray tone with 18% reflectance. See also, gray card.

midtone

The tone that appears as medium brightness, or medium gray tone, in a photographic print.

overexposed

When too much light is recorded in the image, causing the photo to be too light in tone.

pan

Moving the camera to follow a moving subject. When a slow shutter speed is used, this creates an image in which the subject appears sharp and the background is blurred.

plugin

Third-party software created to augment an existing software program.

pre-flashes

A series of short duration, low intensity flash pulses emitted by a flash unit immediately prior to the shutter opening. These flashes help the TTL light meter assess the reflectivity of the subject. See also, TTL.

Program mode

In Program exposure mode, the camera selects a combination of shutter speed and aperture automatically.

RAW

An image file format that has little internal processing applied by the camera. It contains 12-bit color information, a wider range of data than 8-bit formats such as JPEG.

RAW+JPEG

An image file format that records two files per capture; one RAW file and one JPEG file.

rear-curtain sync

A feature that causes the flash unit to fire just prior to the shutter closing. It is used for creative effect when mixing flash and ambient light.

RGB mode

Red, Green, and Blue. This is the color model most commonly used to display color images on video systems, film recorders, and computer monitors. It displays all visible colors as combinations of red, green, and blue. RGB mode is the most common color mode for viewing and working with digital files onscreen.

S

See Shutter-priority mode.

saturation

The degree to which a color of fixed tone varies from the neutral, grey tone; low saturation produces pastel shades whereas high saturation gives pure color.

Shutter-priority mode

An automatic exposure mode in which you manually select the shutter speed and the camera automatically selects the aperture.

slow sync

A flash mode in which a slow shutter speed is used with the flash in order to allow low-level ambient light to be recorded by the sensitized medium.

synchronize

Causing a flash unit to fire simultaneously with the complete opening of the camera's shutter.

thumbnail

A small representation of an image file used principally for identification purposes.

TIFF

Tagged Image File Format. This popular digital format uses lossless compression.

TTL

Through-the-Lens, i.e., TTL metering. Any metering system – ambient exposure or flash – which works through the lens. Such systems require sensors built into the camera bodies with beam splitters to transfer incoming light to the sensor systems.

vignetting

A reduction in light at the edge of an image due to use of a filter or an inappropriate lens hood for the particular lens.

VR

Vibration Reduction. This technology is used in such photographic accessories as a VR lens and reduces camera shake and vibration.

Index